Setting Foot on the Shores of Connemara
& Other Writings

THE ARAN ISLANDS AND NEIGHBOURING COASTS

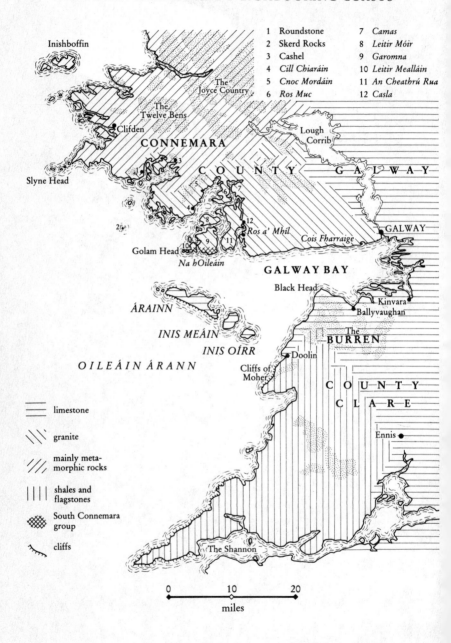

1 Roundstone
2 Skerd Rocks
3 Cashel
4 *Cill Chiaráin*
5 *Cnoc Mordáin*
6 *Ros Muc*
7 *Camas*
8 *Leitir Móir*
9 *Garomna*
10 *Leitir Mealláin*
11 *An Cheathrú Rua*
12 *Casla*

Inishboffin

The
Joyce Country

The
Twelve Bens
Clifden

CONNEMARA

Lough
Corrib

Slyne Head

C O U N T Y   G A L W A Y

Ros a' Mhíl
Cois Fharraige

GALWAY

Golam Head

Na hOileáin

GALWAY BAY

Black Head

Kinvara
Ballyvaughan

ÁRAINN

INIS MEÁIN

INIS OÍRR

The
BURREN

Doolin

Cliffs of
Moher

OILEÁIN ÁRANN

C O U N T Y

C L A R E

Ennis

limestone

granite

mainly meta-
morphic rocks

shales and
flagstones

South Connemara
group

cliffs

The Shannon

0   10   20
miles

Setting Foot on the Shores of Connemara
& Other Writings

Tim Robinson

THE LILLIPUT PRESS
Dublin

First published 1996 by
THE LILLIPUT PRESS LTD
4 Rosemount Terrace, Arbour Hill,
Dublin 7, Ireland.

Reprinted with corrections 1997.

A CIP record for this
title is available from
The British Library.

ISBN 1 874675 74 0 (pbk), 1 874675 79 1 (hbk)

*The Lilliput Press receives financial assistance from
An Chomhairle Ealaíon/ The Arts Council of Ireland.*

Set in 10.5 on 12.5 Ehrhardt
by Verbatim Typesetting & Design Ltd
Printed in England
by Redwood Books of Trowbridge, Wiltshire

Contents

Preface

Now and again during the twenty or so years of work on *Stones of Aran* and my maps, I was invited to give a talk or write an essay on some particular topic, and accepted if the occasion could be turned into one for me to step back and think about what I was chiefly at, or think at a slight angle to my main heading. The book and maps now being finished, it is time to sort through the pile of shorter works, edit out a few overlaps, and offer them as a collection. I thank the various publications mentioned in the sources, and the BBC, for permission to reprint.

Most of these writings relate to the ABC of earth-wonders – Aran, the Burren, Connemara – that I have been spelling out in the maps; some go farther into holes and corners, others fly off into wider spaces. 'Landscape' has during the past decade become a key term in several disciplines; but I would prefer this body of work to be read in the light of 'Space'. Since as an artist and a student of mathematics I was a votary of abstract and imaginary spaces long before I engrained myself in landscape, I can only wonder at the amplitude of actual Space, in which one can without real contradiction build deep-eaved Heideggerian dwellings and revel in the latest scientific speculations about its twenty-six dimensions of which all but the three everyday spatial ones and that of time are so tightly rolled up no perception of ours can ever enter them! However revelatory the current theorizing of somatic space, perceptual space, existential space and so on, ultimately there is no space but Space, 'nor am I out of it', to quote Marlowe's Mephistopheles, for it is, among everything else, the interlocking of all our mental and physical trajectories, good or ill, through all the subspaces of experience up to the cosmic.

Tim Robinson
Roundstone, June 1996

I

Islands and Images

The geography of Aran was explained to us on our first visit by an old man: 'The ocean', he said, 'goes all around the island.' A few days' rambles confirmed that fact, and revealed another: that to explore an island is to court obsession. We returned to live in Aran as soon as we could leave the city.

There is something compulsive in one's relationship to an island. A mainland area with its ambiguous or arbitrary boundaries doesn't constrain the attention in the same way. With an island, it is as if the surrounding ocean like a magnifying glass directs an intensified vision onto the narrow field of view. A little piece is cut out of the world, marked off in fact by its richness in significances. So an island appears to be mappable. Already a little abstracted from reality, already half-concept, it holds out the delusion of a comprehensible totality.

The island is held by the ocean as a well-formed concept is grasped by the mind. But the analogy breaks down, or is diversified; the ocean has broken down Aran into three islands, each in its own relationship to the other, to the mainland and to the ocean itself. These three islands of Aran (Oileáin Árann in Irish) are called Árainn, Inis Meáin and Inis Oírr. I give them their proper names rather than the anglicized ones of Inishmore, Inishmaan and Inisheer, because they are of the Irish-speaking region of western Ireland. The three islands sail in line-astern across the mouth of Galway Bay. First the biggest, Árainn, with a population of about nine hundred and the islands' chief village, the fishing port of Cill Rónáin. The landfall for its trawlers is Ros a' Mhíl on the Connemara coast, but the steamer brings in bread and tourists from Galway near the head of the bay, a three-hour sail if the weather favours. The next is Inis Meáin, the loneliest one, and the last is the smallest, Inis Oírr. About three hundred and twenty people live on each of these two, which have more to do with the Clare coast than with Connemara.

The three islands are the divided remains of a single limestone escarpment extending in a north-westerly direction from Clare. The ridge-line running from end to end of the group forms another division, transverse to the sea-straits, and is a natural axis for thought about the islands. North-east of this line: terraces bearing a mosaic of crops and pastures, villages, roads (and even too many cars, on the big island), and views across the sound into the multi-coloured depths of Ireland. South-west of the line: bare stone acres, cliffs and surge, the Atlantic horizon. This parallelism of community and solitude is most marked on the big island, where one can walk all day (making a map, perhaps), meeting nobody, getting lonely, and knowing that only twenty minutes away over the hill is a different world where every walk is a linear social occasion.

It was no doubt the common knowledge that I spent so much time exploring the unfrequented parts of the island that prompted Máire Bn. Uí Chonghaile, the postmistress of Cill Mhuirbhigh in Árainn, to suggest I make a map of it: tourists were always asking her for a map, and it was an embarrassment that the island could not provide one. In fact, the only maps covering Aran were the six-inch Ordnance Survey sheets, which broke the islands up into five awkward bits and were no less than seventy-five years out of date, and the skimpy half-inch map of the whole of Galway Bay. I produced a rough design for the map that same evening, the project appealed to me with such urgency. First, it would involve all the things I liked doing: walking, drawing, asking questions. Secondly, it fitted in with ideas I had been hatching about the effects of tourism on such communities. Aran has suffered a loss of confidence over the last few decades; the reasons for this go deep, and the summer invasion of visitors often critical of the islands' ways and uninformed of their excellencies is a mere aggravating factor; yet it did not seem useless to commend the islands' fragile uniqueness to the protection of the greater world, and this was a task a map could begin, if it could be made expressive of as well as informative about that uniqueness. Finally, a vague cloud of ideas about maps and their relationship to the place mapped, some of which I had half-realized in artworks before now, could perhaps be worked out in practice; thus the project appeared as a step in an interior evolution, and its execution as what I think of as a private work of art.

The making of a map, I soon found out, is many things as well as a work of art, and among others it is a political, or more exactly an ideological, act. The old Ordnance Survey shows this clearly. Whereas the nineteenth-century surveyors meticulously recorded every crooked wall on the islands, they handled the placenames with a carelessness that reveals contempt, often mishearing them and even misplacing them on the map, and crudely transliterating them in English phonetics. To the colonial administration of that time rents and rates came before any other aspect of life, and the language of the peasant was nothing more than a subversive muttering behind the landlord's back. This historical insult stings the sharper in Aran because Irish is its first language, and although with each generation some of the placenames are forgotten or become incomprehensible, thousands of them still bring their poetry into everyday life. This made it intolerable that the barbarisms of the OS be perpetuated. Was it possible to make amends? For me, a beginner in Irish, it was a considerable challenge, but fortunately I didn't realize that until I had become fascinated by the problem. A thesaurus of local history, anecdote and myth was to be deciphered among these stones; each farmer driving his cows from a field to a well, each fisherman setting his lobster-pots off a rocky shore, held the key to part of it – but I was soon to discover that persuading him to turn out his mental pockets and produce that key, however rusty, bent or broken, had to be a work of patience and cunning.

I was anxious to get on with the actual mapping as soon as possible, though I had little idea of how to go about it. It was to be a summer of unprecedented rains. Between showers I set off for the remotest village, Bun Gabhla, a group of ten dwellings in a hollow of the north-western shoulder of Árainn. One cottage-length seemed a unit good enough to let me sketch the layout of the village without obtrusive peering-about; back at home I could then identify the older cottages on the OS, and by a little deduction pinpoint the more recent ones. I sat on a wall and opened my notebook; a few drops of rain soon added their blurring commentary. On my way back up the hill I turned to look down on Bun Gabhla and check my work. A sea-mist had silently encircled the village, leaving it in a pool of light. A woman running out to the clothes-line behind her cottage, two children playing in the street, a goose stretching its neck in a little meadow, were all living in a world so small and detached I could almost pick it up and examine it; yet as I stood wrapped in semi-invisibility on the hillside I felt that my task was impossible, that no scale of miles could express the remoteness of this place. Often during that summer, struggling along briary paths in the rain, or on the cliffs trying to sketch the headlands with the wind ripping my notebook apart in my hands, I felt that this obstinate isle was not returning my love. It was only after my return the following spring with the completed and printed map that Aran rewarded me with a period of golden calm.

Most days of the mapping took me to and fro between the two aspects of the island, the convivial and the solitary, corresponding to the sheltered terraces of the scarp slope, and the dip slope inclining towards the afternoon sun and the Atlantic storms. Working along the main road that links the villages was my opportunity to talk to everyone, the women who run the little shops or who put up summer visitors (for I aimed to make the map a sort of gazetteer as well), and the farmer, fisherman, publican and priest I had to consult about placenames. All along the way men were at work, erecting the first factory of the islands, digging the trenches for an extension of the water supply, building houses, preparing a site for the generator which would give us electricity for the first time. The transformation of this face of the island was going ahead at an exhilarating and alarming pace; I saw that my map, recording a moment in a time of unprecedented changes, would quickly date.

From the main road the rough grassy side-roads or boreens lead across the terraces of little fields down to the northern coast or up on to the creigs (*craga*) as the bare rocky areas are called. The scale of these terraces is domestic; the tiny fields succeed each other like wry and tilted suites of rooms, and the boreens and 'roadeens' (*róidíní*) just wide enough for a cow that branch off from them, are more like hallways and staircases than public thoroughfares. Almost the entire area of the island is divided up by drystone walls into a maze of fields reached by a bewilderment of

4

paths. Each field can feed two or three cows for a certain number of days, and this network of paths is mainly for driving cattle from one field to another, or to and from a spring, a job I was sometimes called upon to assist in as I came by. Because the paths branch so frequently, the number of ways a few bullocks can go astray when driven from behind by one child rapidly approaches infinity, and the task is complicated by the fact that the field entrances are closed not by gates but by short stretches of specially loosely-built wall, to be knocked down and then rebuilt when the cattle have passed through. After an hour of running and shouting, and piling and unpiling of stones, the outsider is tempted to think that there must be an easier way. But Aran is virtually treeless; stone is the only material to hand, and that in disheartening abundance. This dizzy multiplication of walls has come into being through the centuries as the solution to various problems: clearing the ground of loose stone, protecting stock and crops from gales, the control of grazing, the marking of new boundaries when land was subdivided. There are said to be two thousand miles of wall on the islands! Sometimes as I forced my way along an ancient overgrown *róidín* now bypassed by a wider and more convenient way, I felt moved to record it as an act of piety to the disregarded generations that created this system of fields and paths, an image of human labour in all its wearisome repetitiousness and tireless spontaneity.

Here and there in sheltered hollows among these fields are the roofless ruins of tiny mediaeval churches, reminders of the time of 'Aran of the Saints', when these islands played a role comparable with that of Iona in the advance of Christendom. These churches must always have been humble places, and now, reduced to the few and spare gestures of their simple architecture – pointed door-arch of two curved stones leaned together, deep-set slit window, blocklike altar – they serve to focus vision on what is most delicate in this introspective landscape, the violets in spring and harebells in summer growing in and around the ruins, the wren scuttling like a mouse in the chinks of the field-walls.

The wren may be king of the birds north of the ridge-line, but south of it the raven rules. Often when I was crossing the bare grey plateau that slopes almost imperceptibly down to the cliff edge, the only sound apart from a loose stone rattled by the wind would be the croak of a raven circling high above. The thin pasture of these crags is used for winter grazing and in that season one sometimes sees a man carrying a sack of turnips to his cattle or a child with a milkcan, but in summer this can be an unnervingly desolate region. There are acres of bare limestone scattered with strangely perched boulders of Connemara granite brought over by the last Ice Age. Glaciation has polished some areas into natural dance-floors and moulded others into successions of whale-backed ridges. In places the limestone is so closely divided by long parallel fissures it is like a series of knife-blades underfoot. Where the joints are wider and deeper they are filled exactly to the brim with vegetation, for wherever there is shelter from the wind the moist Atlantic climate encourages a vigorous growth, and the flora of these barren regions is paradoxically rich and various. Southwards the creigs stop in mid-air, and breakers crash on the rocks two or three hundred feet below. Corresponding to the little Christian ruins in the sheltered hollows of the terraces, a series of great pagan forts dominate these windy spaces. Two of these drystone 'dúns' are actually on the cliff edge; the largest, Dún Aonghasa, lording it over a stormy sea from the brink of a three-hundred-foot sheer drop, stands out against the sky like a diagram of 'the sublime'; its appearance is entirely adequate to the romance of the theory that it was the stronghold of a defeated people driven to a glorious last stand on the outermost rim of Europe. In fact these so-called forts, that crown the heights of Aran like vast reservoirs of legend, were the combined stockyards, follies, citadels, temples and places of assembly of long-settled and prosperous Iron-Age or Early Christian farming communities.

I spent much time perched on promontories drawing the cliffs, as I intended to show them in perspective on my map. The strata of shale interleaved with the limestone, which have led to the formation of wide terraces on the more sheltered side of the island, show up on the cliff face as deeply cut ledges, in which during the nesting season rows of guillemots, razorbills, kittiwakes and fulmars are shelved like books. I had heard many stories of the men who used to be let down on ropes to kill the seabirds as they came in to roost, and be hauled up again rigid with cold in the dawn. While a few men still catch rockfish with long lines from the clifftop, nowadays most islanders shun the cliffs and quite rightly regard them as treacherous. They are, in fact, deeply undercut and collapses are not rare. In one place a pillar of rock has become detached and leans out over the sea bearing a little green field on its head as if caught in the act of filching a bit of someone's farm; when it falls, I shall have to revise the map. I met nobody during the days I spent working along the cliffs, peering over the edge and trying to work out how the strata run. After a spell of this it was often a relief to turn away from the wind and the aboriginal clamour of the gulls, and recross the creigs to the other side of the island, the cherishing side, of cups of tea in friendly kitchens, Guinness in pubs the colour of Guinness, and lifts home by pony-car or minibus.

After a few weeks I got into my cartographer's stride, and often finished off the day's work by walking part of the northern coast, where the fields come down to a varied shoreline of sandy bays, shingle banks and rocky promontories. This shore is more frequented than the other, and here and there I would meet a man pulling rye for thatch or spraying potatoes against the blight, who would be ready to talk. Most farms here are of twenty or thirty difficult acres and only support perhaps an old couple whose children have gone away to America or are off with the trawlers, or one of the many bachelors too old to marry now, and for these people farming is a life of solitary days. One evening I met an elderly man who showed me where the sea-kale, almost extinct in the wild in Ireland, still grows. After viewing this prehistoric-looking cabbage thrusting up through the heavy shingle, we stepped over a little wall into a field where he had a few heaps of carraigín, a seaweed gathered between the tides which makes a sort of blancmange when boiled with milk. It has to be left out to bleach for a few days before being packed and sent off to the buyer, and 'I'd leave it out for another night if only I knew it wouldn't rain,' he said. Rain, it seemed, would rot it, and the trouble of picking out the bad bits would be added to that of picking out the winkles, and at the price it fetched it was hardly worth it. He fingered his chin and peered at the gathering clouds; I felt equally forlorn in this ancient dilemma. Eventually we propped the sticky half-dried masses against a wall so that the wind could blow through them, and left it to fate.

Apart from the trawlers there are a number of small half-deckers working out of Cill Rónáin, drift-net fishing for salmon in

June and July, and lobster-potting until the weather breaks up in autumn. I often watched them throwing out the pots as I walked along the shore. One day I saw one of these boats coming into the bay at Cill Mhuirbhigh at an unusual pace, towing something big and heavy. By the time I had hurried round the bay the crew had hauled some sort of a monster out of the water and were hacking it open. It was a basking shark that had become entangled in their nets and which they told me they had 'drowned' by towing it behind the boat. This fish, a harmless plankton-eater that can grow up to thirty-five feet long, used to be harpooned by the islanders for the oil of its liver; Robert Flaherty had reconstructed the hunt for his film *Man of Aran*. There is still a basking shark fishery off Achill Island, and the oil, which has some engineering uses, fetches a high price, while the fins, we hear, go to Chinese restaurants. Recently a Norwegian trawler had been seen poaching for basking sharks around Aran, and our fishermen had decided to take a closer look at one. They spilled out the liver, which would have filled a couple of suitcases, and stuck their fingers in its eye-sockets and twiddled its huge eyeballs; then they tumbled the corpse back into the water before I had a chance to take a bit of fin home for our dinner. This incident led to a brief revival of the fishery in the following year, but fortunately the catch was not even sufficient to cover the cost of the diesel expended in scouring the seas for the elusive prey, and the project was abandoned.

As well as its fishing fleet the village of Cill Rónáin turned out to have more points of interest than I had expected, though I recorded them with mixed feelings as they were mainly relics of the bad old days – barracks, courtroom, coastguard station, pound – all now adapted to better purposes. The contrast between this weighty apparatus of extortion and the resources of the community to which it was applied reminded me of the accounts of armed constabulary being landed on the islands to carry out the eviction of an old woman or the sequestration of a cow, within the memory of some still living. Nowadays two gardaí, seldom in uniform, work from a small room in the huge empty coastguard station, the courtroom is a café and the barracks a pub.

By the end of the summer I had covered Árainn and was ready to leave for Inis Meáin. The Galway steamer calls at the two smaller islands two or three times a week on its way to or from

Cill Rónáin. It cannot dock at either island but drifts offshore while goods and passengers are ferried ashore in the famous Aran currachs – keelless canoes of lath and tarred canvas, nimble as a seal among waves and rocks but alarmingly fragile-looking to the tourist who has to jump into one as it lurches up and down outside the steel door in the steamer's hold. On this occasion I was the only stranger going ashore, and the boatmen extorted a pound from me, saying that it was so rough I wouldn't have got ashore at all but for the fine crew I had.

The landing-place in Inis Meáin is exposed, and the island is more frequently cut off in winter than is Árainn. It is the least visited and least changed of the islands, and here the harshness of Aran triumphs over its milder aspects. It is unbelievably stony; I think of Inis Meáin as the Delos of the Rain God. The north-facing terraces, which in the big island are largely cultivated, here extend below the line of villages in successive rims of bare rock several hundred yards wide, and the 'back of the island' behind the ridge-line is made oppressive by countless field-walls too high to see over. In many of the fields superfluous stone has been built into big rectangular stacks, to clear the sparse grass. All around the south and south-west coast, storms have moved massive blocks of stone, many of them the size of cars or cottages, up the shelving shore, and assembled them into a huge dyke; one can walk outside this 'storm beach' on utterly barren sheets of rock swept bare of loose stone, which towards the very exposed south-western head-land are two or three hundred yards wide. Out on the rim of this lugubrious grey-green desert, a glittering plume of foam leaps up again and again as waves rush into a cavern below. There are cliffs along the west-facing coast, increasing in height as one goes north-wards; here the storm beach is actually on the clifftop, and only fades out where the cliffs are over a hundred feet high and the waves cannot scale them. At this point there is a ruinous structure of rough stone blocks, perhaps once a lookout's hut, called Synge's Chair. Here the writer J.M. Synge used to sit and watch the seabirds circling and screaming below; I often came to rest in the same spot, envying him his stormy creative height.

Synge's coming to this desolation, just before the end of the last century, to find the stories and the language of the plays he was to write in later years, symbolizes the return of Ireland to its origins, for this stony island nourished one of the roots of nation-hood. The Irish language, suppressed, starved and despised, nearly died in the last century; its revival was a necessary step in the fight for independence, and Inis Meáin was one of the places to which the cultural nationalists turned in search of the language through which the nation could rediscover its identity. At that period so many scholars and writers lodged in the one cottage that put up visitors that it became known as Ollscoil na Gaeilge, the University of Irish. One young man who stayed there was Pádraic Pearse, who was to proclaim the Republic in the rising of Easter 1916. How, then, does modern Ireland repay its debt to such places? In the pub, weather-darkened faces are illuminated by the flicker of TV; images of speed and sexuality are received in non-committal silence. On the slip in the driving rain four children huddled together in a plastic sheet watch as the currachs are run out into the waves, taking off the last of the summer visitors. Is Inis Meáin to die? Soon these children will follow, to jobs in Galway, Birmingham, Boston – anywhere but Inis Meáin.

Having seen those last visitors off into the mists, I found myself weather-bound for a few days, and sat in the kitchen deci-phering the blotches in my notebook while the woman of the house huddled in her shawl, knitted and took snuff. Sometimes a neighbouring lad would come in and sit by the range in silence, bending sideways to let his spittle drool onto the hot plate and sizzle into a little pancake. Gathering that I was a 'scholar', another man called in to put his problem to me, perhaps just to pass the time. The lobster season was ended and it was time to tow his wooden tank full of lobsters now moored by the slip across to the Clare coast. There one dealer was offering £1 a pound for full-sized lobsters only, and another was offering 80p a pound for all lobsters above and below the legal limit. Which was the better deal? 'Well, how many small ones have you?' – 'Maybe a couple of dozen.' – 'And how many big ones?' – 'By Jesus, I haven't a clue!' So I had to fall back from mathematical to moral argument, and as the weather didn't clear enough for lobster-delivery during my stay I never heard the outcome. My reputation as a scholar must have survived, however, for when an unprecedented event occurred one Sunday I was urged to record it, because 'That day should be in History!' Every Sunday the curate from Inis Oírr is brought across by currach to celebrate mass in Inis Meáin, and the honour of this sometimes dangerous task devolves upon each of the Inis Oírr households in turn. Recently a new household had come into existence, a lay community of young Catholic enthusiasts, men and women, collectively known as 'The Danes' because their leader was Danish; they sang psalms at all canonical hours of day and night, fished from a catamaran, built their own currachs to a modernized design, and in everything they did were a source of endless speculation to the islanders. Then they claimed their right to bring the curate across, and the curate, who was new to the islands, accepted the offer. The men of Inis Meáin who went down to the slip as usual that day to greet him were amazed and amused to find that his crew included two girls. He himself was unaware of the sensation caused by this jolting of ancient observances and prohibitions. As the procession to the chapel passed the cottage I was staying in, a lad broke off from it to run in with the news: 'There were women in the curate's boat!' – and I was told that it would be worth my while writing it down, which I now do. And as an historian should, I note the date of this event: 15 September 1974.

There is quite a lot of social interchange between the two small islands, and my hosts' cottage, at the top of the road leading down to the slip, was well placed for observing it; the lady of the house spent much time scanning the seaways through binoculars. One misty evening – my last in Inis Meáin – we were all at the door anxiously watching the return of a currach with some lads who were banned from the Inis Meáin pub because of 'blackguardism' and had gone to do their drinking in Inis Oírr. Their progress was slow and irregular, but they made land at last, and came up the hill past our cottage all clinging to the cab of a tractor. Shortly afterwards they sent a child down to us to borrow a butcher's knife, which the man of the house handed over with evident reluctance. When next we looked out into the gathering murk, they were down on one of the great creigs below the village, with a cow and a shotgun. One of them took uncertain aim at the cow's forehead, there was a bang, the beast fell, kicking and slithering on the wet rock, and toppled off the conveniently flat place they had chosen for their butchering into a deep gully. They leaped down to finish her off with a hammer, waving at us to come and help; we shrank back into the doorway. For an hour or more they were hacking and tugging at the carcase, and later that evening on our way to the pub we passed them standing in the drizzle by the roadside, with a heap of raw meat that steamed in the cold air, drinking mugs of Guinness out of a white plastic bucket; I recognized them as the brave crew that had brought me safe to shore. The next day, as I was saying goodbye to my host, we saw a raven circling above the creig, and he observed sagely, 'Nothing happens unknown to the raven!'

I crossed to Inis Oírr by the trawler that takes over the interisland connection when the steamer is withdrawn for servicing at the end of the season. As at Inis Meáin, the currachs come out to ferry travellers ashore; on this occasion there were few passengers – an Icelandic geologist, an elderly man from the Folklore Commission, and myself – and only one currach was launched, which had to go to and fro several times. The landing is on a wide shelving beach, giving the island a welcoming aspect; as the currach nosed into the sand two men grasped me by the elbows and flew me ashore. When I think of boat-days on Inis Meáin's dismal shore I remember a dog on the rocks howling at the breakers crashing in out of the fog; Inis Oírr's boat-day, however, I see as a sort of garden-party, a talkative gathering on a brilliant expanse of smooth sand watching the trawler or the steamer beating to and fro offshore, and the currachs bounding in over a festive sea. White houses scattered in a wide arc around the foreshore, and behind them a bright craggy hill bearing a picturesque ruined castle – a gleam of sunshine on all this transports one for a moment to the Mediterranean. But beyond the skyline begins the same grey criss-cross of walls and scraggy fields, slowly declining to a storm-battered shore. A monument to the power of the sea, there is the sixty- or seventy-yard-long hulk of the *Plassy*, a freighter that struck a notorious rock off the east coast of the island a few years ago and eventually drifted ashore. Successive storms have lifted her higher and higher and now she stands boltupright on the storm beach several yards above normal high tides, and appears to be sailing across dry land. Her hull is broken open and one can step into the hold; her cargo for this motionless voyage is huge boulders.

Behind the livelier aspects of Inis Oírr as compared with Inis

Meáin – the better-stocked shops and less spartan lodgings, the animation brought by children from mainland schools who spend a summer month here learning Irish – there is the same sad wasting-away of a community losing its lifeblood through emigration of the young. The girls go first; it is easier for them to get jobs in hotels and shops. Not long before my visit the socially conscious young curate had written an appeal to the authorities to do something about this desperate situation, instancing the fact that there was just one girl of marriageable age left, to twenty-six young men. I fell into conversation with an island girl soon after my arrival, and asked 'Are you she?' No, she was not; she was just home for a holiday from her job in Galway, and anyway, she said, 'I couldn't marry any of those lads; they're all my first cousins!' An exaggeration no doubt, but one that points up the problems facing a dwindling community. This year the curate has to report that there are no marriageable girls at all in Inis Oírr.

The islanders tend to mistrust the offices of the outside world, on the whole with good cause, and as this was my first visit to Inis Oírr I felt it more than ever necessary to explain to everyone what I was up to. Maybe I imagined an initial reserve, but in any case it dissolved as news of my activities got round, and my explorations were interspersed with hundreds of conversational encounters, from the barrel-shaped old salt directing four men stretching canvas over the framework of a currach in his boatyard on the foreshore, to the lighthouse keepers in their isolated quarters at the back of the island, from Seán an Siopa (Seán of the shop), the unofficial king of the island, sitting massively by his fireside and rolling forth grand diplomatic utterances with his eyes shut, to the blue-robed zealots, the 'Danes' (Mary's Followers of the Cross, they call themselves), who questioned me closely about the times of mass in the big island.

Then it was time for me to leave the islands to their motionless voyage and stony cargoes, and go to London, where I would have space to piece together my sketches, notes and sodden OS sheets. A motorboat was to take me across to the Clare coast, but as Joe the boatman lingered in the pub watching a football match on television, and the sky darkened, I became more and more doubtful about this first step of the journey. I had seen the little fibreglass boat battering about in the waves against the quayside for some days with a fender sagging loose and the canopy hanging on by one bolt. A couple of tourists in the pub were also in two minds as to whether to leave or not, but Joe persuaded them to stay, saying that he would be back for them in the morning. Eventually we set off down to the quay, and as we looked out into rain and prancing waves Joe surprised me by saying, 'That's the last they'll see of me!' It seemed that the weather was breaking up and that if we had waited for them to make up their minds it would have been too late to cross before dark. The only other passenger was a pretty little American girl besotted with the rugged Joe. It was to be a wildly exciting crossing. Once we had left the shelter of the island nothing was visible in the mist but huge waves chasing up from behind us. I watched how Joe negotiated our way through the seas: holding to his course through the smaller waves, keeping a lookout over his shoulder for swells breaking at the top, and when one of the regular successions of three big seas came, steering away from the first, letting the second lift us stern first – they were much bigger than the boat – and pivoting on its top to head down the other side and face into the third. The only time he faltered was when the girl started to caress his knee; a mass of water exploded into the boat, and he pushed her aside with an oath. After an hour or so the Cliffs of Moher loomed up out of the gloom, and soon we were running into the little cove of Doolin through a narrow gap between a rocky peninsula and an islet smothered in breakers. We spent that evening listening to the famous local folk-musicians in the pub, and when we came out a gale was howling. Two rather drunk youngsters drove us down through lashing rain to see how the boat was faring; it was swooping to and fro agitatedly, and a violent sea was threatening to break over the quay and swamp it. Outside the feeble circle of light from my torch I could see nothing but huge white-topped swells rushing past. Joe put on a lifejacket, clambered down and sprawled on the nose of the lurching boat hanging tyres over its bows. With the lads larking about among mooring-ropes in the darkness, I was really frightened that my adventure would end in tragedy, but I pulled them back from the edge, and with much shouting and hauling and tying and untying of ropes we got the boat turned around and moored bows outwards, and nobody was drowned. I slept that night in a caravan that seemed about to take off from the foreshore, and woke to sunshine and the roar of top-pling breakers. Then I hitched a lift to Shannon, and flew to the cloistral calm of London.

My task now was to make good my analogy of the 'well-formed concept' and to objectify it as a map. Because I knew little about normal cartographical procedures, the problems of conveying information intelligibly were not to be solved by ready-to-hand techniques; rather they appeared as opportunities for expressing my feelings about the islands. In choosing line-weights and type-faces I had in mind not so much legibility as the Aran landscape, the beauty of which lies in its crystalline delicacy of detail always on the point of dissolution into vast luminous spaces. The com-mercially available mechanical tints seemed inadequate symbols for beautifully shelving beaches and the ever-changing interpenetra-tions of rock and water, and I preferred to let my pen run on for hours in minute lyrical effusions of dots and twirls. All around the coast, a fiction, the high-water mark, posed a similar problem; rather than indicate it by a line I relived with my pen the hourly give-and-take of land and sea. Drawing the cliffs was a strange experience; as I reconstructed them from my sketches I found myself becoming dizzy over these half-inch abysses; no doubt it would have been easier to search out aerial photographs, but my instinct was to keep as close as possible to my experience of them. I had tended to think of my approach as consisting in the closest possible identification with the object, but that, I now came to bel-ieve, is not quite the case. While I was exploring the islands my dreams expressed the process in sexual metaphor; my distinctness from the object was preserved, but at a limit beyond which lay a threat of self-loss. Now in the act of drawing my aim was to achieve the same intimacy of physical contact with the emergent image as I had reached with the reality. – But all this is to formal-ize in retrospect a practice that was tentative and instinctual, and indeed to fill up with ideals the blanks on the resultant map.

In the basic geographic act of mapping I find three conjunc-tions: that of the place mapped with the one who maps it; that of the mapper with the map itself; and finally that of the map with the mapped – this last a confrontation that tests the worth of the first and second. I returned to Aran in the spring with the first printed copies of the map, which have been on sale here since. It is too early to say much about the outcome. In a superficial way the map has been a success with tourists; in fact I sometimes wonder if in many minds I have merely substituted concept for reality. Last year when I met visitors they were usually lost and making a difficult acquaintance with the island, whereas this year I pass group after group huddled over the map with their backs to the view. As for myself, I have become a minor object of touristic interest, perhaps the only one not marked on the map. As I sit at my desk writing this, I hear the driver of a passing jaunting-car pointing out our house to his 'load' of tourists: 'The man who made them maps lives there!' Individual visitors have told me the map has enhanced their appreciation of the islands, which is gratifying, but more important to me is the generous response of the islanders, who have examined it minutely and with no trace of a wish to find fault. I know that the map has been 'read' to old men by their sons or grandsons, and I am always relieved to hear that one or other of the fishermen has confirmed my naming of rocks and inlets he has known all his life. Finally, I know that many copies have been sent off to 'the exiles' in Britain, Australia and the USA, and this makes me both proud and sad.

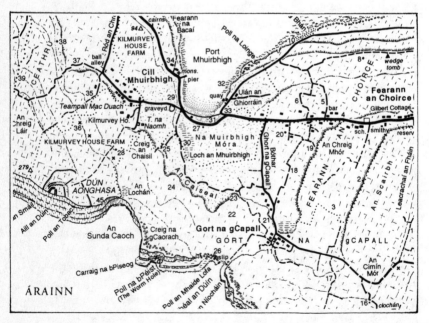

2

Setting Foot on the Shores of Connemara

THE TANGLED TIGHTROPE

For some years I have spent a few weeks of each spring and autumn walking the southern coast of Connemara. It is a strange region. Granite, harsh-edged, glittering, shows its teeth everywhere in the heathery wastes and ridged potato fields, and even between the houses of the shapeless villages. The peaty, acidic soil is burdened with countless boulders left by glaciers that came down from the mountains immediately to the north during the last Ice Age. The land has been scrubbed raw, by the ice, by the Atlantic gales, by poverty.

South Connemara was very sparsely peopled in early times, judging by the fewness of its archaeological sites. To the merchants of mediaeval Galway it was a lair of pirates, of the 'Ferocious O'Flaherties'. Some of those dispossessed of better lands by the Cromwellians in 1650 or hunted out of Ulster by the Orangemen in 1795 settled in this unenviable quarter. By the nineteenth century a teeming and periodically starving population was crowded into a narrow coastal strip, fishing, gathering molluscs on the shore, growing potatoes in tiny plots of black waterlogged soil which they fertilized with seaweed, and cutting turf, the only fuel this treeless land affords, from the vast bogs that made the interior almost impassable and otherwise sterile. The sea's deeply penetrating inlets were their lanes of communication and bore the trade they depended on, the export of turf to the stony and fuelless Aran Islands, the Burren in County Clare, and to Galway city. By the beginning of this century the bogland near the coast had been stripped to bare rock.

Modern times have introduced other resources – tourism, some light industry, the teaching of Irish in summer schools, the dole – but the pattern set by that old coastal folklife, a human tidemark between the two sustaining desolations of the sea and the bog, has not been obliterated. From the little mounds of shells left by Neolithic winkle-pickers, to the newest bungalow, a daydream of California's blessed clime, sprouting between two knolls of wet rock and already weatherstained, the dense record of life has been scribbled in the margin of the sea. Only the very shoreline itself, now that the main roads passing by half a mile or so inland have drawn habitation away from it, has been left a lonely place, a long graveyard for the black skeletons of the wooden boats that used to throng the waterways.

This shoreline is of incredible complexity. The two little fishing villages of Ros a' Mhíl and Roundstone are only about twenty miles apart, but, even estimating from a small-scale map and ignoring the fifty or more sizeable islands in the bays and off the headlands, there are at least two hundred and fifty miles of coast between them. It was this strange geography, like a rope of closely interwoven strands flung down in twists and coils across an otherwise bare surface, that brought me to the region; I had a conception filling my head of the correspondingly strange map I could make of it, in which all the density of reference would cluster along one line between two almost blank zones, and that line so convoluted as to visit every square inch of the sheet. And having selected this particular stretch of coast because its near unmappability perversely suggested the possibility of mapping it, I had felt the idea of walking its entire length impose itself like a duty, a ritual of deep if obscure significance through which I would be made adequate to the task of creating an image of the terrain.

In the first month of days of walking I covered perhaps a quarter of the way; the going is not easy. At that stage I wrote some pages which I have now looked over, as I pause between the end of walking and the beginning of drawing, and try to recall those first steps towards the heart of Connemara.

* * *

I carry with me on this tangled tightrope of a journey the dozen sheets of the six-inch Ordnance Survey map that cover the area, on which to note my finds – a few rare plants, a number of archaeological sites, endless hundreds of tiny landing-stages, and above all the Irish placenames I collect from the people of the region. As these maps were last revised eighty years ago I also have to mark in new buildings and paths, which sometimes involves compass-work and the pacing-out of distances. But on the whole the mensurational side of cartography is not my concern; in my efforts to see a little farther into this terrain I stand, if not on the shoulders of giants, then on those of an army, for the original Survey, made in the 1830s, was carried out in the style and with the manpower of a military operation, which in various of its aspects is just what it was. This horde of men who tramped over the countryside with theodolites and chains so adequately measured its lengths, breadths and heights that I am free to concentrate on that mysterious and neglected fourth dimension of cartography which extends deep into the self of the cartographer. My task is to establish a network of lines involving this dimension, along which the landscape can enter my mind, unfragmented and undistorted, to be projected into a map that will be faithful to more than the measurable.

The principles of this subjective triangulation of the world are only now beginning to become expressible for me as I work on this, my third, map. I can throw a glancing light on them by saying that the base-triangle of the system is that formed by the three church-towers of Proust's Martinville, and for the discovery of its other significant points I have to rely on the sort of magical illumination that produces sometimes poetry and sometimes jokes – but when I use the word 'magical' of my procedures it is only as a blank to hold a space open until I find some more penetrating adjective.

Magic is a tool more easily mislaid than a compass. In my anxiety to miss no tricks on the exactly scientific level, I sometimes go out overburdened with the desire to find classifiable elements of the scene, which I can post off in the form of neat lists to the helpful experts who advise me on archaeology, botany, geology, placenames and so on; and then I merely succeed in blurring for myself the location of those more elusive places, the rivetholes through which I will be able to fasten my experience of the territory to my expression of it on paper, that are only spotted through a mobile reposefulness of mind. In fact after the first week of tramping arduous miles of solitude, with a very thin file of reports to show for the effort, having forgotten the ritual element in this endless walking and come to regard it as merely a means, which was proving inefficient, of finding curiosities, I was almost ready to admit that this wearisome muddle of land and sea was unmappable by my pedestrian methods. Worse still, the inner recesses of these bays, which from the various hilltops I climbed to get a conspectus of the country looked like the roots of a marvellous silver tree winding far into the rich darkness of the hinterland, had, when investigated in detail, slimy shores of black mud tidemarked by gigantic heaps of khaki seaweed, which seemed to multiply the miles by the accusation of insanity.

But by degrees, under the hypnosis of repetitive days, my perceptions changed, and all that had seemed to stand between me and my object – the steep rocky promontories, the ankle-turning shinglebanks, the slithery penetralia of the inlets – became instead part of what I was there for, the shore itself. Then the various incidental difficulties such as the field-walls and drainage ditches that came right down to the water's edge, and even the banks of seaweed, no longer impeded me psychologically, and my body ceased to notice them as physical obstacles. I saw with interest how the walls were continued onto the foreshore by little ramparts of piled boulders linking outcrops of rock, to stop the cattle wandering at low tide. I heard the drainage channels beginning to murmur as an exceptional tide of the autumn equinox, silently brimming and gleaming along the land's edge like the rim of water about an over-filled glass, reached into them and perturbed their stagnation. And the incredible bulk of seaweed itself took on an explanatory role as I realized the influence it has had on the fine structure of the coastline – for in the old days it was the only fertilizer used on this sour land, and there is a spot corresponding to each cottage and in places to each field where boatloads of it used to be landed, so that long stretches of the coast have been remodelled in ways so slight they eluded my eye at first, by the removal of a few stones here to make a navigable passage to high-water mark and the piling up of a few stones there to make a tiny quay.

Thus, in this region commonly said to be bare of archaeological interest, the shore revealed itself as a human construct, the work of numberless generations, in which it was tempting to discern the superimposition and entanglement of evolutionary sequences. There are landing-places even more primaeval-looking than those little hummocks of boulders at the field's edge, for where the thick blanket-bog of the interior comes down to sea level it ends in strange soft black cliffs which collapse here and there to form little muddy harbours, out of the walls of which the gnarled roots of long-buried forests protrude as weird but handy bollards. Farther up the scale are more substantial dry-stone jetties built by energetic families, and the handsome masonry piers, famine-relief work of the last century, some of which have been given a twentieth-century topping or cladding, and finally the huge and precisely geometrical concrete acreage of the new EEC-grant-aided harbour works at Ros a' Mhíl, which has probably come into existence over the centuries by progressive improvement of some little alignment of boulders or a twisted bog-oak root now reburied deep in its foundations.

But beyond all these fascinating explanations of itself, the shore drew me on by the mesmeric glittering of its waters; the days of walking became a drug, until I felt I was abandoning myself to the pursuit of this glittering for its own sake, that I welcomed every conceivable complexity of interplay between land and sea. I devoured distances, although I was working in finer and finer detail. Such a labour of mind and body is at first crushingly exhausting, rises to bliss as the activity fuels its own source of vigour, and then a point of satiety is reached rather suddenly, it is time to break off, go home, and lie for a spell under waves of tiredness.

WALKING OUT TO ISLANDS

'Interdigitation' is the fine term I overhear the scientists using for the way in which one natural zone meets another along a complex boundary of salients and re-entrants; the close-set come-and-go of its syllables is almost enough to convey the word's meaning, but etymologically it is a little inadequate to such cases as this Connemara coastline where land and sea not only entwine their crooked fingers but each element abandons particles of itself temporarily or permanently to the clutch of the other.

An outline map of this area showing nothing but the boundary between land and water might well be misread unless it indicated which was which. To the bays that ramify into inlets and creeks correspond the peninsulas with their subsidiary headlands and spits; the lakes of the bogland are sometimes linked into archipelago-like sequences, as the major islands are joined by causeways; there are matching ambiguities too, lakes that become inlets at high tide, and islands that can be reached on foot when the tide is out. This last category appealed to me even more than the true islands I had to hire a boatman to reach.

When a few years ago I was mapping the Burren uplands on the south of Galway Bay, and even earlier during a time of walking in Provence that found expression in a series of geometrical abstract works rather than a map, I had become aware of certain experiences of the traveller that do not depend on anything in the nature of the terrain apart from its topography. The most easily conveyed of these is that high point of awareness one reaches in crossing a pass, where the line of the knowable, leading over from the lowland already traversed to that just being revealed, is intersected by the axis of the heights on either side which are left unvisited and unknowable by this journey. The completing of a circuit of an island is another of these purely topographical sensations, the promises and illusions of which I am exploring at length on the Aran Isles. In Connemara I identified a third, this visiting of quasi-islands by foot.

A little anxiety sharpens the business. Such a visit is an island in time too, a narrow space allotted by the tides; will the slight pressure one is under help to crystallize one's impressions or merely crumple them? Sometimes one has to wait for the parting of the waters as for the curtain-up of a play, which wakes high expectations. Some of these intermittent islands of Connemara are still inhabited, but only by one or two people, and so to visit them is to visit a person, and the topography of 'walking out to islands' becomes an image of personal contact, a metaphor one lives out in concrete reality. I remember vividly two such intertidal episodes, one played out in a suite of green fields beached on wide sands, the other on a rocky pyramid among plunging, folding, silvery rivers of ebb and flow.

I had chosen a day of spring tide for the first of these occasions, and although I suppose this made little difference to my ration of time to be spent on the island, it certainly heightened the stealthy drama of the unsheeting of the sea's bed. I loitered about the deserted strand wondering where was the best point from which to strike out for what was still an island half a mile offshore. The seaweedy rocks I picked my way along did not link up into a route, the sandy-bottomed pools between them were too deep to wade, and nothing seemed to be changing. Then far away on shining levels near the horizon, I saw a pair of little figures trudging outwards – women going to gather winkles round the island. I had been aiming off at entirely the wrong angle; I went back along the shore and followed in their steps over freshly rippled sand and fleeting shallows. The island put out a gangplank of damp gold towards me, but as I approached it seemed to retire behind the pale sand-cliffs of its dunes.

I had already heard of old Tomás, the last of his family, who still spent most of his time on the island although he often slept in the houses of various mainland relatives and would probably soon settle down in Ros a' Mhíl. As I crested the dunes I saw him in the distance on a slight rise, looking about his empty fields, and it was immediately clear that this was how he passed most of his island hours. He was the only moving object in my field of vision, and I in his, though his movements as he watched me approach were merely a scarecrow's slight turnings and leanings with the wind.

He greeted me courteously when I spoke to him in Irish, and invited me into his house which stood nearby, a little apart from the line of roofless cottages that marked the long axis of the island like the vertebrae of a beached carcass. It was a stone-built cottage of the traditional type, its thatch replaced by roofing-felt, with a loft above each end-room and a central kitchen open to the gaunt roof-space. I sat on the only chair by an empty hearth while he boiled a kettle for tea on a ring set on the nozzle of a gas cylinder. There was nothing in the room except the frayed and bleached wares of the strandline, of which he showed me from a collection of little things on the windowsill a wave-worn cigarette lighter and a small disc of mica. I would be welcome to stay the night, he told me, but when I explained that I had to return 'by this ebb' he stood up immediately to show me round the island. As we went out he showed me the trophies he still wins every year for dancing jigs at the local festivals. He moved lightly before me over the low and broken stone walls of the pallid autumnal fields, in which the twisted rootstocks of wild iris showed everywhere among the scant grass. We looked at the unfenced burial-ground with its graves marked only by little boulders and unnamed except in the oral record which would soon leave the island to fade away with this old man, and of which I jotted down a mere scrap: that the grave in the north-west corner is of a woman, said to have been the first settler here, who was drowned when coming into the island on horseback, three hundred years ago.

We crossed the grassy street of the skeletal village and took a barely discernible path, once called The Scholars' Road, down to Schoolhouse Beach. Rabbits, flourishing unhunted, had under-mined the walls of the deserted schoolhouse and it had totally col-lapsed. To the south, the ocean-face, a third of the island was smothering in sand as the rabbits tunnelled the dunes and then ate them bare until the winter gales broke them up and set the sand marching. Tomás showed me where the lads used to play football on green fields when he was young; but the fields had fled since then, revealing low foundations of ancient habitations and the heaps of limpet, mussel and winkle shells left by some shore-folk of the island's dateless past. On the way back to the house we lin-gered along the strand and examined the offerings of the last high tide. The writing on a plastic bottle we decided was Hungarian. A lavatory-brush puzzled Tomás until I explained its use, which however did not much interest him, and it was for its appearance that he carried it home.

When we reached his house he suddenly dodged inside before me and ran to rap on the bedroom door, shouting, 'Get up! Get up! Are you all in bed yet?' – and then turning to me with a laugh-ing face flung open the door to show me the room empty save for a blanket or two on the floor. The only adequate response to his joke would have been to promise to stay with him there for the rest of his life, indeed to have settled down, repelled the sands and repop-ulated the island. But the tide of my life was set in another direc-tion, and it was already time to walk out of his world.

* * *

The second of these little domains with their lunar schedules of opening and closing hours was named after a saint of ancient times who sailed there from Aran of the Saints itself, and I hoped for miracles from it. It stands in the mouth of a bay near An Caiseal and is reached by the Road of the Islands, a sequence of fords improved into causeways of piled boulders, which links three islets into a mile of tortuous path. Only three people still lived on the saint's rocky steeps, an old couple too infirm to leave home and a man who preferred to row across to a farther shore of the bay to do his shopping; thus through disuse the Road of the Islands had become – as the woman of the house I was lodging in at the time had told me in her horribly corrupted Irish – 'cineál rougháilte', kind of rough. So I had allowed myself plenty of time for it, and came down to the shore to find no sign of it beyond a little jetty of black stones slanting down into the broad and steady outflow from the bay. I sat down to wait for the way to open, which it did, not mechanically like a toll-barrier or park gate, but as a flower does, by change so slow that it lulls, entrances and eludes the attention and thus appears as a number of separate instantaneous and miraculous leaps from stepping-stone to stepping-stone across the flow of daydream. The river-like shifting of water into which the way descended between the shore on which I lay and the islet a hundred yards away was every time I remeasured it with my eye narrower than I had remembered, but its present state seemed so unchanging as to throw doubt on the memory.

Eventually the flood looked as if it might be fordable, so I walked out over the roughly piled and seaweed-covered boulders of the causeway and planted my foot in the current, which pressed against my wellington boot and rose in a silvery bow-wave that warned me to withdraw, to be patient. And over the next ten minutes stones added themselves onto the length of the causeway, appearing like dark mushrooms growing up through the water. When one or two more had made themselves available in the middle of the dwindling gap I made a few splashy bounds, and the farther part of the causeway took me safely to the shore of the first islet. There was no obvious path across it and I had some tussles with thickets; a few cattle in a marshy hollow looked up but did not finish formulating a reaction to my presence before I was making my way over the ford between their islet and the next. That and the third crossing were no obstacle, but on the outermost islet I got into almost impassable complications of sloughs and thorns and reefs of rock, and the ultimate causeway was a long penance of round boulders wrapped in wet seaweed. I was hot and tired as I climbed the grassy lane that ran straight up from the end of the causeway to the cluster of gables near the top of the saint's island.

Life has so far withdrawn from these marginal places, leaving few except the old, that I had not expected to find a man entering upon his prime here and still less one who appeared to embody the ideals of those visionary revolutionaries of the turn of the century who dreamed of and fought for a Gaelic nation, alive to its ancient traditions and fiercely independent of the corruptions of modern Europe. This man, another Tomás, thoughtful-looking but open-faced, just returned in his boat from Sunday mass, was sitting in his neat sunny cottage smoking his pipe and contemplating the sally-rod baskets he had been making during the week. Before the door was the framework of a currach he was building for the Pattern Day boat-races on another island. We fell into easy conversation, as if it had been my daily habit to drop in on him. I was a little disappointed to hear that the baskets were merely to decorate a pub. However, his contentment with the island life that gave him space for his crafts, and his ready response to my inquiries about old burial grounds, holy wells and such matters were genuine enough. He led me with the leaping strides of one of Synge's Aran men down the rough flank of the island, while his dog flitted and circled, not so much the man's shadow as the shadow of his attention as he cast the automatic glance of a farmer about his fields. In a hidden hollow he showed me a little burial-ground, long disused and very overgrown, unrecorded on the map, nameless, its graves marked by mere boulders we found with our feet in the long grass, with a pine-tree he had transplanted there flourishing over it and a bit of thornbush in the gap in the wall to keep the cattle out. He thought that most of the graves were of children but that there were some adults buried there too from the *drochshaol*, the 'bad time' of the Famine. He asked me, as the Connemara man of Patrick Pearse's unearthly paradise would not have done, whether I thought the Council would give him a grant for looking after the place, and I told him I imagined they would not, knowing as I do into what extremely small pieces his executors have torn Pearse's will.

While I made my notes – for such a 'children's burial ground' might well be the site of a forgotten Early Christian church, or even some spot of prehistoric sanctity – and puzzled out by means of the field-walls where we were in the spider's web of lines on my old Ordnance Survey map, we discoursed of other wonders. I asked if there was a holy well on the island, and after some thought he said that there was not, but that there was a well about which there was a doubt as to whether it was holy or not. He offered to show me two strange marks on the rocks on the way to it; one, he said, looked like the print of a heel of a huge shoe, and the other like that of a great bird's foot. These sounded promising. Curious marks in the rock seem to be less common in granite Connemara than in the two limestone areas I had mapped, Aran and the Burren, in both of which I had trampled miles in searching out the imprints of the hoof of a mythical cow, of St Benan's foot, St Bridget's knees, St Ísleamán's hands, St Colmkill's fingers and even his ribs, as well as the marks left by an entire dinner service down to the pepper and salt whisked away through the air from a king's banquet by St Colman. In those two wonderful regions where neither the aboriginal rock nor the ancient lore is much obscured by later deposits, it seems that every irregularity underfoot has both a scientific cause and a legendary one, but when I pestered the geologists for more details of the formation of these 'solution hollows' it appeared that although they had been classified according to various discordant schemes they had not been fully understood, and that the geological system of explanation was hardly less dubious than the hagiographical one. Nevertheless such oddities were for me something more than the faintly comic after-images of the wondering mediaeval vision of the world that still persists in such places and that I find so sympathetic, for at such spots two modes of understanding intersect, giving as it were an accurate fix on a point of reality, which therefore could become a reference-point of my own intuitive surveying.

But today I was to be disappointed. The first of the two marks the islander had to show me, the heel-print, in a stone of a field-wall near his house, appeared to be natural, but I could add nothing to his description of it and he had no legend to account for it. The second, the bird's footmark, was in a sheet of bare rock at the highest point of the island, and I could tell him it was the bench-mark which the old surveyors carved on points the heights of which were given on the map – and that here we were therefore exactly so many feet above sea-level. But for my purposes a secondhand trig-point would not do.

The dubiously holy well was in a field largely of bare rock not far away, and as soon as I saw it I knew how the doubt had arisen, and that it would play a part in my own mysterious triangulations even if it would not appear on my finished map. Many of the holy wells of the west of Ireland are not true springs but mere hollows in the rock that hold a little rainwater, sometimes through such long droughty periods that it is easy to share the old folks' belief that they never run dry. Now only a few days earlier on another island I had seen such a well, dedicated to St Ann, which was a perfectly triangular hole just a few inches across. The granite of this region is cut through by long slanting fissures that run in various directions, and there three such planes, happening to intersect just below ground-level, had left a tetrahedral piece of stone isolated between them to be plucked out by the glaciers that scoured the region during the Ice Ages, or dissolved away by trickling rainwater in subsequent millennia. The puddle we were now looking at was another, rather larger triangle, and just as it had immediately appealed to me as being custom-built by Nature for my personal system of co-ordinates, it must always have seemed to the old folk of the island to relate to the St Ann's well which they would have visited, and therefore to bear some significance, which in this case it appears had never become explicit, for there were none of the usual accumulation of little objects – pebbles for counting the 'rounds' of prayer, coins, holy medallions, teacup-shards, horseshoe nails – that mark a well at which wishes are efficacious, and the young man had no qualms about letting his dog drink from it. And although I am acquiring a reputation in these countrysides for my devotion to the cult of blessed wells, I did not feel I could pronounce on the genuineness of this one, precious though it would be to me.

By the time the islander had finished naming for me all the inlets and headlands visible from this height, the state of the tide was on my mind. I said goodbye and thanked him, and walked on down to have a quick look at a cluster of roofless cottages on a steep slope above a little bay. The overgrown kitchen gardens and lanes around them trapped me in brambles and ambushed me with tottering walls, and it took me so long to work my way through them and around the coast to the beginning of the Road of the Islands that I felt I should hurry. Then the three islets flustered me with clifflets and pockets of bog, and in the end I went so far astray on territory disputed between marshland and seabed that I began to imagine that the final causeway to the mainland must already have been submerged, and that I would have to bellow until someone launched a boat to fetch me off. But then the causeway came in sight, a broad firm path still well above the waters, with the look of one saying calmly, 'You could have taken another hour, or half an hour at least,' or even, reproachfully, 'By hurrying you risked something more than being stuck on an islet for a few hours. You might have blotted the ironies of your meeting with today's Connemara man, or even mislaid one of the co-ordinates of your dream.'

3

The View from Errisbeg

In my face, the Atlantic wind, bringing walls of rain, low ceilings of cloud, dazzling windows of sunshine, the endless transformation scenes of the far west. Underfoot, dark crystalline stone, one of the many summits of a dragon-backed hill, the last, beyond which the land tails off into a bleak peninsula, clusters of foaming rocks and a lonely lighthouse. And spread below, to the north, a bewildering topography of lakes lost in bogs, across which scarcely less comprehensible maps of cloud-shadow race inland, towards mountain ranges. Eastwards, a wrinkled golden spread half unravelled by the sea, dotted with the tiny white rectangles of human habitation; off this, to the south, islands, the nearer ones gold too, those on the horizon grey-blue; finally, closing the south-east, another land, of hills the colour of distance itself.

The hill is Errisbeg, which shelters the little fishing-village of Roundstone from the west wind, in Connemara; the portion of the world's surface visible from its summit comprises the suite of landscapes grouped around Galway Bay which it has been my wonderful and wearying privilege to explore in detail over the last fifteen years, the Burren uplands in County Clare, the Aran Islands, and Connemara itself. Most recently I have been enquiring out the names of those lakes that lie on the dark plain below like fragments of a mirror flung down and shattered. The elderly men who used to herd sheep, fish for brown trout or shoot the white-fronted Greenland goose out in that labyrinth can recall about two dozen of the names of the larger lakes, and there are a similar number whose names I am beginning to despair of, not to mention countless little ones, all within an area of about thirty square miles. One is called Loch Beithinis, birch-island lake; for while the lakes themselves are often hard to find among the slight undulations of the bog, the wind-shaped domes of the dense little woods on their islands are visible from greater distances. Crows nest in most of these islands, and the occasional merlin; some are heronries, and the trees of one have been reduced to skeletons by the droppings of generations of cormorants. The vegetation of these ungrazed patches suggests that but for the omnipresent sheep at least the better-drained parts of the low-lying blanket boglands would be covered with a forest of sessile oak, holly, yew, birch and willow. As elsewhere, it is human activity that determines the texture of what appears at first glance to be untouched wilderness, a fact that complicates the conservationist case somewhat. However, this area, which is becoming known as Roundstone Bog, having been spared by forestry and commercial turf-cutting so far, should most certainly be preserved as it is; apart from its ecological uniqueness, it harbours one of the rarest of resources, solitude.

One road winds across this bog, along which the traveller can enjoy a sky undivided by wires. I can just make it out from Errisbeg, clambering around the knoll called Na Creaga Móra, the big crags, famous in botanical literature as the station of a heather, Mackay's Heath, discovered here by the self-taught Roundstone botanist William McCalla in 1835, and otherwise only known from Donegal and Oviedo in Spain. The other rare heathers of Roundstone Bog are the Dorset Heath, of which half a dozen tussocks here constitute the entire Irish population, and the Mediterranean Heath, which grows in the streaming valleys of Errisbeg's northeast flank, and in Mayo, and is otherwise restricted to Spain and Portugal. It is the warm breath of the Atlantic that fosters such southern exotics in this almost tundra-like terrain.

Following that road with my eye, I see it disappear north-westwards, where the Protestant spire and the Catholic spire of Clifden show above low hills, the western decrescendo of a symphony of mountains all along the skyline. Due north of me, the Twelve Bens huddle like sheep; there are in fact eleven summits of between 1700 and 2000 feet in height, with names like Binn Bhán, white peak, and one which is not a peak but a massive lump, called Meacanacht, probably from an obsolete Irish word meaning a lumpy thing. While the sharper tops are of quartzite, a rock resistant to weathering and inhospitable to vegetation, Meacanacht is of kinder stuff, a schist that breaks down into clayey soil; its southern face is green, and rare alpines lurk on its north-facing precipices. Farther east and separated from the Bens by the majestic Inagh Valley are the Mám Tuirc mountains, a line of peaks forming the boundary between Connemara proper and its eastern province, the Joyce Country. Mám Tuirc itself, the pass of the boar, towards the northern end of the range, is hidden from me by the Bens, but I can make out the broad saddle of Mám Éan, the pass of birds, near the southern end, where the ancient Celts used to celebrate the festival of Lughnasa at the beginning of harvest-time. Later this site was Christianized, and legend brings St Patrick there to bless the lands west of it from that vantage point. For the Pattern Day festivities that succeeded to Lughnasa, Connemara and the Joyce Country would meet there, to pray, to drink poitín, to enjoy a blackthorn-stick fight. A few years ago the clergy imposed the alien rite of the Stations of the Cross on Mám Éan, but even while the priest is conducting the ceremony folk faithful to the old ways still clamber into St Patrick's Bed, a hollow of the steep hillside only a few feet away from the new marble altar, and turn round seven times, sunwise.

Although the clustered Bens and the oblique line of the Mám Tuirc peaks look unrelated when one clambers among them, their essential unity is clear in this view from Errisbeg. They are the remains of one great ridge running from east to west, which dates from the Caledonian period of mountain building some 450 million years ago, when two of the plates that make up the earth's surface were slowly driving against one another, the resultant crumpling being the origin of the mountains of Scandinavia, 'Caledonia, stern and wild' itself, the northern half of Ireland, and Newfoundland. A sandstone of even earlier date was pinched in the interior of a giant fold here, and recrystallized under immense pressure to produce the unyielding quartzite of the Connemara peaks. Clay and limestone materials caught up into the outer layers of the fold were metamorphosed into the softer schists and marble that have worn down since then to form the lower land south of the mountains, the corresponding but narrower valleys north of them, and the broad north-south corridor of the Inagh Valley. The blackish crags of Errisbeg itself are of gabbro, a dense basic rock that came up molten from the earth's mantle some tens of millions of years before the Caledonian convulsions. The lovely cone of Cashel Hill rising from the head of the bay east of Roundstone is of the same rock, and there are a few similar dark hills north of the Bens, including Dúchruach, the 'black stack', that lowers over the wooded valley and lake of Kylemore, a sympathetic backdrop for the nineteenth-century gothic fantasy of Kylemore Castle. Thus there are dark hills both north and south of the pale quartzite mountains, preserving the approximate symmetry of Connemara about its east-west axis.

The Ice Ages, starting about one and a half million years ago and perhaps not all past yet, have carved up all these variously resistant rocks into the welter of forms that meet the eye today, excavating the valleys between the mountain ranges and the great fiord of Killary Harbour that divides Connemara from the Mayo uplands to the north. Some of the material removed by the glaciers was dumped when they melted back, in the form of the low rounded hills of boulder and clay called drumlins by geographers. These isolated hills, usually of green, arable land, contrast vividly with the dark level bogs on which they are stranded, and they all have individual names. In western Connemara such a hill is an *imleach*, perhaps from their rather sharply defined rims (*imeall*, a rim). From Errisbeg I can identify several of them, including Imleach na Beithe, the drumlin of the birch, and Imleach Caorach, sheep-drumlin, near Ballyconneely to my west.

So, one prehistoric collision of continents, a few hundred million years of erosion, and my almost equally drastic geological oversimplifications, suffice to explain the look of things to the north of Errisbeg. But this tousled fringe of Connemara to the east of me – can any generalization hold it together? Immediately below is Roundstone Bay, most of which is occupied by an island, Inis Ní, which is not quite an island since there is a causeway and a bridge leading into it, and even before that was built people could walk into it over the seaweed-covered rocks when the tide was out – though, on the other hand, very high tides still overrun its lower parts and make three islands out of Inis Ní. And Roundstone Bay is only a side-issue of Cuan na Beirtrí Buí, the bay of the yellow oyster-bank, which goes on to divide again, facing the incoming salmon with a choice between the outlet of the famous Ballynahinch River fishery on the west and Cashel Bay on the east, which delivers them into the Gowla River and the hands of the Zetland Hotel's guests. Beyond this dilemma is a broad headland with the ancient name of Iorras Aintheach, the stormy peninsula; it carries the villages of Carna and Cill Chiaráin, and to the south spawns various islands, some isolated and deserted since a generation or two ago, others linked to the mainland by causeways and still populated, others exactly halfway between these two conditions, being accessible at low tide and occasionally reoccupied by the last of their former inhabitants, who gather winkles round their shores or take cattle out to graze their sandy wind-eroded pastures. A little farther out is the most precious stone of all this stony littoral, the bare low dome of St Macdara's Island, with its minute oratory dating back almost to the age of the hermits who sought out such inaccessible retreats all around the coasts of Connemara. Eastwards again, more ramifying bays, with islands strung together by causeways or proliferating out into the waters of Galway Bay itself, delighting and defying the map-maker.

All this topographical extravaganza has been carved out of granite, which was intruded into the pre-existent rocks a little over 400 million years ago, at the end of the Caledonian mountain-building period. It is criss-crossed with joints and faults, which the sea has exploited to bite off archipelagos and prize open the creeks that traverse it in all directions. Without these seaways, as I will show, it would be as sparsely inhabited as the boglands and mountains farther inland, whereas in fact it is the most densely peopled region of Connemara. But in spite of the cottages and bungalows strung out along its web of roads and boreens, this is an intimidating landscape, of glinting pinkish or golden-brown rock-sheets polished by the Ice Ages and strewn with glacial boulders, interspersed with tiny saucer-shaped tillage plots of black waterlogged soil, and interrupted everywhere by dark stony or muddy shores on which high tides pile unbelievable masses of yellow seaweed. This growth of knotted wrack or yellow-weed as it is called locally is one of the factors that has made life possible on the acidic granite, for large amounts of it were harvested, both for fertilizing the land and for burning to kelp, the main source of industrial alkalies in the eighteenth and of iodine in the nineteenth century; it was the money paid out by the agent of a Scottish kelp-firm resident in Cashel that kept hundreds of families just above starvation level in the 1880s. Even today one can see rafts of weeds being towed into quays all round that intricate coast, for sale to a factory in Cill Chiaráin as a source of the alginates used in thickening agents for foods, paints and cosmetics.

Another resource of this apparently unfavoured coast was its covering of bog, which had developed on the impervious granite as it had on the metamorphic rocks inland. That covering is almost entirely stripped away now, through generations of cutting of the turf that was shipped out of hundreds of little harbours to be burned in Galway city or on the other side of Galway Bay where there is no peat covering the rocks. But to develop this theme of the strange process by which the bareness of one landscape made another bare, I must now look south, to those islands that lie like clean steel blades along the horizon, so utterly different from the rusty twistings of south Connemara.

Seeing the three Aran Islands from Errisbeg, wrapped in their mist-coloured cloaks of monkish remoteness and simplicity, it is hard to credit that fifteen hundred people live out there, manning an up-to-date trawler fleet, profiting from tourism, and farming those obdurately stony little fields reclaimed from the bare crags. As I watch, a line of light seeping under the islands from the bright horizon seems to be easing them free of even what tenuous relationship to mainland realities the sea can mediate, and floating them back to the time when *Ára na Naomh*, Aran of the Saints, was a source of inspiration to the monasteries of western Europe. The tall cliffs of Árainn or Inishmore, the largest of the islands, are turned away from the mainland to the south-western Atlantic spaces; remembering the many days I spent exploring them, I feel the thunder of the billows in their recesses and hear the fierce clamour of a peregrine falcon sweeping along their sheer faces. And beyond the islands is the Burren, with its flower-strewn hills rising in sweeping terraces to breezy plateaux, cross-hatched by four thousand years of wall-building! Marvels beyond description! I turn again to geology, mother of earth-sciences, for some unifying approach to them.

The essential oneness of the three islands and the Burren is clearly discernible from Errisbeg; the islands are built of a number of thick, horizontal layers of rock that correspond to those of the Burren and have evidently been separated from it by long-acting agencies that have otherwise not disrupted their strata. Whereas the visual turmoil of Connemara is a memory-trace of the mountains' travail, those sober levels to the south are the petrified after-image of a long-departed sea. A hundred million years after the Caledonian events, this area lay under a subtropical ocean, the waters of which pullulated with shelled creatures, from dot-sized foraminifera to brachiopods as big as saucers. Their remains, piling up together with the corals of the sea-bed for countless generations and compressed into limestone under their own weight, eventually totalled a thickness of over half a mile. Earth movements evidently changed the depths of those Carboniferous period seas from time to time, as there are thin strata of shale, formed from the mud of shallow coastal waters, between the strata of limestone, and even beds of clay, showing that the surface occasionally rose above the water long enough for a soil to form, only to be submerged again. Eventually, some 270 million years ago, a final upward heave abolished that sea, and since then climates ranging from the tropical to the glacial, and the surges of the modern Atlantic, have been eating away at the limestone, leaving the three islands and the dissected plateau of the Burren, which are even now being reduced in level by half a millimetre or so every year through the solvent action of the rain.

Subsequent movements of the earth's crust, perhaps connected with the opening up of the Atlantic Ocean, have exerted lateral forces on the limestone beds, fracturing them in a system of vertical cracks of astonishing regularity, the major ones running south-south-westwards, the minor set at right-angles to them. Flowing rainwater has enlarged these into fissures of all widths up to two feet or so, subdividing the rock outcrops into rectangular slabs, or, where they are very close-set, a rubble of small blocks. So the surface, with whatever shallow soil it carries, is extremely efficiently drained. But while the limestone is vulnerable to rain, the shale and clay bands are more impermeable. On a hillside it is the limestone exposed between two of these bands that will be removed first, while that overlain by the bands will persist longer, so the hillside is eaten away into great steps; such at least is one scenario that has been proposed to account for the terraced formation of the Aran Islands and the higher regions of the Burren. Therefore the clay and shale is exposed all along the feet of the steep scarps or low cliffs that run across the hillsides, and the rain-water that sinks through the creviced limestone layers and is then conducted sideways by the impervious shale bubbles out in springs at the foot of these cliffs, washing the shale or clay out with it to add a little soil to the attractions of these particular levels. Even from Errisbeg I can see how the lines of white dots, the cottages and bungalows along Aran's roads, follow the terraces, keeping their heads down below the ridge-line that shelters them from the prevailing south-westerlies.

As neighbours, the Aran Islands have come to be closely relat-ed in culture to south Connemara; most importantly, both speak Irish, and indeed between them they carry most of the language's hopes for the future. But ecologically and archaeologically Aran belongs to the Burren, limestone being the determining factor. Nearly all the Burren's famous flora is shared with the islands; the mountain avens is absent from Aran but most of its other alpine or northern species such as the spring gentian are present, while the roseroot (in Connemara exceedingly rare and found only on certain cliffs near the mountain-tops) flourishes on some exposed areas of crag right down to sea-level. There are plants peculiar to Aran too. In the wind- and rabbit-mown sward of the highest clifftops one can find the purple milk vetch, recorded nowhere else in Ireland and which is perhaps a relict of the tundra vegetation of immedi-ately post-glacial times. And since modern agriculture can hardly enter Aran's tiny fields, some weeds still occur that have been exterminated almost everywhere else; I have even found the penny-cress, whose transparent disc-shaped capsules used to delight children of previous generations in many rural areas.

Despite such multicoloured mitigations, though, much of Aran is a desolation of bare stone, like the Burren. But in both places the sheer number of prehistoric monuments shows that this cannot always have been the case. For instance in the islands there are five megalithic tombs of the type known from their shape as wedge tombs and usually dated to the Late Neolithic or Early Bronze Age. Then there are no fewer than seven great stone cashels, including the promontory fort of Dúchathair and Ireland's most spectacular prehistoric site, Dún Aonghasa, whose three roughly concentric semicircular ramparts abut onto the edge of a dizzy cliff above the Atlantic, and which is visible in silhouette even from Errisbeg. Both these forts have arrays of set stones before them, an apparently defensive feature that suggests, by analogy with similar cases in Iberia, an Early Iron Age date. The dozens of stone huts or *clocháin* and scores of stony mounds that could well be ruined huts, suggest that the Early Christian period here was settled and prosperous. In mediaeval times the O'Briens, the dominant force in Munster, had three tower-houses on the islands (which they lost to the O'Flahertys of Connemara in the 1550s). The O'Briens also added a Franciscan friary to the already venerable monasteries of Árainn. The record of settlement in the Burren is similarly continuous, and recent studies in environmental archaeology (such as the analysis of soil material from beneath ancient walls and tombs) is tending to reinforce the impression that the limestone lands remained fertile and productive long after bog had begun to form elsewhere, and that their present bareness is not so primordial as it looks.

The story in Connemara is intriguingly different. Here, early cultures left abundant traces, but then the trail almost peters out. Middens of seashells, looking much like those in the Dingle peninsula now thought to be of Late Mesolithic or Early Neolithic date, occur on several of Connemara's shores. Just below Errisbeg, for instance, the sandy spit between the back-to-back beaches of Dog's Bay and Port na Feadóige (the bay of the plover) was evidently a resort of those early food-gatherers, for in the eroded dune-faces one can see blackish layers full of bones, winkleshells and the heat-shattered stones of hearths. And whereas only a few years ago the received opinion was that Connemara has little to offer the archae-ologist apart from a small number of megaliths in the north-west, a spate of recent discoveries has shown that in the Neolithic and Bronze Ages the valleys giving onto the bays of Streamstown and Ballynakill were almost as populous as the Burren. This Atlantic coastal area was then, as it still is, the most prosperous part of Connemara, because of its deposits of glacial till and scattered out-crops of metamorphosed limestone. Some of these finds have been revealed by turf-cutting, and close to many of them one can make out the walls of fields that predate the growth of the bogs. It was perhaps the arsonist clearance methods of these early farmers, coinciding with a climatic change from a warmer, drier post-glacial period to the cool, wet times we still enjoy today, that proved too much for the great forests that formerly covered the land and whose roots can be seen in the bottoms of the turf-banks.

However, the evidence for later settlement is more scattered and ambiguous. There are about a dozen promontory forts, stone cashels and earthen raths, nearly all on or near the western coast, none of them comparable with the great forts of Aran. More characteristic of the region is the widely scattered score or so of crannogs (cashel-like lake-dwellings on wholly or partly artificial islands). Perhaps there were unenclosed forms of settlement too, that have left little trace, or perhaps the onset of bog development was already concentrating life on the teeming trout-lakes south of the Bens. In any case, it is as if Connemara had become a quieter place, when the Burren and Aran were humming with energy. After the Iron Age, settlement seems to confine itself to the coast. The monks of the island hermitages and seashore communities were notoriously averse to neighbours – tradition repeatedly tells of them departing out of hearing of one another's bells – so the ragged periphery of a deserted Connemara must have suited them well. The seven tower-houses (chiefly of the O'Flahertys) were all on the coast, with the exception of one centrally placed on the lake-island of Ballynahinch, and as far apart as could well be. The bogs, by sealing off the interior, had deprived the coast of its supportive hinterland, and vast tracts of central Connemara remain virtually desolate to this day. But while Connemara was wrapping itself in bog, the Burren and Aran remained hospitable throughout, until continuous millenia of intensive farming reduced them to naked rock, perhaps as recently as the Middle Ages. The difference between limestone on the one hand and metamorphic or igneous rocks on the other has been a dominant factor in this divergence of the fate of these two lands throughout the rainy centuries of the Atlantic regime: limestone drinks water, granite hoards it.

But then came a strange reversal of fortunes. Since at least the seventeenth century the only source of fuel for the limestone side of Galway Bay has been the peat covering the granite side, and throughout the centuries of Ireland's huge population growth every niche of the south Connemara coastline sheltered a tiny harbour exporting the region's turf to Galway, to Kinvara, to some little landing-stage corresponding to each village of the Aran

Islands and the Burren coast. The nineteenth century was the hey-
day of the Galway hookers, the tar-black wooden workboats with
their famous tannin-brown sails, capacious bellies and lines honed
by generations of experience of lee Atlantic shores. In 1836 there
were just over three hundred sailboats working out of harbours
from Roundstone to Ros a' Mhíl, engaged in fishing, general
trading, and the carriage of turf; the seaways of south Connemara
were brimming with activity. Even today elderly Aran Islanders
look back nostalgically to the beautiful sight of the approach of the
turfboats bringing their winter warmth. Many other goods crossed
the bay in the hookers too: Aran potatoes in payment for turf,
poitín from Connemara, limestone itself brought back as ballast in
the empty boats and burned in kilns on the seashore for lime to
whiten the houses and sweeten the land of Connemara. Cattle
from the mainland used to be taken across to winter on the
islands, where they fared better on the dry crags than in the
sodden rushy fields of home. On the other hand the Aran farmer
used his (Connemara) pony mainly in the winter for carrying
fodder to the cattle out on the 'back of the island', and for carting
seaweed to the fields as fertilizer or to the stacks for kelp-making;
in the summer when grass and water were short he could send it
back to its native hillsides. Invisible goods were carried in the turfboats too: stories, songs, love even, mixing the folklore and the
gene-pools of granite-country and limestone-land. As two different
metals dipped in acid can power a voltaic cell, so all this life-force
was generated by the differences between granite and limestone, in
the common medium of scarcity.

But it was a precarious symbiosis, as the view from Errisbeg
reminds me. Just across Roundstone Bay I see a cluster of roofless
walls on a desolate promontory: Rosroe, An Ros Rua, the reddish
peninsula. 'Rua' is a common placename element here, and the
reddishness is that of poor, bracken-infested, land, of nitrogen-
deficient vegetation. Rosroe depended entirely on its turf trade,
and got its potatoes in Aran rather than plant them at home; so,
according to local oral history, it 'went down' in 1845, the first
year of the Great Famine, while other villages survived longer. In
those years many Connemara people fled to Aran, lived in little
caves of the inland cliffs and worked for their keep, until the
bailiffs drove them out; for it is said that Aran, with its better soil,

its degree of insulation from potato blight, and its variety of sea-food sources, lost nobody through hunger, while in south Connemara in particular the famine grave in the thicket or among the stones of the foreshore is a constant if obscure element of local geography. And as the recurrent years of 'distress' settled into the chronic misery of the 'Congested Districts' of the turn of the century, the winning of turf proceeded with ever greater desperation; by the late nineteenth century the outer parts of the south Connemara archipelago known simply as Na hOileáin, the islands, had not even fuel for themselves, and the stoniness of the limestone lands had been brought back like an infection to An Cheathrú Rua, the 'reddish quarter', and the other peninsulas pointing out to Aran like ever bonier fingers.

It is a dreadful story that is legible in the hard face of south Connemara, but it has a brave footnote, with which I will close; a brown sail in the bay below brings it to mind. The working life of the hookers dwindled to an end only as recently as the 1960s, though by then most of them were mouldering away in obscure creeks, irrelevant to the age of lorries, which had rendered the old seaways of Connemara obsolete, and of the various fuels that were reducing turf to a historical curiosity. But since then there has been a remarkable revival of interest in these fine boats; several have been prised out of the mud and restored, and a new generation of boat-builders is recalling almost lost traditions of craftsmanship. All summer long the hookers, one or two centenarians among them, sail from regatta to regatta around Connemara, with visits to Cill Rónáin, and, the high point of their season, to Kinvara for Cruinniú na mBád, the 'gathering of the boats'. This movement, which might seem to be of merely specialist interest, is one of the psychologically most important developments of recent years in these communities, putting the wisdom of the old side by side with the energy of the young, and undoing that dire equation spelled out by Synge between hateful poverty and all the old graces of Connemara life.

4

Crossing the Pass

Seen from the Aran Islands, from Galway city or from Kinvara, the Burren imposes itself as an entity; its battered walls, rising steeply from the waters of the Atlantic or Galway Bay, or from the stony plain of Gort, which is almost as low and level as the sea itself, admit no doubt as to where it begins. Ambiguity creeps in only from the south, with the gentle rise of the shale-and-bog country and its irregular cessation, revealing the limestone strata underlying it; hence towns like Lisdoonvarna and even Lahinch can quibble their way into the region. But the word *boireann* means a rock, or a place composed of rocks, and to be true to ancient intention one should confine the name to the limestone region, with the reluctant inclusion of the shale-capped back of Slieve Elva, which runs into it from the south and rises just a little higher than the rest of its hills.

However, once one is within the Burren, this geological prescription is not enough to guarantee a sense of its unity. The region is a plateau sundered by valleys, some of which open onto the sea and others close in on themselves, and its heights are all so close to the thousand-foot mark that none offers a panorama of the whole. In my initial explorations I felt that the place was out-manoeuvring me, that wherever I penetrated, it withdrew and lurked elsewhere. But then, one still, sunlit, autumn day (a day, it turned out, that had come down through hundreds, perhaps thousands, of years) I was privileged to hear the vast, slow heartbeat of this place of rock. I had been visiting the ruins of Corcomroe Abbey, where in the early thirteenth century the Cistercians had coaxed the stones of the Burren into conformity with the spirit of Gothic Europe, and I was walking back to the farmhouse I was staying in at Lough Rask near Ballyvaughan. As I climbed the pass from Turlough, a herd of cattle was being urged up the rugged track ahead of me; the cries of men and barks of dogs rang to and fro between the bare hillsides. At the saddlepoint their way diverged from mine and wound on up into the heights. I paused to let the afternoon achieve its perfection, and felt the wholeness of the Burren like a fruit mellowing on the branch.

I learned later that this was one of the two dates upon which the Burren year hinges, for it is the uplands that provide 'winter-age' to graze the cattle on, while in summer they are kept near the houses in the lowlands, where they are more easily watered and their calves tended. It was a pattern I was familiar with from the Aran Islands, though there the seasonal movement between the crags and the little patches of improved land around the houses is of smaller compass. Perhaps it was the Celts, whose unit of wealth was the heifer and whose stonework is everywhere in the Burren, who initiated this alternation between upland and lowland pastures, or rather the particular form of the custom that marks this region. For what I saw that day was the exact opposite of the ancient practice once general in western Ireland.

The two seasons of the Celtic year were articulated by the movement of cattle and their attendants between winter quarters in permanent lowland settlements and the mountain pastures habitable only in summer. In Connemara, for example, the O'Flaherty chieftains and their retinue took up residence in temporary dwellings every May, and this custom of 'booleying' (from *buaile*, a milking-pasture) persisted among the peasantry until late in the last century, it being the womenfolk who spent the milking and buttermaking season in little huts of stones and sods on the hillsides while the men attended to the tillage, fishing and kelp-burning below. But the Burren is different. A spell of hot weather that would make the Connemara hills delightful will reduce the Burren's uplands of thirsty limestone to waterless deserts; conversely in winter when Connemara's hillsides are streaming quagmires, the Burren's are relatively dry underfoot, and the Burren farmer can take advantage of the residual Gulf Stream mildness that plays around his land, and leave his cattle out of doors.

Of course the visitor who drives into the region past its northern hillsides, which from a distance look like the flanks of giant salmon closely armoured with silvery-grey scales, or from the south along roads that cross square miles of the bare rock-sheets so aptly called 'pavement', must wonder how any human or animal could survive on what such a terrain has to offer, winter or summer. But as it happens the harder, purer limestones that take on such a hostile polish occur mainly on the lower and intermediate levels, and so make a disproportionate contribution to one's first impressions, while the upper strata are of a dolomitic limestone, richer in magnesia, and break down into a light soil supporting a nutritious vegetation. Also, even the barest-looking areas have pockets of lush grazing here and there around the springs and seepages at the feet of the scarps that run across the hillsides.

This pass that, crossed with a time-hallowed day, gave me a hint of the specificity of the Burren, is called Mám Chatha, the pass of battle, for history has penetrated it, as I shall tell. A walk that winds through it will supply themes enough for this brief evocation of a region that exceeds it in all dimensions. I begin at Turlough, the village south-east of it, and end at Lough Rask, to the north-west.

A *turlach* is a hollow in which a lake comes and goes, not fed by streams but filling and emptying from below through openings in its bed as the general level of groundwater held in the fissured rock fluctuates in sympathy with the rainfall. Since the phenomenon is almost unknown outside the limestone region of western Ireland, the Irish term has been adopted generally, anglicized as 'turlough' on the natural but mistaken assumption that the second syllable has something to do with *loch*, a lake. The village is named from a fine example of a turlough, and there is another just northwest of it; between them they exhibit most of the strange features of this unusual landform.

Since different plants can tolerate different degrees and frequencies of immersion, the flora of a turlough is arranged in zones that follow the contours of the hollow. Where a turlough is surrounded by hazel scrub the diminutive forest will stop short around its rim as neatly as if trimmed by a landscape gardener, and its inner face will be embellished with flowers of hawthorn, rowan and guelder rose. Slightly lower comes a contour line of a blackish moss with the musical name of *Cinclidotus fontaniloides*, which is diagnostic of periodic flooding. The grassy bowl within is usually well grazed and rich in flowering herbs; the common sorts of violet are replaced at the lower levels by the pallid *Viola persici-folia*, a rarity in Ireland, where it is almost restricted to this specialized station in life. In the centre, pondweeds grow in the muddy dregs around the natural drainholes.

Sometimes in summer one finds that the empty bowl of a turlough is sheeted in what looks like whitish blotting-paper laid over the vegetation; I remember being baffled by the phenomenon when I came across it for the first time in the Aran Islands. It is made up of the matted and bleached remains of microscopic algae, which have multiplied countlessly in sun-warmed water and then been left high and dry when the turlough emptied. Algal paper, as it is called, can appear with mysterious suddenness; in Germany, where it has been recorded only about a dozen times, it is called meteor paper, as people imagined it had fallen from the sky.

A bare limestone landscape without surface streams, in which the drainage is subterranean, is termed a karst, from the name of such a region in Yugoslavia. The Burren is a karst that has been worked over by glaciation; the bowls of these turloughs are depressions that have been gouged out by the glaciers, or are formed in deposits of glacial drift. Other karstic and glacio-karstic features of the Burren can be seen on the hillsides around Mám Chatha, such as, to the east of the pass, a row of steep conical pits which were once swallow-holes of some long-vanished stream, and a ravine formed by the collapse of a cavern excavated by water flowing underground. These impressive works of water date from a time when the shale strata that still overlie the limestone farther south were much more extensive than they are today, for erosion is slowly stripping them away. A stream running off the impervious shale will be acid with bog-water, and on reaching the limestone will soon (*i.e.* over many hundreds of years) dissolve itself out a swallow-hole by eating away at the fissures and enlarging them; the rest of its journey to the sea will be underground, with perhaps some reappearances in turloughs and springs. As the area covered by shale contracts, the stream will abandon its first swallow-hole and punch through another one closer to the retreating boundary of the shale; one can see the process at work today around the margins of Slieve Elva (and it is because of their creative implication with the limestone topography that one must include such shale areas in the region to be thought of as the Burren). This is the location of the famous potholes and caves of the Burren, which the wet-suited experts can follow for, in one case, over eight miles. Their latest discovery has been of a section of dry cave near Doolin, which can only be entered through an opening on the sea-bed and a quarter of a mile of submarine passage; the river that formed this system must have been flowing when sea-level was much lower than it is now, perhaps at the end of the last Ice Age. For the family party on a Sunday outing there is Aillwee Cave south of Ballyvaughan, farther west along the ridge from Mám Chatha; here one can stroll through over quarter of a mile of tortuous caverns, sprigged with tastefully illuminated stalactites.

Just east of the summit of the pass are the scars of old opencast mining of fluorspar, the glossy purple crystals of which can still be turned up in the spoil. Fluorspar is formed out of calcite (the pure white and crystalline form of calcium carbonate) by the action of hot fluorine gas, and the fact that at one time there were such fumes rising through the fissures here is part of the evidence for the existence of granite deep down under the limestone. In fact it seems that the Burren is underlain by an extension of the granite that is exposed on the north side of Galway Bay. Perhaps it was because of this solid basement that the limestone strata were so little disrupted by the Hercynian uplift, some 270 million years ago, that left them as a plateau with just a slight southwards inclination. Only at the two ends of the upland area is there substantial folding or faulting; the giant steps with which the last hillside of Árainn descends into the sea are slightly warped and cleft by little rift valleys, while the terraced sides of Mullach Mór, a hill in the south-east of the Burren, are so curved as to make it look like a layer-cake that has sunk in the cooking.

But it is on the nature of what is immediately underfoot, the broken stone of such hillsides as these around Mám Chatha, that the Burren's paradoxical fame for barrenness and floral luxuriance is grounded. The limestone offers plants some very specialized habitats, of which two form a strikingly complementary pair. Down in the grykes, as the enlarged fissures are called, all is shadowy, still and dank; ferns such as the hart's-tongue and maidenhair thrive in this atmosphere from a Victorian bottle-garden. But the horizontal surfaces (the clints) between the grykes are dry and brilliantly sunlit, exposed to strong winds and searchingly grazed by cattle, goats and rabbits. Wherever a thimbleful of humus has accumulated some plant will root, of a sort adapted to these spartan conditions rather than to, say, the hurly-burly of a buttercup-meadow. Thus, close to the maidenhair fern, which is a plant of the mild, Atlantic side of southern Europe, one finds here species associated with severe sub-arctic or alpine climates, such as those two stars of the late May Burren show, the vivid blue spring gentian and the delicate, ivory-silk-petalled mountain avens. A profusion of the usual lime-loving plants, notably thyme, various saxifrages, eyebrights and orchids, occur on all but the barest surfaces; even the most uncomfortable-looking rubble puts forth woodsage and the lovely burnet rose. Right next to these one finds plants such as heathers that prefer more acidic conditions colonizing deeper, better-drained pockets of soil from which the high rainfall has leached out the lime. Sheltered slopes of neglected land carry dense hazel scrub, and it is worth fighting one's way through its outworks of bramble to see the miniature forest glades, dim, green, bewitched by moss and lichen, where wood-anemones flower virginally in the spring and the rarer broad-leaved helleborine more sophisticatedly in high summer. It is easy – but sometimes rewarding – to get bewildered and go wrong by 360 degrees, in such viewless thickets. When I was exploring around the turloughs described above, in the course of making my map of the Burren, I got lost in the hazel, and decided to work my way up slope to climb out of it. After an hour or so of disentangling myself from endlessly intricate snares, I emerged high on the hillside south of Mám Chatha at a point that would no doubt very seldom see a human being. There, something stirred in a bush ahead; I froze, and after a few minutes a badger came out to root and snuffle about in the rough grass. It took no notice of me as I stepped lightly after it, stopping when it did and waiting for it to move on, as if I were walking a wheezy lapdog in a park. When I went round ahead, it came within a yard of my toecaps before backing off with a throaty hiss of surprise, but then carried on foraging as before. Eventually I had to tear myself away from the occasion – and just a hundred yards farther up the hill found a grove of tall flowers that I did not immediately recognize; they were in bud, and I unrolled one enough to glimpse yellow within: *Meconopsis*, the Welsh poppy, never recorded in the so zealously botanized Burren before, and miles from any possibility of being a garden escapee. That was one of my best crossings of those hills; I flew down to Lough Rask as if winged with delight, and later I commemorated both encounters on my map, with a just detectably four-footed emblem of the animal, and the Latin name of the plant, secreted among my penwork clints and grykes.

On another crossing of the same hills, I was groping my way down in torrential rain to Mám Chatha from the south when I came across an ancient stone-walled enclosure about a hundred yards across, which was not marked on the Ordnance Survey maps nor mentioned in the almost exhaustive one-man survey of the Burren 'forts' conducted by the Clare archaeologist T.J. Westropp in the 1900s. It consisted of a very dilapidated and irregular semi-circular arc of wall springing from the face of a steep scarp crossing the slope just above the saddlepoint of the pass. Whether its purpose had been military, watching over the pass, or peaceable, for the coralling of cattle at a half-way stage of their seasonal migrations, I could not tell. It is only one (but a very large and unusual one) among hundreds of walled enclosures, some of them magnificently situated and visible from afar, others so degraded and enmeshed with more recent fences that it takes a trained eye to distinguish them from the fields around them.

The majority of the three or four hundred ringforts in the Burren are roughly circular and often about twenty yards across, with simply built drystone walls a few feet thick, and they served as cattle yards around small huts, the individual farms of Iron Age and Early Christian times. But a number of them are more imposing, with walls up to five or six yards thick, rising in two or three terrace-like steps inside; a few of them still retain their lintelled doorways. Some are surrounded by one or two outer ramparts, while Baile Cinn Mhargaidh near Kilfenora has an abattis of set, slanting stones around it like the two cliff-forts of Aran. Despite such forbidding externals these great cashels may not have been built with warfare in mind; their outworks may have reflected communal prestige; their interior terraces, it has been suggested, are better adapted to viewing ceremonials within than repelling the foe without. Perhaps such monuments served various purposes, sacred and profane – but since the Celts who built them could not confide their intentions to writing, less is known about the cashels of the Burren than about the pyramids of Egypt. Cathair Mhaol, the 'low-topped (*i.e.* dilapidated) fort', at the foot of the slope just west of Mám Chatha, is typical of these almost anonymous ruins. Like so many others it is deeply obscured by thickets; to fight one's way through them, groping to and fro until one can stretch out a hand to the mighty masonry, is to experience the past in all its difficulty of access and indubitable reality: here was the pride of some well set-up community, and it lies overthrown among thorns.

But it is not just individual monuments, the scores of cashels and hundreds of lesser ringforts, that lie waiting attention in the Burren; there are webs of ancient field-walls, large tracts of the agrarian landscape from which such monuments drew their suste-nance, a stone document of the life of that Late Iron Age and Early Christian period, still legible despite all the layers of over-writing. And interwoven with that message there are earlier ones, from the Bronze Age and the Neolithic, smudged and torn but not indecipherable. Not one of the Burren's sixty or so wedge tombs has been investigated, but the famous 'dolmen' at Poulnabrone, a portal tomb with a huge and rakishly poised capstone, which has had the misfortune to be adopted as a touristic mascot of the region and featured in a thousand vapid come-ons, has been exca-vated and turns out be five hundred or a thousand years older than had been thought, dating from the Middle rather than the Late Neolithic. Modern archaeological techniques could well over-turn all current assumptions about the course of settlement in the Burren, but the prospect of anything more than a cursory survey of the monuments of this, one of the world's richest and most complex prehistoric landscapes, are fading for lack of funds.

However, since the Burren has scarcely been picked over by

the professionals the amateur has every chance of making worth-while discoveries, or at least of bringing to the notice of academia what has long been known to the locals. Coming down from Mám Chatha once, I stopped to poke around two grassy mounds, each by a spring. Unable to make anything of their outward appearance I kicked a bit of turf off one and pulled out a small stone; it crumbled in my hand, and had evidently been in a fire. A farmer I met farther down the slope told me that these mounds were *fulachta fia*, the cooking-places traditionally attributed to Fionn Mac Cumhaill's warrior band. On looking up the subject later on I learned that such mounds of burned stone are common field-monuments in many parts of Ireland, that they are usually horseshoe- or kidney-shaped (as these are), with traces of a wooden trough in the indentation of the perimeter; the water in the trough was brought to the boil for the cooking of meat by dropping heated stones into it, and periodically the debris of shattered stone would have to be dredged out and flung aside, so building up the characteristic heap around the site. When I mentioned these particular cooking-sites to an archaeologist I was told that, no, the Burren was not *fulacht* country; although a few had been discovered recently near Kilnaboy where the Burren merges into the lakelands south of it, in general they were features of wet lowlands east of the Shannon, and not to be expected on limestone hills. However, having learned to recognize them I noted several more in the north of the Burren, and a geologist who was working along the spring-lines for his own purposes began to record them almost throughout, wherever water surfaces. The only Burren *fulacht* to have been studied properly is close to a turlough south of Carran; it was found to date from the later Bronze Age, about three thousand years ago.

All this interwoven Burren lifeworld of ruined cultures and exuberant nature is uniquely beautiful and interesting, but not very profitable for the landowner, who naturally is tempted by the availability of EEC grants to have his hillsides sprayed with fertilizers by helicopter, the result being a more mundane but productive farmland, at least in the short run. The financial, legal and moral persuasions necessary to preserve the Burren from such 'improvement' have not yet been discovered. In too many places, I observe, the land-clearing bulldozer is busy, steered by ignorance and fuelled by greed.

Finally I come down to Lough Rask itself, a lake that is responsive to the tides although it is a quarter of a mile inland, and which occasionally shows itself to be a turlough by disappearing into its own muds. Herons nest in the tall trees around it, and bee orchids flower on its banks. It is a beautiful place, but its legend is horrific. In 1317, when two chieftains of the O'Briens were vying for supremacy in what is now County Clare, one of them, Donough, passed the lake with his army on their way to the fateful battle of Corcomroe. They saw a loathsome hag washing a heap of severed limbs and heads in the lake (the description of her in the mediaeval account of this campaign, *The Triumphs of Turlough*, is one of the foulest passages of literature I have come across); she told Donough that her name was Brónach Boirne, the sorrowful one of Burren, that the limbs were those of his army if he pressed on to this battle, and that his own head was in the middle of the heap. They tried to seize her, but she flew up and hovered above, spewing curses on them. But Donough told his men that she was the demon-lover of his rival Dermot and was seeking to discourage them; so they marched on (through Mám Chatha, the placename suggests), accompanied by wolves and ravens, and by nightfall most of them were dead and laid out in the abbey of Corcomroe. The battle was not without consequence, for having consolidated his power Dermot went on to defeat de Clare, the Norman lord of Bunratty Castle, in the following year, and it was another two hundred years before the region ceased to be under Gaelic rule.

Passes are impressed upon the physical landscape by great forces of nature – in this case the glaciers of the Ice Ages. Subsequently, history follows these ways of least resistance and scores them into the cultural landscape of lore and placename. In one's own mental map of a region it is the weight of significance they are made to bear that incises the passes so deeply. Mám Chatha stands in my mind for two complementary rites of passage: the indefinitely repeated seasonal transit of cattle between upland and lowland, and the crossing of a threshold between prophecy and the reality of death upon a particular day in history. Tracking the past and present of this landscape through Mam Chatha, I meet 'the sorrowful one of Burren', and it is under her shadow that I think of its future. For Brónach Boirne is not just a ban-shee, the time-serving otherworldly retainer of a local dynasty; she is the reapparition of the Celtic divinity of the territory, a night-mare to the usurper, a vision of beauty and fruitfulness to the one who cherishes it. Should she make herself visible to our exploita-tive generation it might well be as the evil prophetess of doom. Indeed our heads could be in the middle of the heap – for if we cannot save such a place as the Burren from spoliation, there is nowhere safe on the surface of the earth.

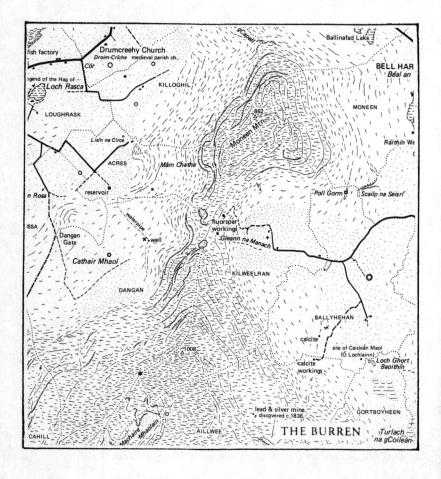

5

Space, Time and Connemara

Connemara – the name drifts across the mind like cloud shadows on a mountainside, or expands and fades like circles on a lake after a trout has risen. Fittingly, there is no official boundary to the land under the spell of this name. It is also true that real landscapes, unlike painted ones, contain their frames, so that each is potentially world-embracing. But such a name as this cannot be left to dissipate its powers of evocation like a scent unstoppered; the topographer, rather, should delight in its sparing, subtle and elusive application.

On the one hand, a modern and commercializing tendency is to call everything west of Galway, Connemara. But the territory so defined is best called, in modern Irish, Iarchonnacht, for it is that described, with the bitter exactitude of regret, by Roderic O'Flaherty's *West or H-Iar Connaught*, written in 1684, not long after his clan had been dispossessed by the Cromwellians. His book traces its bounds from Lough Corrib to Slyne Head to Killary Harbour (and embraces the Aran Islands 'as in a sea-parenthesis', to borrow his pleasing phrase). On this classic definition, Iarchonnacht includes Connemara, but exceeds it eastwards.

On the other hand, the territory of the O'Flahertys' early mediaeval predecessors the Conmaicne Mara (which is the historical kernel of Connemara, both place and name) is too restrictive, for it lay west of the Mám Tuirc watershed and the Inbhear Mór, the 'big rivermouth' near Ros Muc, and so did not contain the full essence of Connemara, a prime ingredient of which is given by the Irish-speaking granite-and-waterlands further east and south. This last area, though, is culturally continuous with Cois Fharraige further east again, and aspires to unity of social action with it under the name of Conamara Theas or South Connemara. Ó

Bhearna go Carna, from Bearna to Carna, is the phrase favoured by Gaeilgeoirí to delimit this linguistic homeland – but most Bearna people would direct you back westwards if you enquired for Connemara there, being close enough to Galway city to share its sense of Connemara as wilderness and westernness itself.

The problem, then, is exemplary, and insoluble. Place flows into place, or holds rigidly distinct from it, according to one's mode of thought. My mode, to declare it at the outset, is that of the discriminating earth-worshipper. For me, Connemara is the land that looks upon the Twelve Bens, that close-knit, mandala-like mountain range, as its stubborn and reclusive heart.

Connemara has had a degree of independent existence for about 460 million years, according to recent theories. Before that time the landmasses and ocean basins, carried on the slowly drifting plates that constitute the earth's surface, lay in configurations quite different from today's. The Atlantic did not yet exist, and an ocean the geologists call Japetus separated two continents, one comprising what was to become North America and the north-west fringe of Europe, and the other, the rest of Europe. The future Ireland was as yet in two pieces, half of it on the north side of the Japetus ocean basin, and the other half on the south. What one might call proto-Connemara lay on the coast of the northern half, 200 miles or more west of what is now Donegal. Its rocks had largely been laid down as sediments of various sorts 200 to 100 million years earlier in the Dalradian (Late Cambrian) period, during the birth of Japetus; subsequently a three-mile-thick layer of the basic rock, gabbro, coming up molten from deep in the earth's mantle, had been forced between its strata. As the two continents now moved towards each other, squeezing Japetus out of geography, the rim of the northern one was crumpled into long ridges, the eroded remains of which are today's 'Caledonide' mountains, that is, those of Norway, Scotland, the north of Ireland, Newfoundland and Appalachia. In this upheaval proto-Connemara's rocks were repeatedly folded, faulted and thrust to and fro, until it became completely detached and was driven eastwards by the oblique collision of the two landmasses. As the two halves of Ireland were finally rammed together, proto-Connemara was slid southwards over volcanic rocks of the southern shore of Japetus, and welded into its present position.

By then Connemara's rocks had been kneaded and baked to various degrees. A thick sandstone layer, pinched inside a complex fold running east-west across the region, was recrystallised into a quartzite of great hardness; clayey materials that ended up on the outside of the fold were metamorphosed into less resistant schists, while strata of ancient limestone were transformed into marble. Erosive aeons later, the quartzite stands high, giving us the silvery, glittering peaks of the Twelve Bens and the Mám Tuirc mountains; the softer schists have been worn down to form the lowlands south of the mountains, the narrower transverse valleys north of them, and the broad corridor of the Inagh valley separating the two massifs. Connemara's famous green marble crops out here and there along the southern flank of the mountain ranges. The dark-toned hills of Cashel and Errisbeg to the south, Dúchruach and Currywongaun to the north, are forged out of the contorted layer of gabbro. In the final stages of the collision, 400 million years ago, several great domes of molten granite were intruded from below; when exposed by erosion of the rocks above them, they proved vulnerable to weathering, and now form the knobbly sea-invaded plain of south Connemara, and low-lying islands such as Omey on the west coast. In one small area known to geologists as the Delaney Dome, north-west of Errisbeg, all the original substance of Connemara has been worn away so that the underlying floor appears as through a hole in a carpet, and one can stand on rock that formed the land south of Japetus.

A few great fault-lines roughly delineate the Connemara of this essay. An east-west trending fault lies off-shore to the south, blanketed by the carboniferous limestone from which the Aran Islands and the Burren have been carved. To the north the mountains of Connemara are separated from those of Mayo by the dramatic fiord of Killary Harbour, excavated by glaciers in the recent Ice Ages out of a zone of sedimentary rocks weakened by another fault. The Maam Valley, to the north-east, has been similarly enlarged by fault-guided erosion. Finally a less obvious feature, the Shannawona fault, running from near Scríb southwards across the granite regions, may explain the striking difference between Cois Fharraige to the east, with its uplands descending in orderly slopes to a straight sea-coast, and the fantastic filigree of peninsulas and inlets west of Ros a' Mhíl: the latter region has been downthrown by over a mile relative to the former, and the more fractured upper levels of the granite brought within the erosive influence of the sea, in which they now lie half-drowned.

During the last Ice Age the snow, piling up on the shadowed lee-side of the mountain peaks, congealed into glaciers; inching downhill, plucking stone out of the slopes behind them and so excavating corries, these glaciers contributed themselves and their load of rock to a sea of ice grinding outwards over the lowlands and stripping them of their covering soils. When the ice finally melted back, from 15,000 to 10,000 years ago, a raw landscape was revealed of polished rock strewn with countless smooth-worn stones of all sizes. The south is particularly burdened with huge boulders, some of which are individually named landmarks today, one of the largest being forty feet high. In certain areas just south of the mountains, and further west, the glacial debris was moulded by the ice flow into the streamlined mounds called drumlins; these now stand out on the brown levels of the bogs as isolated, grass-green hills, or on the western shores as islets and promontories with cliffs of boulder-studded clay.

In due course a tundra growth of least willow, soon followed by dwarf birch and crowberry heath, crept forth across this waste-land, to be followed as times mellowed by woods of birch and hazel, and then great forests of oak and pine. It seems to have been human agencies – fire and the stone axe – that put an end to these woodlands, around 2500-2200 BC, perhaps in conjunction with a deterioration in the climate. Heathers, sedges, bog asphodel and sphagnum moss flourished, forming a blanket bog that spread and deepened, creeping down from the exposed hillsides, seeping out from waterlogged hollows, drowning the forest, pickling its roots and fallen trunks in bogwater. Now, when the accumulated layers of peat are cut away for fuel, ghostly grey armies of tree stumps come to light.

For how many tides have Connemara folk gathered shellfish on the strand? It may be that some of the scattered heaps of whelk-, limpet- and oystershells, laid bare wherever dunes are eroding, date like similar shell-middens in the Dingle peninsula from the Middle Stone Age, 6500 years or more ago. These first stranders would also have gathered nuts and berries in the forest margins, and stalked the network of rivers and lakes after wildfowl and fish.

(Their stone implements have been found at Oughterard recently, but not so far in Connemara proper.) It may have been another 500 years before settled farming began. In one place that 'Neolithic Revolution' has been dated with astonishing precision, thanks to the fact that Connemara's mildly acidic lake sediments and peat bogs preserve any pollen incorporated in them and so keep a diary of changes in the flora of the vicinity. A core was taken out of the bed of a little lake in Sheeauns near Cleggan in 1987, and the organic residues at various levels in it dated by the radiocarbon method. By analysis of its pollen content, the following sequence of events was reconstructed. Unbroken forest of oak and hazel surrounded the lake until about 4100 BC, when small clearings were made in which wheat was sown and weeds such as plantains sprang up. A hundred years later this forest lost its few elms; in fact the elm was in decline all over Europe at that time, perhaps because of a fungal epidemic like today's Dutch Elm Disease, spread by growing human traffic. At a level in the core corresponding to shortly after this elm-decline of 4000 BC, tree-pollens are largely replaced by those of grasses and meadow flowers; the forest had been almost totally removed and tillage superceded by cattle-ranching. Finally, in about 3800 BC, the lake was deserted, and forest returned. Whether agriculture continued elsewhere nearby, having merely shifted its location, is unknown, pending further research, but it seems that the shores of Lough Sheeauns lay in wilderness until the end of the Bronze Age, almost two thousand years later.

These pioneer farmers thought much about death. Successive (or perhaps contemporaneous) groups of them disagreed on the matter and set their differences down (illegibly, alas, to us) in the various styles of communal tombs, built of weighty rock-slabs, that are their lasting memorials. About thirty of these megalithic tombs are known from Connemara; twenty-one of these have been identified only in the last few years, along with a spate of other discoveries that have totally undone the received idea that the region is archaeologically a virtual desert. These lapidary but opaque statements in their ruin still cause dissension. I have seen seminars of archaeologists arguing fiercely among such heaps of tumbled stones, like would-be heirs over a garbled will. An established school of thought has evolved a fourfold classification of these monuments into passage tombs, court tombs, portal tombs and wedge tombs. The first type, best known from the stupendous round tumuli of the Boyne Valley, does not occur in Connemara. In the others, the roofed chamber or chambers in which the burials and grave-goods were placed constitute a roughly rectangular gallery, covered by an elongated cairn which is usually now much reduced. Court tombs have an open, crescentic forecourt defined by upright stones at one end of this cairn, presumably for ritual purposes. In the closely-related portal tombs, the chamber is roofed by an often gigantic capstone, poised on two tall jamb-like pillar stones in front and a smaller stone behind. Wedge tombs are so called because their lintel-roofed galleries are lower and narrower at the rear than at the front, which usually faces west. Each of the four types has its own distribution pattern, its cultural affinities and presumed origins in the wider megalithic scene of western Europe, and its allotted hour in a hypothetical account of the evolution of the Irish Neolithic. A residue of the incomprehensibly dilapidated or unaccountably odd is relegated to a non-category of 'unclassified megalithic tombs'. But here in Connemara, the rebellious younger archaeologists point out, court, portal and wedge tombs crop up apparently ecumenically, while over a third of the total, including some impressive and moderately well-preserved examples, are numbered among the despised and neglected unclassifiables. So these discoveries are further backing for those crying 'Down with the fourfold theory! Let us have a new Neolithic, of which the cornerstones will be those rejected by our elders.' It is likely that this emergent theory will assign a much earlier date to the wedge tombs than their present niche at the very end of the Neolithic, and will emphasize regional and independent developments in tomb-style.

Nearly all these tombs lie close to the long sea-inlets of Omey and Ballynakill parishes; this north-western area, with its comparatively widespread marble outcrops and glacial deposits, was then as it is now the most fertile and prosperous quarter of Connemara. And the distribution of monuments presumed to date from the Bronze Age – mainly standing-stones, single, in pairs or in alignments of up to six – is very similar. The impressive alignment on the crest of a drumlin near Renvyle has long been known, and sufficient finds have been made recently to establish north-west

Connemara as comparable with south-west Munster and mid-Ulster, the principal foci of the distribution of such monuments. Elsewhere in Connemara the most striking example is an alignment of six small boulders on the ridge of a moraine in Gleann Eidhneach, which I came across in 1986. Several of these new sites have been revealed by turf-cuttings; and to see the pair of milk-white quartz boulders newly exposed in the black trench of a turf bank on a hilltop in Crocknaraw, north of Clifden, and to realize that at least half-a-dozen other standing-stones and several other megaliths are or were visible from that point, is to be given a glimpse of a cultural landscape the meaning of which has been lost beneath the bogs.

In many parts of Ireland the most typical monuments of the pagan Iron Age and Early Christian periods, the so-called 'ring-forts', are very numerous; but in Connemara they are strangely rare. The three dry-stone cashels and two earth-banked raths of north Connemara, the two earthen promontory forts on peninsulas of the west coast and the fragmentary stone ones in Inishbofin, probably represent Iron-Age militarism. The twenty or more cran-nógs or lake-dwellings that have been identified with some cer-tainty in the western and southern lowlands of Connemara may be the local equivalent of small ringforts, the circular stockyards around the isolated huts of Iron Age or Early Christian farmers. Perhaps the growth of bog, overwhelming the hillside pastures, forced the evolution of a lake-culture, or of unenclosed shoreline settlements now marked only by great shell-middens. Certainly Connemara was far from deserted at this period, which pollen-records from various sites show to have been a time of increase in cereal crops and their weeds.

However, it seems that the pattern of a populated coastal fringe and an empty interior, which largely obtains today, was established by the early Middle Ages. Connemara's radiating peninsulas and its islets broadcast in the ocean must have answered to the misan-thropy of the sixth century, when every hermit wanted a desert to himself. Some of the many religious sites on the rim of Connemara are named from figures who seem at home in pure legend, like the fisherman's saint, Macdara, also known as Síothnach, a name that perhaps associates him with squalls of wind, as do several folktales told of his powers. Other foundations are attributed to personages who appear convincingly in history, such as St Colman, who retired to Inishbofin after losing the argument between the Irish and the Roman Church over the true date of Easter at the Synod of Whitby in AD 665 (thus initiating the sequence of Celtic causes in retreat to Connemara, which continues to the present day, and of which he should be the patron saint).

The roofless late mediaeval chapel and ancient graveyard, still in use, that mark the location of St Colman's monastery, are idyllically sited in a valley-mouth on the sheltered side of Inishbofin, between a reed-fringed lake and a sandy beach. St Macdara's islet, on the other hand, is of elemental simplicity, a low dome of bare granite on which a tiny stone-roofed oratory, the structure of which imitates that of primitive cruck-built wooden chapels, sits as sedately as a winkle on a rock. For the celebrations of the saint's day, 16 July, the fishing-boats of the nearest harbours of south Connemara bring hundreds of people to his island, but for the rest of the year its wind-polished silence and mica-glinting emptiness are perfect luxury to the ascetic soul. But the sea-sanctuary best suited to more turbulent spirits is that of High Island, two miles out into the Atlantic from the west coast of Connemara. It is only accessible on calm days when a boat can edge into a narrow cove at a point where its tall cliffs are climbable, and an Early Christian cross-slab rises from the wind-strimmed sward above. The remains of a little chapel and the monks' corbelled stone huts cluster within a slight cashel wall at the farther, western end of the island, as if to get full penitential advantage of storm-driven spray. The foundation is attributed to St Feichín, also associated with Cong and Omey Island, who is said to have died in AD 664. In recent years the island has belonged to Richard Murphy, who wrote some of his best poems out of his occasional days of retreat there.

Not long after the era of the saints, the Conmaicne Mara appear out of the shadows of prehistory as the secular rulers of the region. The Conmaicne were a people who claimed descent from Conmac, a son of the legendary Fergus Macraoi and Queen Maeve; the branch of them who lived west of the Corrib were known as the Conmaicne Mara, the Conmaicne of the sea, to distinguish them from their cousins further east. The Ó Cadhlas were their leaders; the Annals of Inishfallen mention a Murtagh Ó

Cadhla, chief of the Conmaicne Mara, among those who fell fighting the Norsemen at Clontarf in 1014. Later they were reduced to
historical footnotes by the coming of the O'Flahertys, but their
name (anglicized as Keeley) still occurs in Connemara.

The O'Flahertys, a powerful clan who had given several kings
to the province of Connacht in the seventh century, held the rich
limestone plains east of Lough Corrib until the thirteenth century,
when the de Burgos, the first of the Normans to move so far west,
gradually forced them to retire to Connemara. With the O'Flahertys came dependent clans whose names occur in local history:
the O'Hallorans, the O'Lees, the Duanes. The Joyces, a Welsh-
Norman family, settled in what became known as the Joyce
Country, around the Maam Valley, under the O'Flahertys' protection. By the sixteenth century the O'Flahertys were building tower-
houses on the Norman model, from which, if the oral traditions be
true, they tyrannized over humbler folk. The main stronghold of
the eastern branch of the O'Flahertys was at Aughnanure near
Oughterard. The western branch had castles spread out around the
coastline, at Ard (near Carna), Bunowen, Doon (near Streamstown)
and Renvyle, and inland at Ballynahinch on a former crannóg.
Small communities of Carmelites and Dominicans were established
by the O'Flahertys near this last-mentioned centre of power, from
which, under the Elizabethan dispensation, the old Conmaicne
Mara was renamed as the barony of Ballynahinch. Mere vestiges of
the Ard, Bunowen and Doon castles survive, while the lake-tower
at Ballynahinch has been much altered by subsequent owners to
serve variously as a prison, a brew-house and a picnic-bower. Thus
the best-preserved of the Connemara tower-houses is now Renvyle,
which has been neatly cross-sectioned by collapse, revealing its
simple structure of three square, vaulted rooms one above the
other, linked by spiral stairs in a corner.

The O'Flaherty chiefs ruled Connemara according to the
ancient Brehon Law until Elizabeth's wily soldier-statesmen, who
rarely ventured into the region, divided and seduced them. In
1585 they accepted the agreement known as the Composition of
Connacht, abrogating their Gaelic rights and enregistering themselves in the feudal hierarchy. Thenceforth they were hereditary
landlords rather than the elective custodians of clan territory, and
the chief the Crown wished to see as head of all could call himself

Sir Murrough O'Flaherty. Nevertheless to the notables of the growing merchant-city of Galway the O'Flahertys were still the atavistic lords of a hinterland rank with rebellion, smuggling and piracy. It took the fierce political and religious cross-currents induced in Ireland by England's Civil War to bring Galway's citizens and the O'Flahertys together even momentarily; that was in 1642 when Galway opted for the Catholic Confederation, then campaigning in the name of the King, and called in the O'Flahertys' hordes of 'wild Irish' to help besiege the nearby English fort, which was manned by supporters of Parliament. But King Charles lost the war and his head, and Cromwell came to purge Ireland of its rebelliousness. By July of 1651 one of his generals was encamped before the city of Galway and his ships were in the bay. Iarchonnacht, and especially Inishbofin, then became crucial to the Confederation's hopes of reinforcement from the continent. A small force of mercenaries sent by the Duke of Lorraine landed in Inishbofin in October with arms for Galway, but the city had to surrender, together with the Aran Islands, by April 1652. Towards the end of that year the Aran Islands were recaptured by a force of six or seven hundred men from Iarchonnacht and Inishbofin, but the Cromwellians moved several men-of-war and 1900 foot-soldiers, first against Aran and then against Inishbofin, which ended its forlorn resistance in February 1653.

A few years later the Commonwealth Council ordered the building of a fort in Inishbofin, and started to use the island as a prison-camp for Catholic priests, as an alternative to transporting them to the West Indies. The priests languished there (half-starved, on an allowance of twopence a day, according to a contemporary source) until well after the restoration of Charles II in 1660. After about 1680 the fort was abandoned. It was re-garrisoned by the Jacobites in the War of the Two Kings ten years later, but since then its history has been merely one of stealthy dilapidation. The cut limestone surrounds of its arches and windows have all been burnt for lime, but its curtain walls and the diamond-shaped bastions at each of its four corners still stand, in picturesque raggedness. Visitors sailing into Inishbofin pass under its dark gaze at the narrow harbour mouth, where it sprawls upon a low cliff with a menacing, crablike presence.

In the years following the victory of Cromwell's army the old clan system was finally broken up, and it is said that Connemara was almost depopulated by famine, plague and massacre. One of the O'Flaherty chiefs who had joined the Galway citizens in 1642, Colonel Edmond, of Renvyle, was wanted for murders committed in the course of a plundering expedition he and his men had undertaken as a relief from the tedium of besieging the English fort. A band of troopers was dispatched to Renvyle to find him and was eventually led by the clamouring of ravens to a small cave in a dark wood, whence they dragged the colonel and his wife:

> And truly who had seen them would have said they had rayther been ghosts than men, for pitifully looked they, pyned away from want of foode, and altogether ghastly with feare.

Colonel Edmond was hanged and the other O'Flahertys expropriated as 'forfeiting traitors' for their part in the rebellion. Soon Connemara was being carved up for distribution among Protestants to whom the Cromwellians had obligations and Catholics who had been dispossessed of estates elsewhere and transplanted westwards.

The main Protestant beneficiaries of England's reformation of Connemara were a Sir Thomas Merridith, one of Cromwell's commissioners, who acquired townlands here and there, including Ballynahinch, and soon cashed them in, and Trinity College, Dublin, who remained as landlords of much of the Inagh and Maam Valley areas until the end of the last century. Catholic transplanters included the Earl of Westmeath, who was given the Renvyle area but later regained his former lands and sold Renvyle to a branch of the Blakes of Galway, and the Geoghegans of Westmeath, who stayed on as landlords of Ballindoon parish until ruined by the Famine. Several of the eminent Catholic merchant families known as 'The Tribes of Galway' were granted tracts of wilderness in place of their Galway estates; the D'Arcys found themselves with the peninsulas of Omey parish and the glens of Kylemore, while the Blakes, Frenches and Lynches shared the granite of south Connemara with the Martins, who also acquired the Cleggan. Most of these grantees managed to avoid actually having to come to Connemara, and some regained parts of their old estates after the restoration of Charles II. The Martins, in the person of 'Nimble Dick' the lawyer, actually put together the largest estate in the kingdom and held on to it through the Williamite period despite their Catholicism, virtually succeeding the O'Flahertys as masters of Connemara.

Nimble Dick's great-grandson Richard (known as Hairtrigger Dick from his many duels) from time to time found it convenient to retire from cosmopolitan prodigality into the fastnesses of Connemara, where no bailiff dared pursue him. His father had made a modest house out of an inn he owned on the bridle-path by the lake at Ballynahinch, and from the 1790s this became the court of a mysterious kingdom, reports of which irritated the authorities and entranced the romantic. Its endlessly devious southern coastline by nature took the part of the innumerable local smugglers against the revenue cutter, and the Martins were known to entertain with the finest of wines and brandies. Its craggy glens sheltered bands of outlaws who had fled there from the yeomanry's vengeance upon Mayo after the French-led rebellion of 1798; among those with a price on their heads was the notorious Father Myles Prendergast, whose secret ministrations to his Catholic flock were winked at by the Martins for years, although they themselves like most landowning families were now Protestant. Richard's tenantry would march into Galway to vote for him in its famously turbulent elections; their number was greatly augmented by the refugees from anti-Catholic pogroms in Antrim he welcomed onto his estates in 1796. After the Act of Union in 1801 he was Galway's representative at Westminster, where he won another nickname, Humanity Dick, for his bill against cruelty to animals; at home, tenants who beat their donkeys could find themselves imprisoned in the old tower-house on the lake-isle of Ballynahinch. It is said that when his friend the Prince Regent boasted of the avenue at Windsor, Martin retorted that his own avenue was fifty miles long, being the road from Galway.

But his 200,000 acres were too poverty-stricken to fuel Humanity Dick's spacious capacity for life, and by the time he died, hiding in Boulogne from his creditors, the estate was heavily in debt. His son Thomas, known as the King of Connemara, resided more continuously at what was now called Ballynahinch Castle, and tried to salvage the family fortunes through a copper mine on High Island, marble quarries in the southern foothills of the Twelve Bens, and kelp-burning on the seaweed-rich shoreline. Contemporary accounts portray him as a benevolent and beloved despot, but local oral history retains less fond memories of him. Maria Edgeworth was one of the visitors drawn to Connemara by the Martin legend, and in 1833 she met at Ballynahinch his daughter Mary, 'one of the most extraordinary persons I ever saw'. This elegant and self-possessed young lady, who reminded Edgeworth of a Leonardo portrait, was prodigiously well read in half a dozen languages ancient and modern: 'Do think of a girl of seventeen, in the wilds of Connemara, intimately acquainted with the beauties of Aeschylus and Euripides, and having them as part of her daily thoughts.' Indeed Miss Martin seems to have been all the imagination could require, as the Miranda of these poetic and yet slightly comic realms. She had studied engineering (at the age of thirteen or fourteen!) with the great Alexander Nimmo, then engaged in laying out the roads of Connemara, while from a former Napoleonic officer in exile at Ballynahinch she had acquired a knowledge of fortification, a passionate Bonapartism, and a barracks-room turn to her French. While showing the Edgeworth party the marble quarries, she was attended by a spontaneous aggregation of rustics which she referred to as her 'tail'; when the visitors commented on her ability to communicate with these people, she calmly replied, '*Je sais mon métier de reine.*' A rather sugary version of this engaging heroine figures in Charles Lever's novel *The Martins of Cro'Martin*; a more bitter memory of her was handed down by the local people whom, it is claimed, she forbade to use the ancient burial ground near the Castle because their noisy lamentations disturbed her. The pathetic fate of the Princess of Connemara will be mentioned below.

In the early years of the nineteenth century the idea that Connemara could be civilized and made profitable persuaded others of the old Galway families to come and live on their estates. In about 1814 John D'Arcy projected a market-town and harbour at a spot called An Clochán, the stepping-stones, by the principal rivermouth of the western shore, and began by building himself a Gothic castle and a grotto. Between 1822, when the government engineer Alexander Nimmo undertook both the harbour and the road from Galway to the new town, and D'Arcy's death in 1839, a Protestant and a Catholic church, 185 dwellings, most of them three-storeyed, two hotels, three schools, a police barracks, court-house, gaol, distillery and twenty-three public houses had accrued to its basic triangle of wide, unpaved streets. The population had grown to 1100, and An Clochán had been 'fashionably anglicized' as Clifden. Merchant vessels were bringing in a wide range of necessities never felt as such before; corn, fish, kelp and marble were being shipped out, and this place formerly 'only remarkable for smuggling and illicit distillation' was now yielding considerable excise duties. Daniel O'Connell's 'Monster Meeting' at Clifden in 1843, when he spoke on Repeal of the Act of Union to a crowd said to number 100,000, may be taken as marking the coming-of-age of the capital Connemara had so long lacked.

While D'Arcy was beginning this transformation of his estate, the Blakes similarly were interesting themselves in something more than the rents of Renvyle, of which they had been absentee land-lords since 1680. The O'Flahertys, former lords of the land, having hung on as middlemen there for generations, found them-selves dismissed into still deeper obscurity when Henry Blake was inspired by the potentialities of a newly discovered slate bed nearby to take over their long thatched cabin, give it a slate roof, and install his family in residence. Like most formerly Catholic landowners the Blakes had by then adopted Protestantism and the ideology of progress. The family's *Letters from the Irish Highlands*, published anonymously in 1825, are full of concern for the welfare of their periodically starving tenantry and evince some interest in their culture; nevertheless the little Catholic chapel the O'Flahertys had built near the house was self-evidently objection-able and had to be removed. (In one of the letters describing the ensuing rumpus, Henry Blake states that it was within a hundred yards of the house, whereas in fact it was four hundred yards away; the uncharacteristic inaccuracy perhaps betrays an uneasy conscience about the matter.) Another branch of the Blakes of Galway had moved out onto their estates in south-east Connemara by this period and became the Blakes of Tully. Enlightened trav-ellers on the coast road from Galway would notice a change in the landscape as they approached 'the seat of Mr Blake, whose improvements and clearances give an agreeable repose to the eye, wearied with the interminable succession of rock, boulder-stones, cabins and loose stone enclosures'. The obverse of such commendations is the ogreish role these Blakes play in local folklore, as the best-hated of all evictors and rackrenters.

Alexander Nimmo, having provided Connemara with a rational road-network and planned the piers that were started at Leenaun, Cleggan, Roundstone and other points as relief-work during the 'distress' of 1822, was himself nursing a private project during this optimistic period. At Roundstone, he states in his Coast Survey of 1836,

> ... as the tenant of the farm on which this pier is situated was very clamourous for damages alleged to be sustained by him during the progress of the work, I ventured at my own expense to purchase up his interest in the lease, as the most likely way to settle his claim; I now hold it by lease under Mr Thomas Martin, and expect soon to have a tol-erable fishing village; several people are already settled there, and I am building a store for the purposes of the fishery.

The street Nimmo created there passes above the little cliff that forms the inner wall of his characteristically boldly conceived harbour, and then climbs a hill to admire the much-painted prospect of the Twelve Bens across Roundstone Bay; we owe to him the handsomest of Connemara's villages, the decisiveness of its layout only superficially obscured by modern developments.

These crowded years of progress were tragically terminated by the Great Hunger of 1845-8, a natural disaster which a grossly malformed society could not mitigate. The peasant population of Connemara, much reduced by the want and pestilence of the 1650s, had been augmented by the Cromwellian resettlements, and by refugees from Antrim in 1796 and Mayo in 1798. The biologi-cal rate of multiplication, upon this expanding base, was phenome-nal. Population was rising generally in Europe throughout these two centuries, but in few places was the rise so steep as in the poorest parts of western Ireland. Even the periodic famines caused by dependence on one crop, the potato, liable to fail for various reasons, did not check the giddy compilation of short generations. The Connemara gentry, having long conformed to the Protestant church under the pressure of the penal laws that made it impossi-ble for Catholics to pass on their estates undivided, were now almost as distinct in culture from their tenantry as were the

Anglo-Irish elsewhere. The master of the Big House, being at once landlord, employer, Justice of the Peace and fount of charity, was unchallengeable. His worthy upkeep was provided for by rents that absorbed all the output of his tenants' farming, fishing, kelp-burning and cottage industry, for happily the lower orders could live off their amazingly productive potato-beds alone; their teeming marriage-beds, on the other hand, threatened to overwhelm all estate-improvement schemes, and had to be countered by eviction and assisted emigration. The shading and colouring lent by individual cases to this schematic figure of class-relationships faded into insignificance when the potato blight struck. At that time most Connemara people owned nothing (literally nothing, many of them; no cart or donkey, no boat or net, no chair, lamp or bed); when their sole foodstuff turned to black slime, they became paupers overnight. The limited capacities of the British government, civil service and public to respond to, or even conceive of, the cumulative horrors of the next few years in Ireland were soon exhausted. By the autumn of 1847, in Connemara, the public road-works upon which the stonebreaker could earn the price of a bowl of Indian meal had been closed down, overwhelmed by the crush of desperate applicants; the Clifden workhouse was bankrupt and had voided its hundreds of feverous skeletons to live or die in the open; ragged hordes were creeping into Galway to face the long nightmare of the Atlantic; what happened in the mountain valleys and the islands is recorded only by small boulders marking name-less graves.

At this juncture it was revealed to the rector of Wonston in England that the Lord had chastised the Irish with a view to making them 'come out from Rome', and that in Connemara in particular there was a potential winning of broken and contrite hearts not to be despised. The Reverend Alexander Dallas set up his Irish Church Mission wherever he had the backing of the Protestant gentry; soup was provided for children attending his schools; some hungry souls 'converted', and were damned for it by their parish priests; little colonies of outcasts grew up in the shadow of the rectories, and for three decades, until the venture lost conviction and faded away, the spiritual education of Connemara was the mutual abuse of bigots. One area in the north-west, Letterfrack, was for a time spared this and other post-

Famine plagues through the work of a Quaker couple, James and Mary Ellis, who in 1848 were moved to settle there, to demonstrate by personal example how resident landowners could and should stand between their tenantry and the gales of misfortune. Neighbouring gentry grumbled at their paying labourers eightpence rather than sixpence a day, but the Ellis's farm and its well-serviced estate village prospered while all Connemara was in decline. Sadly, after nine years of struggle, James's ill-health and the death of his wife led him to sell out to a supporter of the Reverend Dallas, and return to England.

In secular matters too, Connemara's agony appeared as opportunity to some English eyes. The Poor Law Extension Act of 1847 had thriftily transferred the whole burden of famine relief onto the local rates, and such top-heavy estates as those of the Martins, the D'Arcys and the O'Neills (as the Geoghegans had renamed themselves) had capsized as a result; the Encumbered Estates Act of 1848 having removed certain legal obstacles, the creditors could now force on sales. The entail of the Martin estate had been broken by Thomas Martin in favour of his daughter, and when he was carried off (by a fever contracted in visiting his former tenants in Clifden workhouse), Mary and her newly wedded husband had fled the avalanche of debt, first to Belgium, and then to America, where she died in a New York hotel after a premature confinement on ship-board. The 192,000 acres of the Martins' former kingdom were put up for auction in 1849. The Bill of Sale stated that, since the drawing-up of the list of tenants, 'many changes advantageous to a Purchaser have taken place, and the same Tenants, by name and in number, will not now be found on the Lands'; but not even this sinister assurance was enough to attract bidders. The mortgagees, the Law Life Assurance Society of London, then bought in the estate very cheaply, and by rackrenting and evictions carried on the Famine's work until 1872, when they sold the lands, with a few small Mayo estates thrown in, for £230,000 to Richard Berridge, a London brewer.

The D'Arcy lands too had been mortgaged to English financiers, the Eyres of Bath, one of whom took over Clifden Castle as his summer residence when the estate fell into their hands. In 1862 the Blakes of Renvyle had to sell off the eastern half of their lands to the heir to a Manchester fortune, Mitchell Henry, who set about taming the wet mountain slopes and housing himself on a princely scale, employing hundreds on his model farm, extensive drainage schemes and the elegant Gothic mansion of Kylemore Castle. Other new proprietors in the relatively encouraging north-western quarter were residents and improvers too, and indeed it is as if an afterglow of the Ellis's Quaker sense of social responsibility has lingered there to this day.

But at the other extreme, in south Connemara, the granite itself was being stripped bare by the ever more desperate 'winning' of turf for sale to Galway city and the turfless limestone areas south of Galway Bay. Here the poorest of Connemara's poor were still mercilessly harried by the Blakes of Tully and the agents of absentee landlords, including the Berridges themselves, whom the increasingly menacing words and deeds of a no-longer acquiescent tenantry kept away from their new home at Ballynahinch. The Land League, originating in the equally miserable oppression of County Mayo, was beginning to organize resistance to evictions, and in the first days of 1881 a great hosting of tenants on the Kirwans' estate at An Cheathrú Rua drove off a server of eviction notices and his police escort. Although the Kirwans were still evicting there a decade later, such events as this 'Battle of Car-raroe' cumulatively extorted reductions in rent and improvements in security of tenure, and forced upon the government a sense that the moral and economic resources of landlordism were inadequate to the needs of these shameful western backyards of the kingdom. In 1891 the Congested Districts Board was set up to further the development of regions that could not in their present state support their populations, and in Connemara it found everything to be done. Over the next thirty years harbours were improved, small fishing fleets subsidized into precarious existence, herring-curing stations built, lace-making schools opened, and, slowly but inexorably, the landlords bought out, the jumbled small-holdings on their estates rationalized, and the labourer given his own field to labour at last.

This history, for so much of its course a river of sorrows, has flowed through and at times almost swept away a singular culture – not that of the provincial gentry, but of the humble farm- and fisherfolk – a culture which conserved ancient words and ways, and had its matted and tenacious roots in a sense, deeper than any economic or legal realities, of being in its own place. As the Irish language withdrew, throughout the century of famines and modernization, to its present lairs, principally in the south of the region, only a proportion of its oral lore was appropriated by English. But where Irish lives, that tradition is still so voluble in story, song and placename, that one wonders if Connemara's days and nights were longer formerly, to hear all that was said and sung in them of Connemara. Around the end of the last century that peasant culture came to represent the true Ireland to one wing of the nationalist movement; through Patrick Pearse, who regularly returned to Ros Muc as to a well of inspiration, its values entered into the veins of the republic he declared and died for in 1916, and works in them obscurely still. Since Independence the Gaeltacht (the areas officially designated as Irish-speaking) has been treated with varying small degrees of positive discrimination by the governments of the day, and successive generations of the dedicated, through Raidió na Gaeltachta, local co-operatives and other organizations, have insisted on Irish as a language of modern society and its arts. Despite compromises, defeats and disappointments, despite even the numbing effect of continued emigration, the stony south is now socially more vigorous than any other part of Connemara, apart from the historically and geographically favoured exception of Ballynakill in the north-west; the little turf-harbour of Ros a' Mhíl has become the county's major fishing port, and An Cheathrú Rua, with its industrial estates run by Údaras na Gaeltachta, the Gaeltacht Authority, is pulling itself together into a recognizable town.

Emigration, though, is the face in the windows of empty houses throughout Connemara. Youngsters go in search not only of work but the conviviality their depleted villages cannot provide. Grants from Údaras or the Industrial Development Authority help to plant occasional industrial projects in this generally unfavouring far-western ground; some survive and even flourish, while others disappear in a whiff of scandal. The traditional livelihoods of fishing and farming are still basic to Connemara. Many households, whether most of their income is from fishing or bed-and-breakfast or a factory, have a few young cattle in a few rushy fields, which they will sell on as two-year-olds to be fattened in the midlands' lusher pastures. Like cattle, sheep attract 'headage' grants; the shepherds drive their battered cars out along rough tracks and sweep the hillsides with binoculars to check how their black-faced ewes, badged with fluorescent paint, are surviving the gales, the rain and the foxes. There are Connemara ponies on the hills too, especially around Cashel and Roundstone, which will be exhibited and sold at the August show in Clifden. Most households have an allotted strip of bog from which to cut their yearly supply of turf, and in places turf is cut by machine on a commercial scale. Fishing from the smaller harbours, other than Ros a' Mhíl, is limited by the size of the boats; few of the trawlers are big enough to follow the winter shoals of herring once they have left the coast. Half-decked boats do the rounds of the lobster and shrimp pots and dredge for scallops in the bays, and in summer net the incoming salmon. Over the last ten years the rafts of mussel farms and the cages of salmon and sea-trout farms have multiplied, first in the sheltered inlets of the south coast, and now, as the engineering is developed, in more exposed positions. Carna and Na hOileáin in the south are suddenly earning comparatively good money from locally, nationally and internationally based fish-farming companies, while western villages like Roundstone have so far tended to resist the intrusion of alien technology into their pure waters. Most lucratively of all, if only for a few brief summer weeks, Connemara unites the harvest and harvest festival of tourism; restaurants and craftshops open, there are dances, deep-sea angling contests, horse races, pony shows and, best of all, the regattas to which the famous old brown-canvassed, tarry-hulled Galway hookers come sailing out of the past.

All that I have briefly told happened within view of the Twelve Bens, an elemental, constant, presence that would, if the status of the Earth had not been usurped, instil our daily ways with a certain thoughtfulness, like a great cathedral among busy streets. The free-flowing beauty of this landform has been more slighted by the material progress of the last forty years than by centuries of neglect; it is time to redress the balance. When in the 1950s the powerlines marched out across Connemara's vaporous spaces, their assertion that the remotest cottage was part of modern Europe did as much to maintain human presence there as the dole, but the landscape shrank under the lash. More recently rectangles of pine forest have reduced some of the finest mountain glens to banality, with little or no prospect of economic compensation – an ugly mistake, which should be undone by removing the worst examples and helping the blemished land tone back into harmony with the rest. Everywhere in Connemara there are potential conflicts over the sharing-out of its resources; the fertilizers and silt washing down streams from forestry plantations are inimical to famous salmon rivers, the traffic to and from new industries breaks down pleasant old roads and bridges, the fencing of sheep-ranges impedes the freedom of hill-walkers, the chemicals and detritus from fish-farming cages may threaten traditional shellfish beds. The present enthusiasm for mariculture could ebb, leaving a tide-mark of dereliction around Connemara's shores. Prospecting licences covering nearly all of Connemara have in the last few years been issued to Irish and international mining companies, who have scented gold, and the ruthless technologies needed to extract it from huge amounts of ore could be unleashed on our hillsides. A current proposal to site an airport in unspoiled country near Clifden focuses a contradiction between the facilitating of tourism and the conservation of what the tourists come for. Another much criticized development, the scattering of cottages and bungalows along the network of roads on the coastal plains, which appals the city visitor who misidentifies it as surburban sprawl, perhaps deserves more sympathetic understanding than it usually receives. As a new social form, much in need of aesthetic education but full of human potentialities, its evolution is traceable from the breakup of the estates, when their clusters of hovels were replaced by iso-lated cottages each on its own strip of land; now those households have moved down to the roadside and acquired cars, or emigrated and sold out to the holiday population that enlivens these areas for the brief summer but leaves them dark-windowed through the long winter.

All these difficulties of Connemara life can be mitigated, and perhaps the present work, that images the oneness of the place and projects the dimension of the past onto the surface of the present, may hint at the spirit in which modern life and its habitat could be reconciled. But there is much more at stake than the rational-ization of land-use, for Connemara is not just the sum of its resources; it stands aside from and ahead of our quarrelsome human purposes, being part of what we live for as well as what we

73

live by. It is in fact something difficult to speak of in our present condition of civilization. How can I indicate this Connemara, but as the edge of brightness that follows a cloud-shadow across the mountainside, or the stillness of a lake before the trout rises?

6

Interim Reports from Folding Landscapes

Although I have been making maps for a dozen years now, cartography, in the sense of a general desire and competence to make maps, remains alien to me. The maps I have so far undertaken cover all the land I can see from where I live, and are elaborated and externalized versions of the mental sketchmaps one makes to situate oneself, cognitively and emotionally, in a new locality. Since it was the disorientating nature of the place I had opted to live in that urged me to map it, I should begin this brief retrospect with a hint of its strangeness to one coming there directly from London. The Aran Islands are three chips of limestone off the Burren, the paradoxical character of which is well indicated by the name of its ruined abbey, 'St Mary of the Fertile Rock'. However, the islands are more on speaking terms with Connemara, sharing with it the honour and burden of a language in retreat, carrying an oral tradition older than Christianity. The Atlantic batters, caresses, bewilders and depresses the two mainlands and lavishes its attentions on the islands in particular. That will do; that is already more than I knew when I arrived in 1972, to live in a hamlet an hour's walk west of the little port of Árainn, the largest of the islands.

To find myself in such a landscape, or series of interlocking landscapes, was, it turned out, to be the business of many years, and has been done principally through mapping and writing. The maps are published under the imprint of Folding Landscapes, the little publishing concern run by my partner and myself, since 1984, in Roundstone, Connemara. The maps produced so far are of the Aran Islands (1976 and 1984) and the Burren (1977); work on Connemara is (endlessly?) ongoing.

I approached mapping as an art-form particularly suited to

ordering large amounts of fact into an expressive whole. My education had been in maths and physics, but my 'formation' was that
of an artist working in abstract and 'environmental' modes in the
London of the late 1960s, while my draughtsmanship was the
residue of a period as a freelance technical illustrator. So I came to
the practice of cartography largely ignorant of its specific techniques, theories and received ideas, not to say deeply suspicious of
its technological and organizational structures that distance the
drawer of the map ever farther from the place to be drawn, alien-
ating the hand from the foot. For me, making a map was to be a
one-to-one encounter between a person and a terrain, a commitment unlimitable in terms of time and effort, an existential project
of knowing a place. The map itself could hardly then be more
than an interim report on the progress of its own making.

However, from the start I found myself in collaboration with a
traditional cartography. These marginal areas of Ireland were last
mapped in detail by the Ordnance Survey in the 1890s and the
eighty-year-old six-inch sheets proved to be the ideal basis for my
own work, for they lent it a skeletal correctitude of topography but
were singularly short of flesh of their own. In the Burren it was
the hope of finding some of the many unrecorded prehistoric sites
that had me quartering the blanks on the old maps. In Aran and in
Irish-speaking south Connemara the Ordnance Survey placenames,
few and far between, had to be discarded as they were anglicized
garblings that smelled of centuries of cultural imperialism; it
became my duty and pleasure to enquire out their original Irish
forms and still vivid meanings, a quest that led me into labyrinths
of folklore and local history.

When it came to drawing my first maps, I restricted myself to
black, and to linear techniques, the better to represent the interweaving of various aspects of the territory. A coloured map, I felt,
could easily fall apart, visually and conceptually, into superimposed
but otherwise separate layers. In devising symbols for different terrains such as rocky shore, sand-dunes, craggy hillside and blanket
bog, I looked for visual equivalents of their feel underfoot, the
internationally standardized ornaments being unknown in practice
and *a priori* unacceptable to me; even the term 'ornament', with its
connotations of superficiality and redundancy, was quite inappro-
priate for these textures that were to be the very substance and

ground of the drawing. Off-the-peg tints and rulings were out of the question too; in any case I found that by consciously position-ing even the minutest specks and flecks (done with a 0.1 mm nib, for reduction 3:2) I could create subliminal clearances around the larger marks such as the dots of townland boundary lines, which enhanced their clarity and compensated for the absence of colour contrasts. It was of course axiomatic that the cardinal features of the territory in question would suggest the layout and presentation of the sheet; I was not in the business of carving up the continuity of the earth's surface into standard portions. For instance I could choose to show the detail of Aran's majestic range of Atlantic cliffs in a seagull's-eye perspective in a way that would have been im-possible and irrelevant in the case of the anfractuous shores of Connemara.

In all these choices I was trying to preserve the texture of im-mediate experience. I had a formula to guide me and whip me on through the thickets of difficulties I encountered: while walking this land, I am the pen on the paper; while drawing this map, my pen is myself walking the land. The purpose of this identification was to short circuit the polarities of objectivity and subjectivity, and help me keep faith with reality.

Some of the more puritanical ordinances of my early practice have been relaxed now, as I revel in the latitudinarian spaces of Connemara. But my basic orientation is the same: a map is a sus-tained attempt upon an unattainable goal, the complete compre-hension by an individual of a tract of space that will be individual-ized into a place by that attempt. A banal little inequality, etched into me by the cartographical experience, asserts that unattainabil-ity. If t is some linear measure of the sheet within which one is to express oneself, T the corresponding measure of the territory one would express, and m a suitable measure of the richness of detail one's pen can make lucid, then M, the measure of reality these chosen means can grasp, is forever limited thus:

$$M \leq mt/T$$

7

A Connemara Fractal

My intention is to spin a few threads of ideas out of my experience of making a map – the map of Connemara – and tie them to some specific features of that map, in the hope that they will lead off into wider territories of thought.

I'm not very interested in maps from the technical point of view, so I will be brief on how I went about producing this one, and move on to the more interesting questions of what is it like to make a map – insofar as I can untangle my memories of the process – and why maps are, finally, so unsatisfactory. For if cartography is not necessarily more helpless than other modes of representation in the face of the world, it has its own characteristic failings, which the blanks on a map, essential to its legibility as they are, reveal with disconcerting candour.

Of course I can afford this attitude of disinterest in certain aspects of cartography because a lot of the mechanical part of the task has been done for me. Connemara, like the rest of Ireland, was very carefully surveyed in the 1830s and again in the 1890s, by the Ordnance Survey, which is in origins and ethos a section of the army. Indeed it took an army of men, lugging theodolites and chains, to measure all the ins and outs of shoreline and bog and mountain, and there would have been no point in, and indeed no possibility of, one person redoing all that. So the basic topography, in its three dimensions of lengths and breadths and heights, was already available to me. Later I was to discover that this tale of three dimensions is entirely inadequate, not just to the subjective dimensions, the ones that pass through the heart of the cartographer, but even to the objective reality of landscape. But before enmeshing myself in the theory of dimensions, I will mention a few practicalities of the business. Although that Victorian mapping was quite accurate enough for my needs, it is ninety years out of

date so far as concerns roads and paths and buildings. So what I
did was to take the six-inch OS maps, which break up Connemara
into about thirty sheets, and walk or cycle every road and track I
could find, marking in the ones that were not on the old maps and
noting all the buildings and anything else that had changed since
1898. This sometimes involved a very rudimentary sort of surveying; I had a little compass, and I quickly learned to judge distances
of a hundred or two hundred yards by eye. However, I soon found
that most new features could be accurately located on the old maps
by reference to things that had not changed, or of which traces
remained; I could usually see where in the pattern of the old field-
walls the new bungalow was set, for instance. It was simple
enough, but it took me a total of several years of walking to cover
the ground, and some of that was a wearisome struggle against
wind and rain and cold. I started when we were still living in the
Aran Islands, and I used to come across to Connemara for a
month or so at a time, usually in early spring or in the autumn,
and stay in a b&b or with friends in some particular area, and
work out from there each day; setting off on my bike, leaving it by
the roadside while I followed some endless bog road up the mountainside, coming down again, cycling on a bit, discovering another
bog road, tramping to the end of that and back again, and so on,
and cycling home again at the end of the day. The wind, it
seemed, was invariably against me. Sometimes the rain held me up
for days; I'd go out whenever it looked about to slacken, hoping it
would stop by the time I reached the point it had forced me to
give up at the day before, and so I often spent hours sheltering
under hedges or crouched behind a boulder on a desolate shore
while wind and rain reduced my OS maps to pulp. Once in Cill
Chiaráin I got so fed up waiting for a clearance that I went out to
map the village itself in teeming rain, with my map, my pen and
my two hands in a clear plastic bag; I remember people peering
out at me, amazed, from the shelter of doorways. That was the
topographical experience – much of it a penance. But in this way I
got the feeling of the place, its obdurate reality, into my bones. I
comforted myself for the loneliness, the cold and the exhaustion I
often felt, with the idea that it was necessary, this endurance test,
to prepare me for doing the actual drawing of the map. For finally
those six-inch OS maps scribbled all over with notes and amendments had to be traced, and the tracings reduced photographically,

and all the bits stuck together to make a skeleton map of the area,
and then a sheet of transparent film spread over that so that I
could use it as a guide to an entirely new drawing of the whole.
Thus the drawing of the map took place at a few removes – of
time and place and mood – from the exploration of the terrain.
And I used to hope that the intensity of my physical experience of
Connemara would burn through all these layers of methodological
tracing-paper into the final drawing, making it not just a factual
record, but an expression of a feeling or a lot of contradictory feelings about the place. Perhaps if I vividly remembered walking
along a certain shinglebank, I would be able to put some echo of
my footsteps into the dots representing it on my map. However, I
have come to think that, if this process transmits anything of the
terrain itself, it is not my limited, personal and changeable
responses to it, but the objective ground of the possibility of that
subjectivity. It is the inexhaustibly densely structured nature of
reality itself that I would like to image, however feebly, however
smoothed out and generalized, in the texture of the map.

It follows that it seemed to me necessary to go everywhere and
see everything, before I had the right to represent anything on my
drawing. That was and is my guiding instinct, however little I
really understand it, and by and large I have stuck to it. There is
scarcely anything on the map I haven't set eyes on for myself. And
of course this insistence on the primacy of personal experience led
to many discoveries that otherwise would not have been made, and
to many meetings with the people of the countryside. As I was
particularly interested in the things that are not well shown on the
official maps, such as placenames and archaeological sites, and
those that hardly show at all on most maps, like local history and
folklore, it was essential for me to meet the people of Connemara,
for much of this material is not to be turned up in libraries
however deep you dig. Also, since I dislike making appointments,
my method of rambling along and greeting people on the road or
on the shore, or calling in at cottages or indeed factories and
hotels, as and when I reached them, suited me, and although it
was not always efficient in terms of information-gathering, it put
the people in their context; I talked to turf-cutters out in the bogs,
to fishermen on the quays, or to *Bean a' Tí* over the breakfast-
table, where their conversation was in its natural surroundings,
comfortable, immediate, alive.

So my map of Connemara is the record of a long walk, an intricate, knotted, itinerary that visits every place within its territory. Some such idea was in my mind when I started, and it was suggested by the extraordinary form of the southern coast of Connemara. It looks so complicated as to be unmappable; it's a challenge to be unravelled. In an essay I wrote a year or two after starting this map, 'Setting Foot on the Shores of Connemara', I said that the distance from Ros a' Mhíl to Roundstone is only about twenty miles, but that the coastline in between is at least 250 miles long, even as estimated from a small-scale map. My unthought assumption here was that if one estimated its length using a larger-scale map, showing more of its details, one would arrive at a figure a bit bigger than that, a more accurate answer. And, finally, that if one actually measured the coastline with a ruler, going round all the irregularities scrupulously, one would get a more accurate answer. still. But this, I was soon to learn, is a naive assumption, and one that short-changes the riches of the natural world. (This question of the length of a coastline is separate from that of the uncertainties and variabilities caused by tides and waves; one can picture the problem as concerned with the edge of an ocean frozen at a moment in time.) When I wrote, I was ignorant of the fact that in the 1960s an American mathematician, Benoit Mandelbrot, had proved that an outline as complex as a coastline does not have a definable length. The idea that one gets a better and better approximation to its length by measuring it in finer and finer detail is false; the series of approximations does not converge to an answer, it just gets bigger and bigger, to infinity.

This disturbing doctrine – disturbing to one who fondly imagined he had walked a coastline with due attention to its quiddity – I first learned of from a newspaper-clipping sent to me out of the blue by an unknown admirer of 'Setting Foot on the Shores of Connemara', who I am sure did not realize its implications, its annihilating critique of my essay's imagery – for such was its effect. A coastline cannot be straightened out, conceptually or experientially, by walking its length; it is not a 'tangled tightrope'.

A related feature of coastlines, I learned when I went into the matter, is that they look roughly the same at whatever scale one examines them. Think of the coastline of the North Atlantic, as it appears in a small sketch-map: a wriggling line with a few loops

1. The North Atlantic coast, and two successive fractions of it.

off it (Fig. 1). Now think of a bit of that coastline, say part of Ireland, drawn to fill a similar area and with the same degree of inattention to detail: it too is a squiggle with a few loops off it, different in specifics but the same in its general crookedness as the first map. And if then one makes the same sort of casual map of a fraction of that Irish coast, such as Connemara, the result is yet another squiggle with loops. The three drawings are much of a muchness; if they were shuffled, only an inspection of specific shapes could establish which represents the largest sector of coast. Of course some coastlines are more complicated than others. Take part of the south Connemara coast (Fig. 2), and then a bit of it drawn on a larger scale, and then a bit of that enlarged again. Again, at first glance these drawings would look equally convincing if presented in any other order. It is as if the first curve revealed more and more detail the closer it is examined, and that this detail is always similar to the whole. In fact the general characteristics of coastlines are the same, roughly speaking, at all scales, from the whole side of a continent down to the margin of a rockpool.

Such shapes are described as 'self-similar'. A simple geometrical analogy to a coastline can be constructed starting from a jigged line (Fig. 3); smaller jigs are added to each straight bit of the original line, then smaller ones still to each straight bit of the result, and so on to the infinitesimally small, so that it one examined any part of it under a magnifying glass or the most powerful of microscopes, it would look the same, jigs upon jigs for ever. Such an entity is

2. *Part of South Connemara,*
and two successive fractions of it.

more than a line, which has one dimension, its length, and yet it is not quite an area either, with two dimensions, length and breadth. In fact Mandelbrot showed that it is possible to assign it a dimensionality of one and a half. It may seem absurd to talk of something having 1.5 or 2.7 or 0.3 dimensions, but it turns out that such concepts are not just the dreams or nightmares of mathematicians; indeed fractional dimensionalities are a feature of many natural entities, from curdled milk to coastlines, systems of geological faults, cloud-forms, and even the distribution of the 200 billion galaxies in space. The reason, very hastily stated, is this: mathematically self-similar structures are the result of applying a procedure to a simple initial entity, then applying the same procedure to the result, and so on – an iterative process, as in the example of jigs applied to the results of previous jigs of jigs, *etc.*; and Nature itself applies its transforming powers again and again to the outcome of previous transformations, thereby bringing into being forms that are self-similar over a wide range of scales and of a degree of complexity that pre-Mandelbrot geometry cannot model. Mandelbrot called such forms – whether mathematical or natural – 'fractals', from the Latin *fractus*, broken. Conventional geometry would indeed regard such things as broken, confused, tangled, unworthy of the dignity of measure.

The difficulty of the concept of fractional dimensions is that our everyday idea of a dimension is a possible direction of movement. Thus within the space of a box, we can move an object from side to side, from front to back, and from top to bottom, that is, in

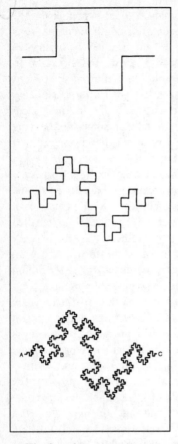

3. The first three stages in constructing a simple fractal; each stage is derived from the preceding one by replacing every straight bit by a reduced replica of the first stage.

three independent dimensions. If the object is to be kept on a table-top, a plane surface, it can only be moved from left to right, say, or from front to back – two independent dimensions; and if it is strung like a bead on a wire we can only slide it to and fro along that line of one dimension. There is no generalizing that idea to cover fractional dimensions; one cannot have two and a half directions. But there are other ways of conceiving of dimensionality, some of which can be stretched to cover fractals more comfortably. To get a taste of one of these, first note that some ordinary geometrical forms are, in a way, self-similar too. For instance a cube can be divided up into smaller cubes, each of which is similar to the whole but reduced by a certain factor, and then the smaller cubes can be dissected in the same way. Think of a cube with sides of unit length, divided up into little cubes with sides of length $1/b$. (Fig. 4 shows the case where $b = 4$.) The number of little cubes fitting along one side of the big one is b, and the total number N of little cubes making up the big one is b x b x b. That is,

$$N = b^3$$

Now think of a square with unit sides, divided up into smaller squares, each of which is the same as the big one but with its sides reduced by the factor $1/b$. The number N of such small squares in the big one is given by

$$N = b^2$$

84

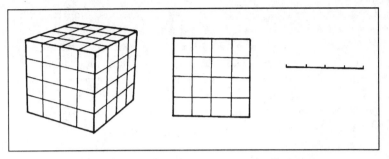

4. The self-similar dissection of a cube, a square, and a line.

And finally think of a line of unit length divided up into smaller sections of length $1/b$; the number of them in the whole line is

$$N = b$$

In each case, $N = b^D$, where the values of D agree with our idea that the cube has three dimensions, the square two, and the line one. Suppose though we take this equation as *defining* what is meant by dimensionality, and ask what result it gives when applied to a fractal form. The simplest case is the jigged form described above, of which any part, however tiny, will look roughly like the last curve in Fig. 3 when suitably magnified. The section of it from A to B, say, is made up of a number of parts such as that from A to C. Each of these parts is similar to the whole section but is smaller by a factor of $1/4$; thus in analogy with the cube, the square and the line, in this case we have $b = 4$. And there are eight of them making up the whole, so $N = 8$. Putting these values into the equation $N = b^D$, we have:

$$8 = 4^D$$

whence:[1]

$$D = 3/2$$

This way of looking at the idea of dimensions thus concurs with our normal ideas about simple shapes like squares and cubes, and gives a result for fractals too; in this case it seems very well to express the feeling that there is more space in the 'jigged line' than there is in an ordinary one-dimensional line, but that it is still something less than an area with two dimensions. One can easily construct examples which have a dimensionality of less than one, or between two and three. And the idea can be extended to cover irregular natural forms like coastlines and clouds, though here the results will be approximations, arrived at by statistical methods. Coastlines typically have dimensionalities of about 1.2; my very crude estimate for an average stretch of the south Connemara shore is 1.25, and the more complicated bits of it would give a higher answer still.

The fact that coastlines are virtually infinitely long had been stated before Mandelbrot, just as the concept of non-integral dimensionality had been suggested by earlier mathematicians; but it is Mandelbrot's collation of the two ideas that opens onto new vistas of thought. A previously obscure topic in mathematics is suddenly important in physics, the earth sciences, biology and astrophysics, is crucial to the new disciplines of chaos and complexity theory, and promises to be a rich source of metaphor and imagery in literature and art. Like all discoveries it surprises us yet again with the unfathomable depth and texture of the natural world; specifically it shows that there is more space, there are more places, on a seashore, within a forest or among the galaxies, than the geometry of common sense allows.

The hints about the subject I gleaned from the newspaper cutting prompted me to get Mandelbrot's book, *The Fractal Geometry of Nature*.[2] It is an unlovely work in some ways (though without the abominable faults of the other principal sourcebook on the subject, *The Beauty of Fractals*,[3] which misidentifies the beauty of science and that of art, and crosses them to produce a hybrid with the virtues of neither). However, Mandelbrot's concern with assessing his own priority in the field does lead him to discuss his intellectual forebears, and I was intrigued to learn that the particular concept of dimensionality he used (and of which I have given a very crude version above) was 'formulated in Hausdorff 1919 and put in final form by Besicovitch'; in fact his mention of the latter name led me into the fractals of personal memory, which eventually spelt out a reason for my obsessive tracings of the Connemara shoreline. The anecdote involves another mathematical construction, the Peano Curve; so I had better clear the ground by introducing this old friend first.

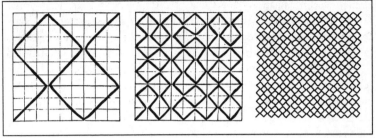

5. The first three stages in constructing a Peano Curve; each stage is derived from the preceding one by replacing every straight section by a reduced replica of the first stage.

We start with a line that zigzags through a square area (Fig. 5). First we replace each leg of it by a zigzag similar to, but smaller than, the first, and then do the same with each leg of the resultant more complex form, and so on, to the infinitely small. My diagram is crude, but drawing even the third stage is a maddening task and the fourth would be quite beyond my powers of attention. Of course the ultimate outcome is impossible to draw, because of the thickness of penpoints and the finiteness of human existence; it is a mathematical concept, like the perfect circle. Peano showed that such a curve actually visits every point within the square. In fact, while a line, however complicated, has a dimensionality of one, this object has the same dimensionality as the square, an area, *i.e.* two. Each little bit of it is a labyrinth in which each detour is a smaller labyrinth, in which each detour is a yet smaller labyrinth, and so on, beyond the dreams of Borges. At the time it was discovered – or created, according to one's view of the nature of mathematical objects – by the Italian mathematician Peano around the turn of the century, it was regarded as a geometrical monstrosity, an exception best disregarded in the name of logical hygiene.

I will nose briefly into just two of the labyrinthine digressions this diagram suggests, in the Irish context, before taking up my story. First: 'How Celtic!' Perhaps one could claim that fractal geometry is to Celtic art as Euclid is to classical art. While the mainstream of European culture has pursued its magnificent course, some other perception has been kept in mind by the Celtic periphery, all the way from La Tène Iron-Age curlicues to Jim Fitzpatrick's kitsch-Celt goddesses. In a word, that a fascinating sort of beauty arises out of the repetitive interweaving of simple

elements. The beauty of Nature is often of this sort. In Connemara, which is pre-eminently the land of 'dappled things' – driz-
zling skies, bubbly streams, tussocky hillsides – one recognizes this
texture. Of course, after a thorough soaking in all this dappled
Celtic bewilderment, one runs for shelter in classical temples, with
relief. And secondly: 'How Ruskin would have liked this!' In his
book *Modern Painters*, which is largely about how Turner achieved
his version of truth to Nature, Ruskin devotes pages to analyzing
such visual phenomena as a mackerel sky or the successive patterns
of striations revealed on the peak of Mont Blanc as the sun moves
round it. But cloud formations and geological fault systems are
often fractal phenomena, and, lacking this concept, Ruskin's
numerical estimates of the number of dabs of cloud that go to
make up the unified spectacle of a sunset sky are heroic but
doomed attempts to render the beauty of the dappled things that
classical art ignored, that it defined itself by excluding.

To return to my personal entanglement in the Peano Curve.
Like various other apparently freakish inventions of turn-of-the-
century mathematics, it was one of the hobby-horses of Besicovitch, who was an elderly and semi-retired professor of mathematics at Cambridge at the time I passed unremarkably through
the place in the fifties. Mere crotchets on the spires of intellection;
so Professor Besicovitch's chosen topics appeared to me, a gauche
would-be aesthete and week-old undergraduate, in the autumn of
1952. His best-known work was a treatise on *Almost Periodic
Functions*, which sounded like a parody of professorial abstruosity.
Besicovitch was to give an exceptional and to some degree extra-
curricular series of seminars to the new intake. In the first of
these, the professor, who had very little English other than mathematical terminology, outlined a number of his favourite problems,
some of which still lacked solutions. An example: a line one inch
long can obviously be turned around inside a circle one inch
across, but what is the smallest area in which it can be turned
around? It had long been accepted that the answer to this curious
query was the area swept out by the line in making a three-point
turn, a sort of concave-sided triangle. But the professor had
demonstrated that in fact it can be turned around inside a shape of
no area whatsoever, provided it is allowed to back off to infinity in
an infinite number of different directions. A typical Besicovitch
result; both ludicrous and mysterious. The image of that line's

minnow-like dartings in all possible directions still remains with me as an emblem of a certain style of thought, and I suspect it also helped me fail my driving test. Having introduced us to half-a-dozen such bizarreries, the professor suggested that some of us might like to divide these problems between us, study them further, and lecture on them to the rest of the group. The first problem on offer concerned a way of representing a Peano Curve by a formula, an infinitely long and curiously constructed series of powers of a complex variable. It was, said Besicovitch, a very beautiful solution. Then he looked off into space rather sadly, and admitted that the curve this formula generated did pass through some points outside the square; nevertheless, it was a very fine solution. Also, he confessed, apparently quite disconsolate, it did pass through some points of the square more than once. But, taken all in all, it was a very beautiful solution. The proof was long, though, so he would suggest two of us divide it between us, to study it and report back to the group. Who would volunteer? He looked at us expectantly *en masse*, and then, as no one responded, he appealed to us mutely, face by face. I had already glanced round the crowded lecture hall at my hundred or more unknown colleagues and decided they were a dull lot; I would have preferred to consort with the lovely and witty beings reading one of the arts subjects; but then for me the only point of art was to practise it, and I was convinced that all pedagogy stultified creativity, whereas I knew I could not climb the cliff-face of mathematics without help, and so had condemned myself to sojourn among these dullards. I recognized, all the same, that most of them had more mathematics than I, for I came from an unassuming provincial grammar school which had not previously aspired to prepare a pupil for Cambridge. But when Besicovitch said 'Please!', in tones of pain and embarrassment, I put up my hand out of impatience with the lot of them. To my relief someone I knew to be better educated than myself in such matters followed me into the breach.

'The Peano Curve and Its Representation by a Lacunary Power Series' was the title of the paper Besicovitch handed to us afterwards. It looked formidable, but such was my ignorance I did not realize how far beyond me it was. My colleague and I met that evening and struggled through a page or two of it, and later called on the professor to have it elucidated. Besicovitch silently admitted us to his small rooms, and enquired our names: Davis and

Robinson; he pondered them for a time and then remarked 'D and R!', with a kindly smile to indicate that he was proffering a joke. (Brezhnev and Khrushchev, visiting the United Nations at that time, had been abbreviated to 'B and K' in newspaper headlines.) Our private sessions with him became a weekly ritual. As our incomprehension drove him deeper and deeper into the problem, I believe he invented new lines of argument that skirted around difficulties too deep for us to ford. We looked over his soft, bulky, Slavic shoulders as his pen hovered and agonized in the air for minutes before inscribing each symbol. We learned a little about him; that he was born a member of the Karaites, a tribe of Jewish faith and Central Asian ethnicity that wandered between the Caspian and Lapland; that he had studied at the University of Perm, where it was so cold that he used to get into a sack to read. What convulsions of history had brought him to Cambridge we did not think to ask.

Eventually we deluded ourselves that we understood the simplified proof that emerged from these tutorials, and the day came on which 'R' had undertaken to expound the first half of it and 'D' the second, to our assembled peers. All were silent and attentive as I blundered on into the valley of death. Besicovitch soon showed signs of concern, though, and at one point where I announced my intention of deducing a certain proposition from another one he interrupted to ask how I intended to do that. 'By the Mean Value Theorem!' I replied, which probably revealed to him for the first time how far out of my depth I was. He put me on the track again and let me limp to my conclusion. I returned to my bench, and 'D' took up the chalk. But he fared even worse than I, and the professor dismissed him from the blackboard and continued the lecture himself. I was overcome by what I self-protectively identified as the absurdity of it all, and sat there snorting hysterically; once or twice Besicovitch's eye rested on me, forebearing, puzzled by this human predicament, before gazing off into the world of forms again.

I do not remember that anyone ever mentioned this dreadful episode to me afterwards, or that I thought much of it myself; it must have vanished into the froth of my rather belated adolescence. But the Peano Curve remained branded on my mentality; it was the original of 'the conception filling my mind of a strange map consisting of one line, and that so convoluted it visited every point of the territory', which I wrote of in 'Setting Foot on the Shores of Connemara'. For a personally researched map that aspires to comprehensiveness must be, as I have said, the record of a walk that covers the ground; therefore the Peano Curve, this topological monster, is its perfect emblem. But it is also a reminder of how far any such map must fall short of success. This fractal nature of the ideal one-person map is both my excuse for the map of Connemara having taken me about five times as long as I thought it would when I set out, and my condemnation for having undertaken an absurdity, an adequate map; for any such thing would have taken not five times but an infinite number of times longer than my naive estimates. And now, when I see the name of Besicovitch in the roll of those of whom Mandelbrot writes, 'These names are not ordinarily encountered in the empirical study of Nature, but I claim that the impact of the work of these giants far transcends its intended scope,' also that 'while Hausdorff is the father of nonstandard dimension, Besicovitch made himself its mother,' I realize that I have wasted some hours of the lifetime of a genius, which is an intellectual crime, and that my penitential would-be fractal journey enacts a double apology – to Besicovitch for my inability to appreciate his self-infolded gigantism, and to the surface of the Earth for the paucity of all our attentions to it.

* * *

Let me now turn to more concrete matters, a tiny selection of the places, experiences, discoveries and surprises that my convoluted walk about Connemara led me through. These are some of the moments that made the endless trudging along muddy shores and stony tracks worthwhile; perhaps my fractal theme will secure them from being mere mementos brought home by polymorphic dilettantism.

I remember one particularly filthy day on the coast south of Ros a' Mhíl. That area is bleak at the best of times, a bare flatland of granite, walled up into the little fields that spell poverty and labour; it used to be part of the estates of the Blakes of Tully, the worst of the rackrenting landlords. It is said that eventually the Blakes were cursed by the priest for their tyrannical ways; he wrote out Salm na Mallacht, the Anathema, against them, and put it in an envelope, which he put in another envelope, and that one in another, seven in all; and gave it to a lad to deliver to the Big House, Teach a' Bhláca, instructing him to leave immediately he had handed it over and put as much distance between himself and the house as possible while Mr Blake was opening those seven envelopes. It seems this moral letter-bomb was expected to devastate all in its vicinity. Indeed the Blakes were soon after embroiled in misfortune, and left the house, which is now roofless and ruined, though for a long time after that the tenants continued to pay their rent to a Blake, who was in the mental asylum at Ballinasloe. It still looks as if the curse had its evil effect on the neighbourhood, which is heartbreakingly dreary, especially in winter. But on this wet, blustery day I met two elderly men there, walking up a boreen past a deserted village, puffing their pipes, having driven their cattle down to some distant field. They were delighted to stop and chat with me even though the rain was teeming down; they hitched their coats up over one ear and started telling me stories. At the time I had just about enough Irish to follow them, but because of the rain I couldn't note anything. They told me about the wicked Blakes, and the strange prophecies of St Colm Cille whose holy well is on the seashore nearby, and then about the giant Conán, the buffoon and glutton of the old legends about Fionn Mac Cumhaill and his warrior band. They said that Conán had emptied out his pocket of winkle shells on the shore at the foot of the boreen we were on, and that it would be worth my while going to see the heap; they called it Toit Chonáin, *toit* being a dialect word for a helping of shellfish. So I walked down to the shore, not very hopeful of being able to find this heap of winkle-shells. And there at the end of the boreen was a hillock of smooth green sward, very conspicuous among the ragged, blackish, seaweedy rocks. Where rabbits had tunnelled into it, thousands of winkle-shells were pouring out. It was evidently a kitchen-midden, marking a place where some prehistoric people had gathered, presumably seasonally over a long period, to live off shore-food. There are many such shell-middens in the west of Connemara, exposed wherever dunes are being eroded; two of them have recently been dated to AD 400 and 700, and it is likely that some contain very much earlier deposits. But none of them is as striking as Toit Chonáin, which is twelve or fifteen feet high, and forty feet long. '*Vaut le détour,*' as the *Michelin Guide* says; the drab shores of Ros a' Mhíl have their gifts, even if they do seem to be hidden within envelope within envelope within envelope, like the priest's curse.

The next day I returned to the same stretch of coast to search for the holy well the old men told me had been made by Colm Cille, who had sailed across from the Aran Islands on a stone boat. The boat is still there, a big boulder like the prow of a hooker, with the saint's huge handprint and marks left by his anchor chain on its deck, and grooves worn into its rim by his oars. The holy well is a rockpool down near the low-water mark, only accessible when the tide is out. There was no one on the shore to direct me, and I spent a long time floundering about among rocks covered in seaweed before I found it. Once seen, it was unmistakable, a big smooth basin, almost circular and with a bowl-shaped bottom, like a baptismal font; in fact (in the sort of fact I was exploring that day, at any rate) St Colm Cille had made this and other similar wells for baptism of the local heathens. However, I was unsure that I was looking at the right rockpool until I put my arm down into it as far as I could reach, and felt something wedged in a crack in the rock – an old penny coin.

This identification by the sense of touch was important to me; it suggested making a mental connection between this particular sort of holy well and the lifestyle of the people who used to frequent them, and still do so to a declining extent. For these are not wells in the sense of being sources of fresh water. They are actually small potholes in the rock, and their formation is so odd that it is no wonder people think they are of miraculous origin. I have been shown about thirty of them on the shores of Connemara, almost without exception on the granite of the south coast. Most of them are about eighteen inches across and two or three feet deep, cylindrical, with a rounded bottom, and remarkably smooth. If you describe one to the geologists they will explain that it is has been formed by a stone getting caught in a crevice and being driven round and round by waves, especially during storms, and gradually, perhaps over centuries, grinding out a hole. However I have found that if you actually take the geologists and show them an example, even their belief in scientific explanation wavers, for the finish and symmetry of such holes are almost incredibly perfect. This type of holy well seems not to have been described in anthropological or folklore studies. Only a very few of them are marked on the old OS maps, and some of these are in the wrong position, perhaps because the draughtsman could not believe the surveyor's report that a so-called 'well' was down at low water level, and moved it onto the dry land. Most of them are only known to a few people, usually the older ones, of the immediate locality, and many are very hard even for them to find, because of the heaps of seaweed covering them. But it is because of this seaweed that they are known at all, for past generations of Connemara people used to gather seaweed to fertilize their potato-crops, and to burn for kelp, which was a principal source of income for almost two-and-a-half centuries from the 1700s on. Each household of the coastal villages had seaweed rights on a certain stretch of shore, and harvested several tons of weed off it every year; in fact it is the sheer complexity, the high fractal dimensionality, of the shoreline that provides habitat for the huge tonnages of seaweed on which the inordinate nineteenth-century population of this otherwise unproductive coastal strip could sustain itself in life, if not in comfort. So every little cranny of the shore was intimately known, by touch, to the families who worked it, and as a result such remarkable features as these potholes were found and named, and acquired their legend.

A woman I met on the road near An Cheathrú Rua told me of one of the holy wells in that area, in which there was a fish that could answer questions about your friends and relatives who had gone to America or England. If you had had no news for a long time, you could go down to this well, and throw in some crumbs, and if the fish appeared swimming the right way up, your absent friend was alive and well; if the fish swam upside down, the absent one was dead. That stark alternative tells us something about the pain of a community forsaken by so many of its sons and daughters, in those preliterate times. Strangely enough, I have actually touched this fish. I asked someone who said he used to know the well in question to guide me to it, and then as he couldn't find it, we went up to the nearest village and collected a couple of local people; they hadn't visited it in years, for seaweed, like religion, isn't so important nowadays, but after a lot of splashing and groping they identified it. The pothole was full of mud, and as we were cleaning it out one of my guides just picked up the fish and

94

showed it to me, a little *donnánach* or rockling, on his palm; I stroked its head, and he put it aside quite casually; there was no question but that it would find its way back into its holy well when the tide came in again, whether by magic or the scientifically well-known territorial instincts of small shore-fish. One of the applications of fractal theory, I am reminded, is to estimating the number of habitable niches available to creatures of different sizes, on a given surface. Here a small area of shore, say an acre, when examined in detail discloses a huge variety of holes and crevices, of a total surface area hundreds of times greater than that of the acre, and within those holes and clefts are smaller ones sheltering smaller creatures, who enjoy areas hugely greater still (not just in inverse proportion to the lesser size of the creatures, but absolutely greater) – and so on, to the well-nigh infinitesimal, the single-celled. If one mentally adds to this natural world endlessly en-folded within itself, the names of places, coins stuck in the cracks of holy wells, saints' handprints on stone boats, and prophetic fish, one begins to feel the ground tremble; plenitude of being dissolves into a mist of fictions. The tidal holy wells in particular have been founts of significance for me, on these waste shores.

Indeed the otherworld is copiously enfolded into this one, throughout Connemara. Because of the oral genius of the folk cul-ture, which is far from dead in these parts, at any moment one can be beguiled into belief systems quite foreign to one's normal mental guidelines or trammels. While I was mapping the boglands and trying to find out the names of hundreds of little lakes from the turf cutters, I heard some wonderful stories. One was about a 'mass rock', a little table-like outcrop on the hill called Cnoc Mordáin, where the mass is said to have been celebrated by an outlaw priest, at the time when the Catholic religion was proscribed. Its story was told me by a youngish man, in Irish, as he leaned on his *sleán* and rested from turf cutting, on a beautiful summer afternoon far out in the bog. I think I remember his words fairly accurately. There was once a man living in An Aird, near Carna, he said, who dreamed that mass was being celebrated in the mountain, at a place he rec-ognized. When he woke up he remembered the dream, and he dressed quickly and hurried over the mountain to the place he'd seen in his dream. A lot of people were gathered there, and he was just in time to see the priest come and celebrate the mass. But he noticed that the priest kept glancing at him as if he was uneasy. Afterwards when the people were dispersing the priest came over to him, and said, 'How did you know there was going to be a mass read here today?' So the man told him about his dream. The priest said, 'Well, no harm to you this time. But in future, take no notice of such dreams. And next time you go to mass, make sure you go to the right one – for we are not people of this world, and this mass was not for the likes of you.'

Interestingly enough, the next day I heard the same story in English, almost a word-for-word equivalent, from a man on the other side of the same hill. But I suspect that this is the exception, and that an enormous proportion of the old lore is lost when the Irish language ceases to be spoken. In this case, though, a rather haunting story had been transferred from the Irish to the English-speaking culture without loss; and now I have transferred it further, into print. That is one function of my work, this translation of the dense web of place-lore out of speech and memory into the world of books and maps, and it is a troubling aspect of the enterprise.

I am of course not the first to have woven Connemara places into the stuff of writing. When I was exploring Ros Muc, and reading Patrick Pearse's short stories, many of which he wrote in his holiday cottage there, I came across an example of how intricately knotted together landscape and literature can be. Pearse often used the topography of Ros Muc symbolically, and almost as if he could assume that everyone else was familiar with it, as Dante could rest on certain commonplaces about Jerusalem and Rome; this was overweening in Pearse, but the quality of his stories is not negligible and there are of course extraliterary reasons for examining them. His story 'Na Bóithre', the roads, is particularly full of placenames; it mentions almost every townland and village in the neighbourhood except Ros Muc itself, which always appears in Pearse's fiction as Ros na gCaorach, the peninsula of the sheep, rather than the peninsula of pigs. Perhaps he felt that sheep were more poetically suited than pigs to his rather pastoral vision of life in Connemara, or perhaps he was just over-sensitive to mindless English or Ascendancy jokes about the Irishman and his pig. In any case it is likely that the *muc* refers to the hogback hills of the locality rather than to pigs. To understand 'Na Bóithre' and to extract

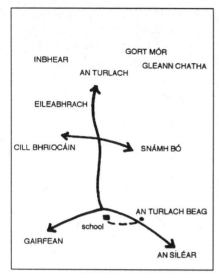

INBHEAR

GORT MÓR

GLEANN CHATHA

AN TURLACH

EILEABHRACH

CILL BHRIOCÁIN

SNÁMH BÓ

AN TURLACH BEAG

school

GAIRFEAN

AN SILÉAR

6. *Places and directions in Pearse's 'Na Bóithre'.*

from it some significances Pearse himself may not have been aware of, it is necessary to go into details of its setting and the occasion that prompted it. Nora, the girl-child heroine of the story, lives in An Turlach Beag, near the school, from which roads diverge. In my diagram (Fig. 6) summarizing the story's explicit geography as a rudimentary labyrinth, I have indicated these various villages with arrows rather than dots, for they are named in the text primarily as places people come from or go to; they are directions, like Guermantes in Proust. These roads represent the choices or destinies life offers. However, Pearse is extremely repressive in the choice he thrusts upon his heroine, and was in fact more concerned with his own destiny while writing this story, as I shall show. The story begins with a *fleá*, a festivity, in the school, organized by a regular visitor known as the Man from Dublin. Nora is told to stay at home and mind the baby while her parents and brother go off to enjoy the fun. Rebelling against her lot, she cuts off her hair to look like a boy, and ventures out into the darkness. She has to hide from the people dispersing from the *fleá*, and then takes the road which would lead out into the wide world. But by the time she has reached a place Pearse calls Eileabhrach she is tired and frightened; she steps aside into a wood there, and faints, and has a vision of Christ's agony in the Garden of Gethsemane. She longs to help carry the cross – but at that moment her father finds her, and takes her home. She is wandering in her mind for a month, but when she comes to herself she asks for the baby to be put in the bed with her, and vows never to leave her family again.

The message is unambiguous: stay at home, girl, and bear children; the excitements and sufferings of the roads of life are

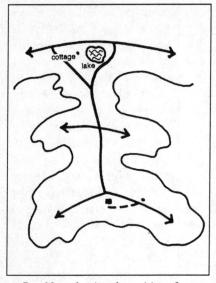

7. Ros Muc, showing the position of Pearse's cottage.

Man's portion. But under this bit of patriarchal indoctrination is another level of significance, only legible in the light of the real-life event that prompted the story, and the detailed geography of Ros Muc – both matters few if any of Pearse's readers could be aware of. First, the event: Pearse himself had organized such a *fleá* in the school of An Turlach Beag, in opposition to some entertainment of too English a tone mounted by the Viceroy, Lord Dudley, who used to come for fishing holidays to Inver Lodge near Ros Muc. Pearse was delighted with the success of his evening, and later based the story of 'Na Bóithre' on it (he finished it only in the summer of 1915 and it was published a few months before the Easter Rising and his own execution). So the 'Man from Dublin' of the story is Pearse himself. Secondly, the local geography of Ros Muc, the next layer of the labyrinth, which I show wrapped around the schematic map of the story (Fig. 7). Eileabhrach is in fact the wooded area south of Loch Eileabhrach – the name is properly Oiriúlach, perhaps from *foithriúil* and signifying a place of thickets – which lies in the angle between the road leading out of the Ros Muc peninsula and the main road passing by from east to west. The Ros Muc road goes around the east of the lake, and Pearse's cottage was rather isolated, on the west of the lake. So, if Nora's hallucination of Christ had been prompted by her actually seeing a man in the wood there, that man would most likely have been Pearse himself, taking a shortcut home after his *fleá*. Since Nora is a fiction, so is her vision, and so is any rationalization of it; the last-named exists only in our reconstruction of Pearse's mind. His self-identification with Christ the Redeemer is well known; here is an unusual demonstration of it, emerging through an interpretation of a projection into a hallucination in a fiction. He must have been full of forebodings of his forthcoming Easter self-sacrifice at the time of writing this story. The wood of Eileabhrach was evidently his Garden of Gethsemane.

A terminological footnote: literary theory is in part a study of intertextuality, the understanding of a given text in its web of relationships to other texts – relations of influence or rebellion, quotation, parody, plagiarism, *etc.* By broadening the connotation of the word 'text' one can include here the work's relationships to other symbolic structures, such as placename systems. But by no amount of stretching can the concept of a text be made to cover the basic topography of an area. There is something the theses of geography are about, of which a conceptualized landscape is an interpretation, that is not a message, not a map; it is not oriented along the vector of intention to communicate which distinguishes messages from many other things we humans like to receive as messages; it stands beyond and behind our desire to make sense of it. I lack a term for the business of explicating a text in its relationship to the non-textual, but I do not accept that the world, or even human life, is texts all the way down.

Returning to Pearse's Ros Muc for a moment: in another of his stories, 'An Bhean Chaointe', the wailing woman, there is repeated mention of 'An Glais Dubh', the black stream. Enquiring locally, I found this to be a muddy ditch now culverted under the main road a couple of miles east of the Ros Muc turning. In the story there is a lonely, crazy widow-woman living just beyond it. She is for ever expecting the return of her son, who will never return as he has died while in prison in Galway. Whenever the narrator of the story encounters this woman, he has just passed the Glais Dubh; it stands for the grief and mental confusion that separates the widow from the rest of the community. As a symbol it works well enough in the fiction; what about its symbolic effect in the real landscape? Well, since nobody except the immediate locals even knows that there is in fact such a place, until now it has had no geographical potency whatsoever. But the insistent and almost systematic use of Ros Muc placenames in Pearse demonstrates his urge to appropriate this landscape, to make it the theatre of his moralities. The project founders on his early death, and on the fixated juvenility of his prose. Nevertheless, the attempt is of historical importance. Had Pearse succeeded in his foundation of

1916 Ireland, Ros Muc might have become its ethical map, its mythic theme-park – for better or for worse.

My business in making maps is not just the recording of all the oddities and singularities I pick up on my way along convoluted walks like this one through Connemara. I, too, want to create meaning, but meaning of a specifically geographical sort. So, I am particularly interested in or excited by the points at which the thread of my explorations crosses itself, as it were, from various directions, and can be knotted firmly, that is, memorably, in a way that elevates a mere location to the status of a place. A good example, all the better for being rather complicated, arises at Garraunbawn, a townland near Ballynakill in the north-west of Connemara. According to the placenames experts at the Ordnance Survey, 'Garraunbawn' is an anglicization of the Irish 'An Garrán Bán', meaning the white thicket, or the fallow thicket; *garrán*, a shrubbery or thicket, is a common element in placenames. However, in the os archives are the original 'field notebooks' kept by the surveyors who first mapped this area in 1839, and in one of these I found a note that the Irish name of this place was 'An Gearrán Bán', the white horse. *Gearrán*, meaning a gelding or small horse, is close in sound to *garrán*, a shrubbery, and the difference between them is lost, like so much else, in anglicization. Further, the old notebook said that the townland took its name from that of a rock, but did not record where this rock was. Also, a very elderly former resident of the locality had told me a story about a white horse that came out of Garraunbawn Lake; a man had caught it and saddled and ridden it, and then he had taken the saddle off and hung it over a rock, and the horse had galloped off and plunged into the lake again. The mark of the saddle, my informant said, had remained on the rock. Unfortunately he didn't know exactly where this rock was, nor its name. Also, I had heard from an archaeologist that there was a standing-stone in this townland, on the top of a hill. There are a number of standing-stones dating from the Bronze Age, about 4000 years ago, in north-west Connemara, several of them on the tops of small glacial hills or drumlins; such a hill occupies most of the townland of Garraunbawn. What the significance of these stones was is, of course, difficult to know; some may have marked important burials, or they may have been ritual sites, or territorial markers.

All this information, fragmentary but intriguing, was already in my mind by the time the thread of my explorations led me through Garraunbawn one beautiful autumn evening. It is a particularly lovely area, gentler than most of Connemara, its lanes sunk between banks rich with wildflowers. I pushed my bike up the lane that crosses the hill, and just at the top of the slope I glanced through a hole in the hedge, and there in a field was the standing-stone. It was about five feet high, of milk-white quartz, dappled with grey lichen. In the twilight it looked exactly like the rump of an old white horse, peacefully grazing. Veins of quartz, formed in more turbulent geological eras by hot water seeping up fault-planes of the country rock from deep in the earth, carrying silica in solution and depositing it in pure crystals, occur here and there throughout Connemara. There is a quartz dyke exposed on the shore of an island near Garraunbawn in Ballynakill Bay, from which big boulders of quartz occasionally roll out as the coast is eroded back by the waves; perhaps some Bronze Age people rafted such a piece across and lugged it up half a mile of hill to set it up in Garraunbawn. No doubt until the last century, and the building of Garraunbawn House, it was the most prominent object in the neighbourhood. In fact I am sure it was the mythical white horse itself; the surviving version of the story in which the man hangs the saddle over the stone is an attempted rationalization of an older magic tale, which surely identified the horse with the stone. So, at that moment, looking through the hedge at the old stone horse cropping the grass on the hilltop, I could tie together a geological and an archaeological strand of Connemara's prehistory, and follow the efforts of later generations to make sense of that stone, first by means of a legend of an otherworldly horse, and later by tidying up a story already half forgotten and fossilized in a placename misunderstood and gelded by officialdom. For this place is not An Garrán Bán, the fallow thicket, but An Gearrán Bán, named from its ancient, perhaps totemic, white horse of stone, which has been ridden over the 4000 years of its existence by various meanings we can only guess at. The restoration of such an icon of a locality's specificity is the deepest gift a cartographer can offer, to our eroded modern consciousness of place.

Such knots of significant place can hardly be conveyed in a map alone; that is why I have combined my Connemara map with a book, which itself is a complicated text dense with cross-references. Even that cannot accommodate such condensed labyrinths as the one I have spelled out here, so there will have to be another book some day, a recursive, self-enfolding coverage of the terrain, for which this paper is a brief trial run. (I have proposed to my publisher this infinitely long book, to appear as an occasional series of volumes or an 'almost periodical', ending only with the end of the author, publisher or reading public; he looked queasy, but did not baulk.) The map itself has taken me about seven years, but it is only a preliminary orientation in the field; as I said, the most revealing features of a map are its blank areas. I think that is one reason I prefer to build up my maps of little dots and strokes of the pen standing separately on blank paper, rather than layers of colour that cover whole areas and implicitly claim to say something about every point within them. In the nature of fractals, the closest and most detailed exploration or mapping imaginable cannot do more than scratch the surface. My mode of drawing is a scratching of the surface of the paper, and makes no claims to comprehensiveness. Because of the psychological carry-over mentioned earlier, from my repetitious footsteps to this repetitious handwork, it is also a caressing of the Earth, a soothing and taming of the fractious fractal itself.

Discourse, too, is fractal; every remark suggests amplifications and amendments, every thesis, critiques and refutations; this fractal nature of intertextuality is the clue to the way the text itself sits into the fractals of non-textual reality. To be true to the nature of fractals, I should go on indefinitely, but in this world of practicalities, I must at this point abandon the tangled tale.

NOTES

1. This step is immediate for anyone who remembers any school algebra; otherwise the quickest way of seeing it is first to square each side of the equation, thus

$$64 = 4^D \times 4^D$$

and note that $64 = 4 \times 4 \times 4 = 4^3$, and $4^D \times 4^D = 4^{2D}$. Hence $4^3 = 4^{2D}$, and so $3 = 2D$.

2. Benoit Mandelbrot, *The Fractal Geometry of Nature* (New York, 1983).

3. H.-O. Peitgen and P.H. Richter, *The Beauty of Fractals* (Berlin, 1986).

8

On the Cultivation of the Compass Rose

PROUSTIAN TRIANGULATION

Is it by chance that Proust twice uses a trio of uprights and their apparent motions as examples of the type of impression that seems to him the most significant? Let me briefly summon up remembrance of the two passages.

Certain sensations seem to the narrator to impose an obligation on him to discover the reason for the intense but obscure pleasure they give him, but usually the distractions of the succeeding moments provide him with an excuse for evading this 'duty of consciousness'. However, on the drive back from Martinville circumstances leave him facing the memory of such an experience and he begins to consider it deeply. Phrases form in his mind which wonderfully augment the initial pleasure, and he writes a description of the changing appearances of three bell-towers he had observed from various distances and angles during the drive. On finishing this, his inaugural work of literature, he is filled with happiness in having acquitted himself of his obligations to the impressions and what they hid.

But we do not learn what they hid. Instead we have two descriptions, one almost objectively topographical and the other full of metaphors and similes in which the towers are shamelessly anthropomorphized.

Later, near Balbec, the narrator recognizes this unique pleasure again in the sight of three trees near the road he is being driven along. But this time he lets the moment slip away without the necessary effort of analyzed consciousness, and as the trees fall into the distance he feels as sad as if he had lost a friend, died to himself, denied a ghost, or failed to recognize a god.

The back-reference from the pattern of three trees to the pattern of three towers, the possibility that it is a submerged memory of the latter that is stirred by the former, is latent in the passage; indeed the narrator wonders if it is because they remind him of something that the trees are so potent, but he soon drops this line of enquiry. And it would merely bring one back to the question of what was so significant in the earlier experience itself. I suggest that since the narrator himself never knew what it was that the trees wanted to bring him, we are at liberty here to look around from this clearing in the great work, and turn away from the infinite regression of Time Past, to a rarer realization, that of Space Present. The towers are described as close neighbours, three birds alighted in the plain, arms waving farewell, three golden pivots, three maidens in a legend; the trees become a round-dance of sorcerers, lost friends waving their arms in despair. But if all these charming clusters of images are blown off them, what terrain may be triangulated, starting from three bare poles?

Sometimes, changes in the relative position or apparent size of objects, caused by our own motion, reveal that motion to us at an unaccustomed level of consciousness, and bring the bare fact of motion, of position itself, into the light of attention. We rush to humanize the perception: the trees are watching us go; the towers are withdrawing resignedly into the night. But we are left with an uneasy notion that something else is hidden in the experience, and hidden the more deeply by our added layer of interpretation. It may be forced upon us that such kinetic geometries are not merely an endlessly reinterpretable stuff for the expression of the cloud-work of the soul, that the world is not just a Rorschach blotter to soak up the projections of our hopes and fears, not just a bottom-less well of metaphor; that behind whatever social or personal sig-nificances we read into them such impressions carry a reminder of something so obvious that to state it seems absurd, so basic that it rarely intrudes into consciousness, so overwhelming that its real-ization might be profoundly therapeutic or psychically crushing. We are spatial entities – which is even more basic than being material entities, subject to the laws of gravity. The barest of bones of the relationship between an individual and the world are geometrical; on the landscape scale, topographical. Our physical existence is at all times wrapped in the web of directions and distances that constitutes our space. Space, inescapable and all-sustaining Space, is our unrecognized god.

I once wrote about a man who consciously obeyed the laws of perspective, an absurdity that points to its opposite banality: like Carroll's sundial we stand in the middle of a 'wabe'. The totality of geometric relations between the individual and the world is more than infinitely dense, and even the mere set of directions from me to other things or places forms an uncountable continuum. Consciousness at its richest can only hold an infinitesimal proportion of them, and so the image of a web is acceptable not as referring to the totality but to the miserable selection from it that our minds can handle. The relationships are always there, constituting our geometrical existence, which is a component of our physical existence and hence of every other level of individual and social existence. The most rudimentary element of geometry, the relationship of topological inclusion, is the kernel of all the complexities of social and ecological belonging. At such higher levels the geometrical is usually generalized out of mind, though there is always the possibility of unusual 'circumstances' imposing its primacy, as in the ballistic space of the battlefield. Perhaps the duty of consciousness in this regard is to be open to a maximal realization, a delicate and precise awareness of one's spatial relationships to the world. (Try it when watching branches swaying in the breeze, one behind another.) But this awareness, if it becomes strained and muddled, soon subsides into the indiscriminate welter of 'being at one with Nature'. Like love, it flourishes best on the very edge of loss of identity, of merging with the object; it is a dangerous leaning-over the brink of the blissfully all-dissolving Oceanic, or of the seasick existential shudders. A cliff-edge experience.

FIGURE IN A MAP

The 'topographical sensations' arising, for instance, from crossing a pass, completing the circuit of an island, or walking out to an island accessible at low water, are privileged moments of spatial awareness, able to bear the heavy vestments of symbolism. The exhilaration of crossing from one valley to another through a pass comes partly from such a journey's being a metaphor for threshold moments in which successive life-stages are simultaneously grasp-able, and past and present support the moment like two giant stilts. But the ground of this feeling is the geometrical configura-tion of the saddle-point, combining the highest and the lowest into a highly defined point of unstable equilibrium, so that you, here, are highly defined as a figure in a landscape. The landscape itself focuses on you, pinpointing a precise 'sense of place'. Such erup-tions of the meaningful into the plains of geometrical existence are themselves distractions from the quotidian inevitability of emplace-ment, the humble submission to the laws of perspective. It is fitting that, on a map, such singularities and discontinuities of topography as mountain summits, coastlines and passes occupy an area tending to zero with increasing fineness of drawing.

The general utility of a map resides in its being a conceptual model of the terrain projected onto paper, a representation of spatial relationships in a symbolism that facilitates calculations; *i.e.* the map is a visual calculus for topography. In my own maps this aspect only arises incidentally and inescapably, the web of self-centred spatial relationships, which one might symbolize by the compass rose, being inextricable from the totality of directions from point to point. We could not use or even bear to look at a map that was not mostly blank. This emptiness is to be filled in with our own imagined presence, for a map is the representation, simultaneously, of a range of possible spatial relations between the map-user and a part of the world. The compass rose represents the self in these potential relationships; it is usually discreetly located in some unoccupied corner, but is conceptually trans-plantable to any point of the map sheet. Its meagre petals are a conventional selection of the transfinity of directions radiating from the self to the terrain. It is a skeletal flower, befitting our starved spatial consciousness.

This irreducible nub of topographicity is my emblem as map-maker. I present the exiguous mystic bloom of the compass rose to the one who unfolds my map and finds herself a point upon it. It comes from a god unrecognized, a ghost denied, a lost friend, a self to whom you had died. Alternatively it comes from something as crashingly obvious as an Ox, and I, imitating the Rosenkavalier, have cheekily appropriated it for my own wooing of the world's wide spaces.

For I do not know that I understand what I have written. No; I am writing blind, as a pilot has to fly blind in fog or cloud, sustained by faith in a compass course rather than by vision of a destination. But this much is clear: the recommended situation for cultivation of the compass rose is on the very edge of the cliff.

9

Place/Person/Book

It begins: 'I am in Aranmor, sitting over a turf fire, listening to a murmur of Gaelic that is rising from a little public-house under my room', and it ends: 'The next day I left with the steamer.' It does not mention why he came, nor what bearing the island of time represented between these two sentences was to have on his further life. Its exclusion of matters relating to the past and the future of the Aran Islands, except as they arose in thought and conversation during his visits, is equally absolute. This self-sufficiency of the book commands respect, and to present some additional information on its subject and on its author, before discussing it in detail, is not to buttress it, but to erect a base on which to display its singularity.

THE PLACE

The word *ára*, literally the kidneys or loins and, by extension, the back, is a common element of Irish placenames, in which it connotes a back or ridge of land, and so Oileáin Árann, anglicized as the Aran Islands, could be translated as 'the ridge islands'.[1] The three islands, when they come into view against the Atlantic horizon as the ferry leaves the shelter of Galway Bay, are clearly the remains of a long escarpment broken through by the ocean. They once formed part of the Burren uplands to the south-east in County Clare, from which they are divided now by five miles of water. The sounds between the islands are each about a mile and a half wide, and ten or twelve miles separate Árainn (Synge's

'Aranmor') from Connemara to the north. Aran (the island group as a whole can be so named, for brevity) is of limestone, like its parent the Burren, and the formations to which limestone gives rise determine much of the character of the Aran landscape and even many features of daily life there. Stone is what meets the eye everywhere. Along its north-east-facing flank the escarpment rises in a few broad terraces separated by low cliffs or scarps, and the treads of these giant steps are level expanses mainly of bare rock, riven by long parallel fissures and littered with broken fragments and boulders in some areas, as smooth as a dance-floor in others. Inis Meáin (Synge uses the anglicized form, Inishmaan) has the most spectacular examples of this extraordinary limestone 'pavement', as it is called, spreading like grey aprons below the villages. In each of the islands, settlement is largely in the lee of the upper scarps, while from the sheltering ridge above the string of villages, uninhabited expanses of rough stony pasturage decline very slightly south-westwards, and in Árainn terminate with dramatic suddenness in vertical or deeply undercut cliffs fifty to three hundred feet high opposing the Atlantic. All the lower shores of the islands, except for a few sheltered stretches facing north-east, carry a stormbeach of shingle or boulders above the high-water mark, which even continues along the tops of the lower stretches of cliff. Again Inis Meáin has the most breathtaking example of this formation. Around its exposed south-western tip countless blocks of up to a few hundred tons weight have been broken by the sea out of the low rock-terrace forming the shoreline, shifted hundreds of yards inland and piled up like a vast rampart; and where the coastline rises into cliffs along the west of the island the stormbeach follows it, diminishing as it gradually climbs out of range of all except the most exceptional waves and fading out at a height of about a hundred feet (at which point the last few stones of it have been at some unknown period formed into a little clifftop look-out shelter, now called Synge's Seat).

Aboriginal soil is rare in Aran; the glaciers of the last Ice Age scoured the rock bare, and most of what soil developed after that has long been lost to erosion. It is likely that the islands were wooded, perhaps until settlement and grazing increased in early mediaeval times, but for centuries there have been virtually no trees apart from low thickets of hazel on sheltered slopes. The little green fields on the northern sheltered flank of the islands are the work of generations of men, women and children who cleared the crag of loose stone and spread it with sand and seaweed carried up in baskets from the shore. The field boundaries are drystone walls, of which there are about fifteen hundred miles in the three islands, so that most of the terrain is a mosaic of fractions of acres. This apparently manic subdivision has its purposes, in shielding stock and crops from the high winds of the oceanic coast, in facilitating the close control of grazing – so that the cow has to eat up all the grass, not just the juicier sorts, before it is allowed into fresh pasture – and in freeing the ground from the litter of stone. Again, Inis Meáin, the stoniest of the three stony islands, has the tallest walls – well over head-height in places, making an oppressive and bewildering maze of the rough tracks that ramify and dwindle like veins throughout the tissue of little rectangular fields.

Nowadays farming on the tiny scale permitted by Aran's vexatious topography is not a paying proposition, and hazel scrub is invading abandoned fields. Because of the small usage of pesticides and fertilizers, Aran's drifts of common buttercups and daisies are such as cannot be seen now in the rundown countrysides of Europe, while her kindly, crannied limestone and mild climate provide habitats for unusual floristic neighbourings, so that most of the wildflowers which surprise with their variety and opulence in the Burren are present here too. It is the Atlantic that dispenses this climate, shipping in constant weather changes from the south-west: interleaved squalls and shafts of sunshine that dress the islands in rainbow after rainbow, halcyon calms that curdle into sea-mist, storms that blow themselves out like candles.

The islands' spider webs of field walls entangle many archaeologies tumbled one upon another: communal tombs from the late Stone Age like big boxes made of limestone slabs, stone-lined cist graves from the Bronze Age, huge drystone cashels of the Celtic Iron Age, primitive oratories and hermits' cells, foundations of once-famous monasteries, roofless mediaeval chapels. The cliff-edge cashel of Dún Aonghasa, with its three semi-circular ramparts, opening onto empty space nearly three hundred feet above the surge of the Atlantic, occupies the most dramatic site of Celtic Europe. This, together with six other great cashels, of which Dún Chonchúir on the central height of Inis Meáin is the most impressive, shows that Aran was for some centuries around the beginning of our era the seat of a settled and prosperous community, for there is no evidence to justify the traditional designation of these mysterious structures as 'forts'. It has been suggested that the cashels were primarily ritual centres;[2] if so, the religious significance of Aran had been long established when St Enda came here some time before AD 489 (according to the much later mediaeval account of his life and miraculous works) and founded a monastery which was to become known throughout Europe. Columcille of Iona, Ciarán of Clonmacnois and Colman of Kilmacduach were among the saints to whom hagiography ascribes the almost obligatory early years of prayer and study in the illustrious and uniquely blessed isles called 'Aran of the Saints'. According to a poem by the ninth-century king-bishop of Cashel, Cormac mac Cuillenáin, it is impossible to count the saints of Aran, the four holiest places in the world are the Garden of Paradise, Rome, Aran and Jerusalem, no angel ever came to Ireland without visiting Aran, and if people understood how greatly the Lord loves Aran they would all come to partake of its blessings. It was not until the decade of Synge's first visits that Aran briefly recovered something of this extraordinary mystic status.

Throughout the early centuries of the growth of the Normans' walled town of Galway, the Aran Islands belonged to the O'Briens, the traditional Irish rulers of Munster. In the 1560s they were captured from them by the O'Flahertys, a former ruling clan of Connacht who had long been confined to the wildernesses of Connemara by the Norman advance. In trying to regain their lost islands the O'Briens appealed to the new system of law emanating from England, and Queen Elizabeth took the opportunity of appropriating the islands, which in the context of her war with Spain were of some strategic importance, and granting them to an Englishman on condition he maintain a garrison there. A fort was built in Árainn, which had its days of drama in 1652, when Parliamentarian soldiers were· crushing the last gasps out of the Irish rebellion which had broken out in response to England's civil strife. Aran had surrendered to Cromwell's general when he took Galway city, and then was recaptured by an expedition from the Confederate Catholics' last strongholds in Connemara and Inishbofin. The Parliamentarians shipped 1300 foot soldiers and a battering piece out to Aran and, having finally secured the castle, proceeded to enlarge it with ancient stone from the ruined churches and the round tower of St Enda's monastery. For some years Aran was a holding-camp for half-starved Catholic priests rounded up by the fanatically Protestant regime of the Commonwealth. There was an English military presence on Aran thereafter until early in the next century, with the result that today Aran's bloodgroup pattern is similar to that of northern England, where Gaelic and Saxon stock have intermingled.³

Aran's population, like that of Ireland as a whole, was at its peak just before the Great Famine of 1845-9, but the islands rode the demographic storm more smoothly than Connemara, for instance, where many villages were totally abandoned. In 1841 there were 3521 persons in the three islands; in 1851 there were 3333. The potato-blight seems to have been less severe in Aran than on the mainland, and it is said that only one person on the islands died of starvation in those years. But the leech of emigration had been applied to the Aran community, which has never since been able to shake it off. By Synge's time the population was 2863 (421 of them in Inis Meáin), and today it is about 1350. The fragmentation of the terrain into tiny fields expresses the desperation of those nineteenth-century generations, hoarding every tuft of grass for their cattle. Inordinate rents drained the community of capital, forced it to live almost exclusively on potatoes and made its life an unceasing struggle, in the stony fields, in little wooden boats and canvas currachs on the sea, or collecting seaweed on the shore and burning it for kelp. As in much of rural Ireland, long-suffering exploded into violence against the exploiters in the 1880s.

The very seclusion of Aran had occasionally attracted revolutionary influences before that date. It is said that after the defeat of the French invasion of 1798 and the rebellion that welcomed it in Mayo, there was a French officer on the run here with numerous United Irishmen, one of whom set up a hedge-school in Árainn. Similarly, one of the hunted leaders of another revolutionary generation, Young Ireland, passed through after their pitiful attempt at a rising in 1848; a stone is still pointed out on the stormbeach, under which John Blake Dillon hid for a time before escaping to America. Later on the Fenian conspiracy had members among the Aran tenantry, so that when the Land League came into existence in 1879 it found in Aran as elsewhere a nucleus of political awareness and even a number of activists armed with guns stolen from the local police barracks. Aran was at this time the property of absentee landlords, the Digbys of Landenstown in Kildare.[4] Its owners knew little of such a remote source of a tiny fraction of their rents as the Aran Islands, which were administered for them by agents who themselves visited only periodically. The more immediate power over the islanders' lives was the O'Flaherty family of Kilmurvey House in Árainn, a dwindled branch of the Connemara O'Flahertys; they had built up a holding of the best of the land, from which other tenants had been evicted for non-payment of rent, and sublet much of it to the less fortunate. Patrick O'Flaherty and his son James, each in his turn chief middleman, Justice of the Peace and representative of civility in the islands, were in a position of almost feudal power, and they bore the brunt of the islanders' accumulated resentments when Aran, like much of the rest of rural Ireland, was shaken by the Land War. In 1881 the Land Leaguers drove the O'Flahertys' cattle over the highest cliffs of Árainn, a deed still remembered but only reluctantly spoken about in the islands. Aran life at that time was further embittered by involved disputes, boycotts and scandals arising out of attempts by the little Protestant elite – the Church of Ireland minister Mr Kilbride, the landlord's agent, an evangelical school-teacher and others – to persuade the lower orders of the sinfulness of papistry. This murky series of events was copiously reported in the Galway press and in such national organs as the *Freeman's Journal*; Aran was well known to be one of the most hard-done-by communities in all the immiserated West. A branch of the National League was founded in the islands in 1886 to organize support for Home Rule, and rapidly became a power in the community. When the government responded to the terrorism of the Land War not only by coercion but by reform, and tried to 'kill Home Rule by kindness', Aran shared in the benefits. In 1885 a Land·Court sitting in the islands' capital, Cill Rónáin, reduced rents by 40 per cent.[5] The Aran fishing industry had dwindled almost to extinction in the dreadful years of recurrent hunger since the 1840s. In 1891 the Congested Districts Board was set up by the government to develop those localities of the West in which the population far exceeded what their productive capacities could support. A steamer service from Galway had already been established in that year, and on this basis of access to markets the Board undertook to nucleate a modern fishing industry, by paying a bounty to boats from Arklow to come and work out of Aran, by inaugurating a telegraph link to the mainland and by improving the harbours.

While thus badgered and solicited by sectarian and secular politics, the Aran Islanders also found themselves elected to a literary and even a metaphysical status by the romantic nationalism which was transforming Ireland's image of itself. Successive generations of Irish thinkers – many of them members of the Protestant ascendancy – were founding their separatist claims on the rediscovery of the Celtic soul, essentially at odds with the mundane progressivism of the Anglo-Saxon. And this ancient, mysterious, spirit guide of the nation was to be called forth from the humble cottages of the last living representatives of Celtic purity, the Irish-speaking farm- and fisherfolk, and pre-eminently those of the western seaboard. Aran, that forlorn outcrop of want, was to become one of the chief shrines of this Ireland of the mind.

The rediscovery of Aran's Celtic and monastic magnificence had been begun by George Petrie, 'the father of Irish archaeology', in 1821; it was consolidated by the excited reports of John O'Donovan in 1839 when he was employed by the Ordnance Survey to record Ireland's ancient monuments, and crowned in 1857 by the visit of the Ethnological Section of the British Association, who, accompanied by many Irish scholars and led by Dr William Wilde, feasted within the walls of Dún Aonghasa.[6] The enlistment of the contemporary islander in the reconstruction of Irishness followed closely. Here all that was most pungently characteristic of this relict state of being had been hoarded, like treasure buried in troubled times, now to be disinterred. Petrie had also collected folksongs, and O'Donovan placenames, from the Irish-speaking natives; the poet Samuel Ferguson and the painter Frederick Burton made the life of the Aran fisherfolk their subjects. The living culture of Aran, it was realized, was a repository of venerable antiquities. The Celticist Kuno Meyer visited Inis Meáin. Foreign scholars – the linguists Pedersen of Copenhagen and Finck of Marburg, the mediaevalist Zimmer of Berlin, the folklorist Jeremia Curtin of America – made the pilgrimage and paid their respects in learned treatises.[7] The islands' ancient monuments were re-examined by an excursion of the Royal Society of Antiquaries of Ireland in 1895, and in the same year the Irish Field Club Union, led by the naturalist Robert Lloyd Praeger, came to marvel at their fauna and flora. The revival of the Irish language, in retreat for centuries, was the dream of such founder members of the Gaelic League as Eoin MacNeill and Fr Eugene O'Growney, who sought out the living language in Aran in the 1880s.[8] W.B. Yeats came in 1896, looking for a setting for his proposed novel, *The Speckled Bird*, which was to oscillate between mystical Paris and peasant Ireland. In the year of Synge's first visit, 1898, the young Patrick Pearse was there and founded an Aran branch of the Gaelic League, and Lady Augusta Gregory collected fairylore. Thomas MacDonagh, later to be Pearse's colleague at his school, St Enda's in Dublin, and to join him in the sacrificial Easter Rising of 1916, also spent time in Inis Meáin, where he organized rifle practice on the crags. Thus by Synge's time Aran, and Inis Meáin in particular, had been widely identified as the uncorrupted heart of Ireland. (This attribution of a particular degree of Gaelic purity to the middle island was first made by Petrie, who thought that the morals of the big island had been contaminated by people introduced to build the lighthouse in 1818, and those of Inis Oírr by its proximity to the Clare coast.) The cottage of Páidín and Máire MacDonncha, in which Synge also stayed, was sometimes so full that the overflow had to sleep within the cashel walls of Dún Chonchúir nearby, and it was very reasonable of the islanders to conclude, as one of them told Synge, that 'there are few rich men now in the world who are not studying the Gaelic'.

Nowadays each of the islands has its airstrip, its small industries and its electricity generators. But the increasing implication of Aran with the outside world since Synge's day has scarcely dulled its alluring legend. The American director Robert Flaherty's famous 1932 'documentary', *Man of Aran*, situated his hero in a timeless world of rock and wave, and the many subsequent treatments in words and images have threatened to bury the little islands Pompeii-deep in interpretations. If Ireland is intriguing as being an island off the west of Europe, then Aran, as an island off the west of Ireland, is still more so; it is Ireland raised to the power of two. Whether the grain of wonderful truth in this can survive the trampling of the hundred thousand tourists who now visit the islands each year, remains to be seen.

THE PERSON

The Synges came to Ireland in the seventeenth century from England, produced a succession of bishops for the Protestant Church of Ireland, and married land. J.M. Synge's father, John Hatch Synge, was a younger brother of the owner of Glanmore Castle in County Wicklow; he inherited a small estate in County Galway, became a barrister in Dublin, and married the daughter of an Ulster-born rector of intemperate evangelical zeal. As landowners and clerics of the Established Church, standing on the apparently natural and divinely sanctioned economic and cultural rights of the Anglo-Irish community in Ireland, families like the Synges were loftily remote from such aboriginals as the Catholic, Irish-speaking and illiterate peasantry of the Aran Islands. At the same time the ties between the two classes were close and necessary (at least to the well-being of the former). The Synges' income derived in part from the rents paid by the small tenants of their Galway estates (as J.M. Synge's mother sharply reminded him once, when his social conscience was troublesome), while for his proselytizing forebears the rural Irish were a field of souls for the harvesting; in fact Synge's uncle had been the Church of Ireland minister in the Aran Islands in the 1850s.

But by J.M. Synge's generation the attitudes of the Anglo-Irish to the peasantry had become more complex and problematic, as the Protestant hegemony cracked before the rise of the Catholic middle classes. Among the Synges' peers were some of the intellectual leaders of the new version of Irish nationalism which found its inspiration in the hitherto despised folk of the countryside – but the Synge family itself had no truck with such an abdication of the duties of civilization.

John Millington Synge[9] was born in 1871 in Rathfarnham, then a village, now absorbed into the suburbs of south Dublin. His father died in the following year, and Mrs Synge, left with five children and a reduced income, moved to a house next door to her mother in nearby Rathgar. John was a sickly, asthmatic child, and laboured under the burden of his mother's vivid belief in hell-fire. An early love of the countryside and wildlife afforded some relief from the fond oppressions of home, but his reading of Darwin (when he was fourteen) introduced the new pain of religious doubt. Within a few years he no longer regarded himself as a Christian but as a worshipper of a new goddess, Ireland. His disbeliefs and beliefs formed rift-valleys of incomprehension between himself and his relatives, though he always preserved his status as a member of the family household. He gulped the patriotic balladry published in a nationalist newspaper, *The Nation*, and scoured the countryside in search of the Irish antiquities he read about in the writings of George Petrie. And in Petrie he would have read:

> The Araners are remarkable for fine intellect and deep sensibility ... If the inhabitants of the Aran Islands could be considered as a fair specimen of the ancient and present wild Irish ... those whom chance has led to their hospitable shores to admire their simple virtues, would be likely to regret that the blessings of civilization had ever been extended to any portion of the inhabitants of this very wretched country. But, fortunately for them, they cannot be so designated; much of their superiority must be attributed to their remote, insular situation, which has hitherto precluded an acquaintance with the vices of the distant region.[10]

Synge's enthusiasm for Irish matters did not close his mind to a wider cultural heritage. He took up the violin, and, while scraping through a second-class degree at Trinity College, which introduced him to the Irish language[11] and to Hebrew, he worked for and won a scholarship in counterpoint from the Royal Irish Academy of Music. It seemed that music was going to be his life. In 1893 a distant relative, Mary Synge, a concert pianist, arranged for him to stay with friends of hers, the Von Eiken sisters, in Oberwerth on the Rhine. After two months of studying music there, he moved to Würzburg. But he came to feel he would never be sufficiently confident to perform in public, and that his compositional talents were of little worth. He moved to Paris, and in 1895 he commenced courses in modern French literature, mediaeval literature and comparative phonetics at the Sorbonne, with the idea of becoming a critic of French literature. He lived the student's life of cold attics and introspective scribbling; he read such subtle adversaries of his mother's simple words of God as Mallarmé, Huysmans and Baudelaire. Holidays with his family in Wicklow alternated with a visit to Rome and further eclectic studies in Paris: the anarchist Sébastian Faure, Marx, Morris, Petrarch, St Thomas à Kempis's *The Imitation of Christ* (a discipline of meditative practice he seems to have tried to adapt to aesthetic contemplation). In Ireland he was pursuing an unpromising attachment to a girl called Cherrie Matheson, the daughter of a Unionist barrister prominent among the Plymouth Brethren; she would not have him because of his atheism. On the Continent he got to know a number of young women with whom he corresponded – all too often, some of them felt, on the subject of Cherrie – and with whom he obviously found it easier to form close friendships than with the men of his aquaintance.

In 1896 W.B. Yeats, who was a member of the secret Irish Republican Brotherhood, and his even more revolutionary muse Maud Gonne were in Paris, founding *L'Association Irlandaise* ('the Irish League') as a focus for Irish nationalists in France. Synge met Yeats in December of that year and joined the League, but soon resigned: 'I wish to work in my own way for the cause of Ireland and I shall never be able to do so if I get mixed up with a revolutionary and semi-military movement.' But other sides of the multifaceted Yeats probably influenced him, through such works as *The Celtic Twilight*, which enlists the fairies and ghosts of the Irish countryside into the shadowy battalions of European mysticism. Like so many others at that period he 'dabbled', as they say, in psychical research, in company with a new friend, Stephen MacKenna. MacKenna, then an impecunious journalist, had already translated *The Imitation of Christ* and was soon to begin his life's great work, the translation of the Neo-Platonist philosopher Plotinus.[12] But whatever degree of objective existence Synge might have allowed to the manifestations of the séances, he was always too much the realist to have shared Yeats's prodigal credences as expressed in *The Celtic Twilight*: 'Everything exists, everything is true, and the earth is only a little dust under our feet.'

It was probably at a meeting of the League that Yeats (according to his own account written in 1905) issued his momentous command: 'Give up Paris, you will never create anything by reading Racine, and Arthur Symons will always be a better critic of French literature. Go to the Arran Islands. Live there as if you were one of the people themselves; express a life that has never found expression.' Yeats had recently visited Aran with Symons, and, as the strategist of the Irish cultural revival, he realized the islands' symbolic importance, but knew that the new recruit would be better equipped than himself for their retaking.

But before Synge could go to Aran, he had an appointment with the disease that was to kill him twelve years later. The lump on his neck for which he went under the knife in December of 1897 was recognized by his doctor and the hospital nurses as a symptom of Hodgkin's disease, a cancer of the lymphocytes; it seemed they did not reveal this to him, and it was eight years before the growth recurred, but in the light of some very specific imaginings of death in his notebooks of the Aran years, it is difficult to believe he did not suspect the truth.

Synge returned to Paris for the first three months of 1898 and, perhaps with the Aran Islands in mind, interested himself in France's own Celtic appendix. He read Le Braz's *Vieilles Histoires du Pays Breton*, and Pierre Loti's *Pêcheur d'Islande*, about Breton fishermen who spend the summer seasons fishing off Iceland. It appears from a draft of his introduction to *The Aran Islands* that Synge intended to form his work on the model of Loti's. How that could have been done is an intriguing question, since Loti's novel is the story of a doomed romance, in which the sea as bride asserts its primacy over the seafarer's village love. But Synge the romantic atheist must have responded deeply to the meaningless but awesome universe Loti draws, in which prayers are not answered, clouds take up certain shapes only because they must take up some shape, wives keep vigil by granite crosses on rocky promontories for husbands who will never return, and even the attitude of the Crucified himself is finally equated to the gesture of a drowning man.

Synge left Paris at the end of April, had a painful interview with Cherrie Matheson in Dublin, and went straight on to Aran; he must have carried with him a heavy freight of moods, ideas and expectations.[13] His diary for the 10th of May reads simply: 'Dans le batteau à Arranmore à l'Hotel.' The grandly named Atlantic

Hotel was a small two-storey building on the quayfront in Cill Rónáin. From there he explored east and west along the road, and then on the third day of his visit he crossed the ridge of the island to the tall cliffs that confront the vastness of the Atlantic. Reliving this experience later on, his notebook gropes among impossible scenarios for a simile:

> I look now backwards to the morning a few weeks ago when I looked first unexpectedly over the higher cliffs of Aranmór, and stopped trembling with delight. A so sudden gust beauty is a danger. It is well arranged that for the most part we do not realize the beauty of a new wonderful experience till it has grown familiar and so safer to us. If a man could be supposed to come with a fully educated perception of music, yet quite ignorant of it and hear for the first time let us say Lamoureux's Orchestra in a late symphony of Beethoven I doubt his brain would ever recover from the shock. If a man could come with a full power of appreciation and stand for the first time before a woman – a woman perhaps who was very beautiful – what would he suffer? If a man grew up knowing nothing of death or decay and found suddenly a corpse in his path what would he suffer? Some such emotion was in me the day I looked first on these magnificent waves towering in dazzling white and green before the cliff.

Strangely, this revelation, equivalent to an instantaneous initiation into art, love and mortality, is not reported in *The Aran Islands* itself. But that slow-acting shock echoes in diminuendo through the four sections of the book, and is re-echoed more distantly in his subsequent works.

In Cill Rónáin Synge got to know an old blind man, Máirtín Ó Conghaile ('Martin Conneely'), who had been a guide to George Petrie, Sir William Wilde and others, and who he realized was therefore one of those fabulous Araners he had read of in Petrie 'years since when I was first touched with antiquarian passion'. This living antiquity gave him some lessons in the Irish of Aran, which Synge must have found very different from the Irish he had learned at Trinity, and showed him some of the island's Christian sites, including the mediaeval chapel 'of the four beautiful saints' whose holy well was to become the source of his play *The Well of the Saints*.

While in Árainn Synge called on the Church of Ireland minister Mr Kilbride and the Catholic parish priest Fr Farragher, and
acquired a camera from a fellow visitor. After a fortnight, finding
that Cill Rónáin had been dragged out of the Middle Ages by the
Congested Districts Board and become as banal as any other little
west-coast fishing village, he left it for Inis Meáin. There he
stayed in the MacDonnchas' cottage, and their son Máirtín (Synge
calls him Michael in his book) became his guide and tutor. Synge
lived for a month on this more primitive island, and also briefly
visited Inis Oírr. He spent his time drowsing on the walls of the
great cashel that looms over the cottages, wandering with Máirtín
or alone, taking photographs[14] of the islands (photographs mysteriously in tune with the moods of his prose), and picking up folktales and anecdotes, including those that were to grow into *The
Shadow of the Glen* and *The Playboy of the Western World*. Twenty-
seven years old and unlucky in love, he was very aware of the
beauty of the Aran girls; in his luggage was Loti's account of one
of his escapades of Cytherian imperialism, set in Tahiti, *Le
mariage de Loti*. He read a lot; other books listed in his diary
include Maeterlinck's *Le trésor des humbles*, *Les grands initiés* by
Édouard Scheuré (an admirer of Rudolf Steiner), an unspecified
work of Swedenborg's, Rossetti's poems, the Irish mystical poet
AE's latest collection *The Earth Breath*, and, as if as an astringent
corrective to these spiritual effusions, Flaubert's *Madame Bovary*
and de Maupassant's novel *Une Vie*,[15] both of them demonstra-
tions of the proposition that (to quote the latter) '*l'être moral de
chacun des nous reste éternellement seul par la vie*'. And above all, he
wrote. A frequent entry in his laconic diary is the single word
'Écrit'. Some at least of this writing was done in little notebooks
that would fit into the palm of the hand and that he could use
outdoors. It is curiously moving to read, in the stillness of the
manuscripts room of Trinity College Dublin, the first connected
passage in these notebooks:

> I am laid on the outstretched gable of a cliff and many feet below
> me great blue waves hurl from time to time a spray that rises in to
> my face ... So much spray is in the air that a soft crust forms on
> the pages of the notebook where I write.

During this first visit Synge witnessed and photographed one of the last – if not the last – eviction raids to be made on the island.[16] His description of it in *The Aran Islands* is a fine piece of engaged reportage; when he writes

> For these people the outrage to the hearth is the supreme catastrophe; they live here in a world of grey, where there are wild rains and mists every week in the year, and their warm chimney corners, filled with children and young girls, grow into the consciousness of each family in a way it is not easy to understand in more civilized places ...

he had already shared such a hearth for long enough to intuit its mysteries. But he also knew about evictions, in their legal and tactical aspects, from the other side, for his brother Edward was a professional agent to big landlords and an efficient practitioner of the art. Synge had had arguments with his mother on the subject, and when he describes an Aran mother cursing her son for acting as bailiff in this eviction, one could imagine Synge's mother rising opposite her to berate her own son for betraying his class by siding with rent-defaulting peasants.

On his way back to Dublin, Synge stayed for a few days at Coole Park, Lady Gregory's home in south Galway, at Yeats's suggestion. Yeats, Lady Gregory and Edward Martyn, her neighbour at Tulira Castle, were then planning the foundation of the Irish Literary Theatre, which later became the Irish National Theatre. One of the two plays with which the new venture was inaugurated in May 1899, Yeats's symbolic drama, *The Countess Cathleen*, excited the anger and incomprehension of the Catholic Church as well as of the Gaelic League, and the boos with which it was greeted foretold the theatre's turbulent future, on which Synge was to ride to his own troubled fame.

Synge visited Inis Meáin for nearly a month in September 1899, finding the island, in the rains and storms of autumn, a darker place, and the islanders dejected after a poor season's fishing. He caught a feverish cold and had fears of dying and being buried there before anyone on the mainland could know of it. He was there again for a month in September of the following year, when he participated in the islanders' grief over a drowning and witnessed scenes of despair and resignation out of which he was to make *Riders to the Sea*. Throughout his Aran seasons he advanced in island proficiencies; he talked and understood more Irish, learned to row a currach, contributed to evenings of fun and music. He went over to Inis Oírr again for a few days during this third trip, and got to know two girls there, one of whom corresponded with him later on. Whether it was she of whom in his notebook he wrote, 'One woman has interested me in a way that binds me more than ever to the islands,' is not known; the relationship, whatever its nature, seems to have come to nothing – but one wonders if later on this woman ever felt she had lost the only Playwright of the Western World?

In his alternative life in Paris Synge was engaged in another profitless love, with an American art student, Margaret Hardon, whom his diary often refers to as 'La Robe Verte'; he sketched a play (later entitled *When the Moon Has Set*) in which a writer loves a nun, whom he persuades to renounce her vows; she exchanges her habit for a green dress and gives herself to him. Reality was not so complaisant, nor was the sketch a success, and Lady Gregory and Yeats when they read it suggested he turn to peasant themes.

By the summer of 1901 Synge had put together the first three parts of his Aran book, which he sent to Lady Gregory; she and Yeats were impressed by it, but thought it would benefit from the inclusion of more fairylore. In late September he revisited Inis Meáin and Inis Oírr for a total of nineteen days. In Inis Meáin several people were ill with typhus, and Synge was horrified at the thought of them dying without a doctor. He would have met the islands' district nurse in Inis Oírr on one of his previous visits – she was later to write a gruesome account of her struggle against the insanitary folk-cures and the filth of those hearthsides Synge found so cherishing [17] – but it seems that no medical help was available in Inis Meáin at this time. In Inis Oírr he collected folksongs with the dedication of a professional, and translated an eighteenth-century version of the ancient legend, *The Children of Uisneach*, which had been published recently; it was to furnish the matter of his last play, *Deirdre of the Sorrows*.

On his way to Paris that November, Synge delivered the manuscript of *The Aran Islands* to a London publisher Yeats had suggested, Grant Allen, who soon returned it. In January 1902 Fisher

Unwin, also of London, similarly declined it. His writing career was depressingly unsuccessful; he was still living on an allowance of '£40 a year and a new suit when I am too shabby'. But he doggedly pursued his commitment to the Celtic by following a course in Old Irish at the Sorbonne, where he was frequently the lecturer's sole hearer. These were his seasons of endurance, and they were at last rewarded by a creative outflow; during the next summer, which he spent with his mother in a rented house in Wicklow, he wrote *The Shadow of the Glen* and *Riders to the Sea*, and began *The Tinker's Wedding*. The two completed plays were very welcome to Yeats and Lady Gregory, for their Irish National Theatre was more blessed with talented actors than with plays worth acting. Synge spent twenty-five days in Inis Oírr in October but did not visit Inis Meáin; it was his last trip to the islands and was not reflected in his already completed book.

Synge gave up his Paris apartment that winter and lodged in London, where he was introduced by Lady Gregory and Yeats to the literary world. John Masefield took note of this new, but not young and rather sombre face:

> Something in his air gave one the fancy that his face was dark from gravity. Gravity filled the face and haunted it, as though the man behind were forever listening to life's case before passing judgement ... The face was pale, the cheeks were rather drawn. In my memory they were rather seamed and old-looking. The eyes were at once smoky and kindling. The mouth, not well seen below the moustache, had a great play of humour on it.[18]

Then he returned to Ireland, and in June 1903 he heard *The Shadow of the Glen* read by Lady Gregory to the actors of the Irish National Theatre. That autumn he visited Kerry instead of Aran, and found there an English-speaking peasantry whose dialect he could more immediately adopt into his plays.

The first performance, in October of that year, of *The Shadow of the Glen* was hissed by an audience which pronounced its theme an offence to Irish womanhood. Arthur Griffith, founder of the nationalist organization Sinn Féin and editor of the *United Irishman* newspaper, was particularly violent in his attacks on Synge and the National Theatre. Synge's fantastic realism was at odds with that cast of mind which, tensed in repudiation of the 600-

year-long slurs that had accompanied colonization, would admit no defect in the life of Catholic rural Ireland and held that an Irish National Theatre should be the vehicle of patriotic propaganda. His plot had been suggested by a folktale he had heard in Inis Meáin in 1898, concerning a husband who pretends to be dead in order to catch his young wife with her lover; he added to it the wife's abandonment by the pusillanimous lover and her going off with a tramp who has by chance been witness of these events. The setting he chose was one of the great sheep-glens of Wicklow he knew so well. In fact, there are sheep everywhere in the dialogue of the play: the productive and individually recognizable sheep of the skilful shepherd who had befriended the lonely wife and then gone mad and died before the action begins, unmanageable sheep escaping in all directions from his incompetent successor the lover, sheep jumping through gaps, leaving their wool on thornbushes, coughing in the fog, stretched out dead with spiders' webs on them, and perhaps even covertly, aimlessly astray in the famously depressing view from the wife's door, of 'the mists rolling down the bog, and the mists again and they rolling up the bog ...'. Indeed, to accept the nationalists' own simplistic account of why they were disturbed by such a weird drift of disorderly feelings as Synge let loose through this play, is to close one's eyes to the psychological wastes he explores in it.

When *Riders to the Sea*, a sombre presentation of the anguish and resignation of Aran wives and sisters successively robbed by the sea of all their menfolk, was given a first performance in February 1904, it was well received by a small audience, and even Griffith's paper had to admit its tragic beauty. Aran must have long been associated in the public mind with death by drowning; Petrie's account of an old Aran woman still grieving for her son lost to the sea, Burton's painting *The Aran Fisherman's Drowned Child* (exhibited at the Royal Hibernian Academy in 1841, and circulated widely as an engraving[19]), the heroine's drowning in Emily Lawless's *Grania: The Story of an Island*,[20] are some earlier treatments of the theme, and Synge's play, the action of which is always on the point of condensing into ritual, was the definitive celebration of the cult. Folk beliefs of hearth and threshold weigh so heavily if obscurely on speech and gesture in this play that the air its protagonists displace seems thickened with symbol and significance. North, south, east and west are so compulsively evoked as every change of tide and wind brings in new anxiety or despair, that the island itself seethes in a doomful infusion of the compass rose. The elegiac rhythms of Synge's dialogue are those inherent in the English of native Irish speakers, an English the grammar of which has been metamorphosed by the pressure of Irish, and the words of which have therefore been galvanized into new life by syntactic shock. As (necessarily simplified) examples: Irish has two verbal forms that both have to be translated by parts of the verb 'to be' in English; *is*, used in identifying two things, and *tá*, used in attributing quality to something; thus '*Is é Beartla atá ann*' translates literally as 'It is Bartley that is in it (*i.e.* there)'. Again, there is no word for 'yes' in Irish; instead one repeats the verb of the question: 'Is it Bartley that is there?' 'It is.' Both these features involve repetition, and thus the possibility of rhythm, when imitated in English. Also, Irish is rich in little tags and pieties that prolong a sentence soothingly. Synge calls on all these effects for the simple, death-hushed syllables of this exchange, when the body of one of the drowned sons is brought in:

> Is it Bartley it is?
> It is, surely, God rest his soul.

Here he has avoided the form 'Is it Bartley that's in it?' which in a lighter context he would have exploited. But where there is poetic advantage in it, he will translate word for word, ignoring dictionary equivalents: in '... no one to keen him but the black hags that do be flying on the sea', those ominous and mysterious 'black hags' come literally from the Irish name of the shag or green cormorant, *cailleach dhubh*. And where poetry would be irrecuperably lost, he does not translate at all: in 'the dark nights after Samhain', the Irish word for November is so much more expressive of wind and rain (the pronunciation being approximately 'sawain') and the reminder of the ghosts of Hallowe'en, *Oiche Shamhna*, so much more immediate, that Synge chooses to rely on an Irish audience's familiarity with the word and its associations, and on an English audience's intuition of mystery. Douglas Hyde, in his translations of folksongs, and Lady Gregory in her versions of legends, had preceded Synge in the literary exploration of the borderzone between Irish and English inhabited by the folk-people of Ireland, but Synge is the only playboy of this western world of words, in which he grew to his full freedom and power. Synge's language is the translation into English not of an Irish text but of the Irish language itself.

The company went on to a great success in London with Synge's two plays, especially *Riders to the Sea*. In that summer of 1904 it took over what was to become the Abbey Theatre, leased through the generosity of an English admirer of Yeats, Miss Horniman, and rehearsals of *The Well of the Saints* soon began. Synge visited Kerry again, and then, instead of going to Aran as planned, took his bicycle down to Belmullet in the far west of Mayo. This extraordinarily bleak and remote peninsula was to become the setting for *The Playboy of the Western World*, although he had picked up the germ of its plot in Inis Meáin. *The Well of the Saints* was performed in February 1905, and evoked the same rage in nationalist quarters as had *The Shadow of the Glen*. Indeed this grim and comic morality of uncaring youth and foolish age, in which even sanctity and miracle appear as tactless intrusions into hard-won if fantasizing accommodations with reality, holds little comfort for anyone. The setting is again Wicklow, but the well of the title, from which a roving saint has brought holy water to cure an old blind couple, is the one Synge visited in Árainn in company with old Martin Conneely. He could have heard tales of such cures told of any of hundreds of holy wells throughout Ireland, but perhaps in the dreamworkmanship of creativity there was a link between his plot – of old Martin Doul (*dall*, 'blind') and his wife being cured of their blindness, regretting it when they discover they are not the beautiful couple they had imagined, and slowly recovering their blindness – and the odd fact of Synge's being shown a well reputed to cure blindness, by a blind man.

In *Riders to the Sea* the young curate is dismissed near the beginning of the play as powerless to avert the impending tragedy, and the comforts of official doctrine are nowhere called on in its aftermath; the miracle-worker of *The Well of the Saints* sees his dissatisfied clients stumble off to make their way through a dangerous world by the light of their own darkness; similarly, in *The Tinker's Wedding*, which Synge was working on at this time, the wanderers of earth finally assert the irrelevance of the clergy to their life-cycles: 'it's little need we ever had of the like of you to get us our bit to eat, and our bit to drink, and our time of love when we were young men and women and were fine to look at.' Synge's tribute to the born anarchs of the Wicklow roads whom he appreciated so much was never staged in his lifetime. The rejection of religious authority implicit in most of his work was acted out in this play, in which the tinkers bundle the venal priest into a sack when he refuses to marry them without his 'dues' being paid in full. In his preface to the text, published in 1907, Synge hopes that the country people, from tinkers to clergy, would not mind being laughed at without malice, but at the time Yeats was not so optimistic; he felt the play would cause too much trouble for his young theatre, and Synge seems to have agreed. The first performance of it took place in London in 1909, after Synge's death, and it was not seen in Ireland until the year of the Synge Centenary Commemoration, 1971.

In 1905, at the prompting of Masefield, the *Manchester Guardian* commissioned Synge to write a series of articles on the distressed state of the Congested Districts. The artist Jack Yeats, younger brother of the poet, was to illustrate the articles, and the two of them explored Connemara and Belmullet in Mayo that summer. On his return Synge wrote to MacKenna:

> Unluckily my commission was to write on the 'Distress' so I couldn't do anything like what I would have wished as an interpretation of the whole life ... There are sides of all that western life the groggy-patriot-publican-general shop-man who is married to the priest's half sister and is second cousin once removed of the dispensary doctor, that are horrible and awful ... I sometimes wish to God I hadn't a soul and then I could give myself up to putting those lads on the stage. God, wouldn't they hop! In a way it is all heartrending, in one place the people are starving but wonderfully attractive and charming and in another place where things are going well one has a rampant double-chinned vulgarity I haven't seen the like of.[21]

This is impercipient, as personal and business relationships in the small towns of western Ireland were not more incestuous than in Synge's own familial or artistic milieus; but then a substantial stratum of Irish life hardly found expression in the works of the Irish cultural revival, which recognized no muse between the ranks of countess and colleen. However, the imposed theme focused his eyes on the miserable obverse of the rural economics that had delighted him in Aran, and he expressed this darker matter of poverty and exploitation with moving directness. The articles were republished after his death in the 1910 edition of his works, despite Yeats's feeling that they were inferior. Jack Yeats was later to illustrate the first (1907) edition of *The Aran Islands* with twelve drawings, some of them evidently based on Synge's photographs and only one or two of them remotely adequate to the subtle and vigorous text.

Synge had been engaged in the tempestuous politics of the Irish National Theatre from its foundation, and in the autumn of 1905 he became one of its three directors, with Yeats and Lady Gregory; as he explained in a letter to MacKenna, Yeats looked after the stars while he saw to everything else. Soon afterwards a number of the more politically oriented actors seceded, and among those brought in to replace them was a nineteen-year-old girl, Molly Allgood, with whom Synge was soon in love. He had been living with his mother – for their close relationship still persisted despite her incomprehension of his work – but now he took rooms in the suburbs of Dublin, both to be nearer his theatre and to see more of Molly. She was a cheerful and comparatively uneducated girl whose frank enjoyment of such innocent treats as picnics with other members of the company came to torment the jealous and serious-minded Synge; his Dublin Albertine used to annotate his multitudinous, obsessive and insinuating letters with brisk one-word judgements: 'idiotic', or 'peculiar', or 'frivolous'. She was also a Roman Catholic, which promised to cause consternation in his family when their affair should become known. But she inspired the love-talk of Synge's most richly realized character, Christy Mahon of *The Playboy of the Western World*. Synge wrote the part of Pegeen Mike in that play with Molly in mind, and she played that role in the first performance in 1907.

The company was anxious about the wildly prodigal language of the play, and presented it to their highly reactive audience with trepidation. Yeats was in Scotland at the time, and after Act Two had been received with attention Lady Gregory sent him a telegram: 'Play great success.' But Act Three provoked such an uproar that she sent off another telegram: 'Audience broke up in disorder at the word shift.' The 'Playboy Riots' were to become part of theatrical legend. As Synge wrote to Molly the next morning, 'Now we'll be talked about. We're an event in the history of the Irish stage. I have a splitting headache...' Large numbers of police – the Royal Irish Constabulary, to the nationalists an arm of foreign oppression – were called upon to preserve a semblance of order for the following performances, which were largely inaudible. Yeats returned hastily from Scotland, lectured the baying crowd from the stage with courage and dignity, went into court to testify against arrested rioters, and within a few days organized a public debate, in which despite personal reservations he spoke himself hoarse for Synge's play against a tumultuous audience. Synge himself was at home in bed suffering from exhaustion and influenza.

The story of the *Playboy* had been developed out of two incidents Synge had heard of in the west: one, of a Connemara man who murdered his father and was sheltered by the people of Inis Meáin for a while, supplied the theme of parricide, and the other, of a Mayo man who assaulted the lady he was employed by, repeatedly escaped from custody, taunted the police in letters and was protected by various lady-friends, added the ingredients of sexual attractiveness and verbal dexterity.[22] Griffith in an editorial described the play as 'a vile and inhuman story told in the foulest language we have ever listened to from a public platform'. While it is clear that audiences came to the play primed by such opinions to be shocked, it should be recognized that *The Playboy of the Western World* is genuinely shocking. We, nine shocking decades later, if we are not rattled to our ontologies by a play, tend to want our money back; but it is hardly surprising that those unhardened Dublin audiences, facing such a flood of bizarre talk and action bursting from depths in which tragic, including Oedipal, themes echo like laughter, found it difficult even to pinpoint the source of their disquiet. When Christy at the peak of passion cries, 'It's Pegeen I'm seeking only, and what'd I care if you brought me a drift of chosen females, standing in their shifts itself, maybe, from this place to the eastern world?' they thought they found the word 'shift' offensive as being an indelicate synonym of 'chemise'; in fact it is the steam-hiss of an exorbitant fantasy compressed into a moment. Synge, to some degree, knew what he was at. As he wrote to MacKenna, 'On the French stage you get sex without its balancing elements: on the Irish stage you get the other elements without the sex. I restored sex and people were so surprised they saw the sex only.'

The play was taken to England in the summer, and although Yeats decided that it was too risky to put it on in Birmingham where what he called 'the slum Irish' might have been organized by the nationalists to demonstrate against it, performances in Oxford and London were very successful. Synge was in London and in good health for the occasion, and was lionized. Also *The Aran Islands* had at last been published (by Elkin Mathews in London and Maunsel in Dublin), and so 1907 gave him his brief summer of glory. July he spent in the Wicklow hills; Molly and her sister came to spend a fortnight at a cottage near his, and they rambled and rejoiced together.

Over the next autumn he worked on a play very different from his four savage comedies. The plot of his tragedy *Deirdre of the Sorrows* is adapted from the ancient Irish tale, a version of which he had translated in Inis Oírr five years before: the lovely girl being brought up in seclusion as bride for the old king who rules at Emain persuades the young huntsman she has seen in the woods to run away with her, but eventually, as if compelled by the beauty of her own legend, returns to Emain and the fate foretold at her birth. Although Synge's setting is of woods and hillsides, references to the clouds coming from the west and south, and the rain since the night of Samhain, soon take us back to the meteorological determinism of *Riders to the Sea*. Deirdre appears at first as the child of nature itself, unpossessable by all the knowledge and power of civilization, and ends in suicide over a grave dug in the earth, mourned by nature: 'if the oaks and stars could die for sorrow, it's a dark sky and a hard and naked earth we'd have this night in Emain'. Perhaps this is the echo of that thunderous revelation, transcending art, love and death, on the cliffs of Árainn; long-delayed, almost too long-delayed ...

For Synge's period of incipient glory was also that of his dying, and *Deirdre of the Sorrows* was never to be quite finished. His neck glands had been troublesome for some time, and in September he had been operated on for their removal. Although he still discussed marriage plans with Molly, and revisited Kerry, his periods of health and good spirits were sporadic now, and there were endless quarrels and schisms within the theatre company to depress him further. His family no longer opposed his marriage, but it had to be postponed when he went into hospital in April 1908 for investigation of a painful lump in his side, and was found to have an inoperable tumour. He was not told of the fatal implications, and for a time felt much better, but the pain returned. The household he was preparing for Molly had to be broken up, and he returned to live with his mother, who was failing too. Writing to Molly, he said, 'She seems quite a little old woman with an old woman's voice. It makes me sad. It is sad also to see all our little furniture stored away in these rooms. It is a sad queer time for us all, dear Heart, I sometimes feel inclined to sit down and wail.' Then, rallying, he went off to Oberwerth to see the Von Eiken sisters once again, and bought works by the mediaeval German poets von der Vogelweide and Hans Sachs with the intention of translating them. His mother died while he was still in Germany, and he did not feel well enough to face the journey home for her funeral. On his return he lived alone in his mother's house, and worked intermittently on his *Deirdre*. He looked through his earlier work and wrote,

> I read about the Blaskets and Dunquin,
> The Wicklow towns and fair days I've been in.
> I read of Galway, Mayo, Aranmore,
> And men with kelp along a wintry shore.
> Then I remembered that that 'I' was I,
> And I'd a filthy job – to waste and die.

By the spring the filthy job was done. He entered Elpis Hospital again on the 2nd of February 1909 and died there on 24 March. At the funeral, his family and his artistic colleagues formed two immiscible groups, and the fisherfolk, tramps and playboys of Ireland of course knew nothing of it.

THE BOOK

Kilronan ... has been so much changed by the fishing industry, developed there by the Congested Districts Board, that it now has

very little to distinguish it from any fishing village on the west
coast of Ireland. The other islands are more primitive, but even on
them many changes are being made, that it was not worth while to
deal with in the text.

Thus Synge in his brief introduction divides Aran into the primitive and the not worth writing about. His text, though, overflows
his programme. In fact on his typescript[23] Synge scribbled, '*Note
If the early chapters explain themselves I would prefer m.s. without any Introduction. J.M.S.*' Obviously the publishers' worldly
wisdom prevailed, but in ideality Synge was right: all introductions
(and introductory essays by third persons) by indicating a perspective reduce the dimensionality of what they introduce, and so
should be read only after the work itself – but by the time one
realizes this, it is too late. Synge lent his European mind to Aran
for a while on generously indefinite terms, and *The Aran Islands*
can be read in many ways. A sentence in Synge's second notebook
insists on one: 'I cannot say it too often, the supreme interest of
the island lies in the strange concord that exists between the
people and the impersonal limited but powerful impulses of the
nature that is round them' – and so the essential matter of the
book is an ecology of moods. Later on he took a more distanced
view (and one can trace this growing detachment in the book
itself, as the divergences of the islanders from his prescription of
them become their most interesting and theatrically engaging
aspect, and a relish for the actual quarrels in him with his thirst
for the ideal); in 1907 he wrote to a friend, 'I look on *The Aran
Islands* as my first serious piece of work ... In writing out the talk
of the people and their stories in this book, and in a certain
number of articles on the Wicklow peasantry which I have not yet
collected, I learned to write the peasant dialect and dialogue which
I use in my plays.' So the book is a stage in the evolution of
Synge the dramatist. It has also been read in a sociolinguistic
mode as 'fictionalized confessional autobiography'[24] and can be
seen as a set of symptoms of the dilemmas of the late nineteenth-
century Anglo-Irish mind. Books shed meanings as trees their
leaves, year after year, in their slow growth and maturation. Nearly
a century has passed since Synge first walked the bare wet rocks of
Aran and his old blind guide put the riddle of the Sphinx to him.

That double-natured and sphinx-like creature, Synge-on-Aran, still proposes its riddle, which is that of our own mortal stance on the earth. Now that our planet has shrunk to an island in space (if not to a Congested District, and with no fatherly Board set over it!), all past efforts to unriddle our being-on-the-earth have to be reread; perhaps Synge's book will reach another maturity in this age of secular eschatologies.

The Aran Islands is in four parts, corresponding to the first four of his five visits. At the start he materializes, as it were, out of rain and fog on to the big island, Árainn, and meets a satisfactorily mediaeval mentor who talks of women carried off by fairies and gives him scraps of lore in which the Celtic hero Diarmaid and Samson from the Bible cohere with classical motifs, as in the detrital culture of the hedge-schools. But he is surprised at the fluency and abundance of 'the foreign tongue', *i.e.* his own language, in Cill Rónáin, and only a few pages after his arrival he removes to Inis Meáin, having come to the conclusion that life there 'is perhaps the most primitive in Europe'. The first sentence of the Inis Meáin pages echoes the first sentence of the book so closely as to give the impression that the latter merely represented a false start and that it is only now that we are really beginning:

> I am settled at last on Inishmaan in a small cottage with a continual drone of Gaelic coming from the kitchen that opens into my room.

We acquire two meagre hints about Synge's non-Aran existence in these preliminary pages. An old islander tells him that he recognized his likeness to his relative who was in Aran forty-three years earlier – and so we learn of the Synge connection with the islands from the lips of an Aran man, not from the author's. The fact that Synge's uncle was the Protestant incumbent is not stated. And on the trip across to Inis Meáin, his crew call out to some comrades that they 'had a man with them who had been in France a month from this day'. Again, we learn a fact about Synge through its reflection (as a wonder) in the minds of the islanders. Thus one of the book's principles of exclusion is early established, and is only underlined by the very occasional subsequent reference to Paris, standing for all that is not Aran. Another of these principles may be induced from the fact that most of the folktales he records are dropped into the text without comment, as they would have cropped up in Aran life, in the course of a conversational walk or an evening's entertainment. Only in the case of the first tale he heard in Inis Meáin, about the man who bets on his wife's faithfulness during his absence, does he permit himself a belletristic excursus on its European antecedents: 'the gay company who went out from· Florence to tell narratives of love', 'the *Pecorone* of Ser Giovanni, a Florentine notary', and so on. The passage has been praised for its skilful condensation of an extensive body of literary lore, but it does not convince one that it was written out of Synge's memory in Inis Meáin, and as a flaw in the appearance of immediacy that controls the rest of the book, it is the one false note in the whole. (The fourth and last section of the book is perhaps even overloaded with this folk-material, which, though interesting in itself, is not fully thought into the texture of the work.) Thus, by opposites as it were, a specification of the book's content is implied; it is the content of the mind of a visitor on the island, not of someone writing about the island from a study on the mainland.

There are other principles of exclusion at work too. A comparison of the contents of his notebooks and the finished work tells much about the rigour of Synge's processes of composition. For instance, a much revised version of the passage about the spray on the leaves of the notebook itself, quoted above (p. 121), is found in a draft of *The Aran Islands*, but it does not occur in the finished work. As it in fact relates to the cliffs on the big island, this, like other omissions, seems to indicate that Synge wanted to truncate his account of the big island and hasten his definitive settling in Inis Meáin. This same passage in the draft is conflated with some inept nature-notes from the first notebook:

> Everything in Aran has a certain rarity or distinction. Dandelion and buttercup here have yielded up their place to pansies with pale yellow lips, blackfooted maidenhair – to translate its [Gaelic] epithet – clings to the rock among the bracken and rooks and daws are replaced by these more graceful choughs.

Since dandelions and buttercups are glorious in the islands, the fern called in Irish the 'black foot' is not the maidenhair,[25] *etc.*, Synge's final decision not to treat of the flora is wise; even his very general comment on it, 'On these rocks, where there is no growth of animal or vegetable life, all the seasons are the same', is depressingly unobservant – but then it is wafted into a magical and melancholy subjectivity by its conclusion: 'and this June day is so full of autumn that I listen unconsciously for the rustle of dead leaves.' Another entry in the first notebook not reflected in the final work is on Dún Aonghasa:

> The antiquarian treasures of the islands are not strictly in the scope of my scattered notes and they have often been described. Some however possess such conspicuous individual beautiful that they come plainly beneath the impressionist. I have just visited Dun Angus a great primeval fortress placed with strong boldness on the edge of the highest cliff in Aran ... The dull leaden grey of the evening though unlovely in itself was fitted to evoke the sense of absolute loneliness here at home. These races who raised the three great circles of concentric walls, what was their real feeling as they gazed in simple raiment from the cliff where I gazed?

In one of the later drafts this train of thought is continued:

> My sadness and delight are older than the walls about me, and have lingered round these rocks since men were hairy and naked, for emotion is as inherent a property to this place as the colour or odour of the waves.

But the attempt at recuperating the emotions of hairy prehistory by means of the dubious metaphysics of their inherence in the rocks is abandoned, together with the description of the site. In fact Dún Aonghasa is one of the most striking absences in the book, and even the huge cashel lowering over Synge's cottage in Inis Meáin is left undescribed except as 'a corona of stone'.

Most visitors to the islands are as impressed by the great cashels as they are by the luxuriance of the summer flowers; but even before these perceptions they are overawed by the presence of stone everywhere. Synge certainly gives one the picture of a bare and stony island, but his account nowhere conveys the extreme stoniness of Inis Meáin, which is remarkable even in the context of the Aran Islands. Two aspects of this feature have been noted above: the sheets of smooth naked rock that extend for hundreds of yards in terraces below the line of villages, and the mighty stormbeach around the exposed southern shoreline and on top of the western cliffs. Synge does not mention these two astounding formations, which insistently raise the question of geological origins, of the processes of time; it is as if he wanted to generalize his island into elemental simplicity and atemporality. Similarly the striking out of Dún Aonghasa from his record amounts to the suppression of the islands' history. Neither the rich corpus of legends and traditions associated with Aran's saints and monasteries, nor the dramas of the Cromwellian conquest, nor the piteous hungerlore of the Famine century, figure in his account. The great echochambers of the past, from the geological birth through the prehistory and history of the islands, are closed off, almost down to the immediately relevant inheritance of landlordism. On the eve of the threatened evictions Synge asks, as if the question had just come into his head, who owns Inis Meáin; and the islanders' answer places the matter in the perspectives of the picturesque: 'Bedad, we always heard it belonged to Miss —, and she is dead.' The islands, then, exist only in the shallow, cyclic time of sunsets and tides and seasons, the rippling weather-like time so accurately metered by Synge's prose style itself. The pathos of this situation, its vulnerability, is expressed in the first of the notebooks, which so often spell out what is left implicit in the book itself:

> The thought that this island will gradually yield to the ruthlessness of 'progress' is as the certainty that decaying age is moving always nearer the cheeks it is your extasy to kiss. How much of Ireland was formerly like this and how much of Ireland is today Anglicized and civilized and brutalized?

All that has happened to our world impends upon his island; the islanders are soon to be evicted from stasis and sent wandering on the roads of history.

Thus some of Synge's omissions merely result from a decision not to be didactic or to waste time in acquiring the low grade omniscience other topographical writers aspire to, while certain themes broached in the notebooks lead him too far into the personal for exposure in the published work. But the grand exclusions mentioned above are definitive of the work itself, and to note them is not to criticize his creation but to situate it, to discover its co-ordinates, the negative ones as well as the positive, and to measure the richness of its austerity by the stringency of its rejections, the magnitude of the sacrifice of material (self-sacrifice, Synge being so at one with much of this material) necessary to carve it into the form it aspires to, which is island-like, extramundane. But what sort of truth does this drastic paring-away of reality leave to his claim in the introduction that he has written 'a direct account of [his] life on the islands ... changing nothing that is essential'? The life-currents that bring him repeatedly to the islands and carry him off again are virtually unrepresented in the book, which suggests that progressive, autobiographical time is as irrelevant as history to the truths he is conveying. And in listening for these truths, one has to be aware of variable distances between his islands and the Aran of our geographies, as well as between the visitor he projects on the islands and the Synge of the biographies. Synge the writer, for instance, had to put down thousands of words on that spray-encrusted paper while in Aran; the visitor's mind retains the most complex sensations and intuitions in their pristine perfection.

The boat-trip to Inis Meáin from Cill Rónáin, that awkward compromise of Aran with the mainland, had given that visitor the 'exquisite satisfaction' of moving away from civilization in a canoe of a model that had 'served primitive races since men first went on the sea'. The middle island is the real Aran, and its indubitable rock soon wears out his boots, so the islanders make him a pair of rawhide moccasins like their own in which he learns the 'natural walk of man'. These initiations into the archaic, this casting off of modern life like a worn-out pair of boots, suggest that for Synge our civilization itself is merely something interposed, for the sake of false decency and craven comfort, between us and the harsh and beautiful truths of our world.

The visitor's description of the interior of the cottage he is to lodge in is aglow with the colours of homecoming. He feels that the handmade articles of local materials not only 'give this simple life, where all art is unknown, something of the artistic beauty of mediaeval life', but seem to be 'a natural link between the people and the world that is about them'. The islanders' way of life, he notes, 'has never been acted on by anything much more artificial than the nests and burrows of the creatures that live round them'. This action on them of the natural, though, is of a Darwinian ruthlessness; great dexterity is needed to bring a currach into land on a rocky shore through the breakers, and 'this continual danger ... has had considerable influence on the local character, as the waves have made it impossible for clumsy, foolhardy, or timid men to live on these islands.' It is particularly in Part I that Synge builds up this picture of a life lived hand in hand with nature, as, for instance, in his accurate observation of how the appearance of the village street changes with the wind's direction, either all the south doors being open, or all the north doors, and so of how his hostess's ability to judge the time depends on whether or not the sun is casting the shadow of the south door's jamb on the kitchen floor. (How strange it is, that Synge's first gift to his hosts on this island of elemental timekeeping was to be an alarm-clock!) And this sympathy between man and nature works both ways, the visitor is forced to believe, after witnessing a burial at which the thunder seems to join in the keening for the dead.

The visitor is not just an observer of the islands' enviable naturalness, but a novitiate; he learns some of their sea-skills, their language. On his second visit he shows the islanders some photographs he took the previous year, and

> a beautiful young woman I had spoken to a few times last year slipped in, and after a wonderfully simple and cordial speech of welcome, she sat down on the floor beside me to look on also. The complete absence of shyness or self-consciousness in most of these people gives them a peculiar charm, and when this young and beautiful woman leaned across my knees to look nearer at some photograph that pleased her, I felt more than ever the strange simplicity of the island life.

Synge's second notebook goes further: 'Another visit is over ... One woman also has interested me in a way that binds me more than ever to the islands. The women are before convention and share many things with the women of Paris and London.' During his first visit he had been reading Pierre Loti, arch-exponent of the temporary marriage both as a form of life and as a literary genre, and had noted for himself, apropos of *Le mariage de Loti*, 'The wanderer has many pains that are known to wanderers only; in a score of places I also have longed to linger for my life and marry me with the woman that has mostly appeared to personify as a central life each new system of sensation.' The personification of the island as a woman comes no doubt from the promptings of a young man's blood as well as from the august precedents of Celtic myths in which the king marries the tutelary goddess of his realm. The notebook is more visceral than anything in the published text: 'With this limestone Inishmaan ... I am in love, and hear with galling jealousy of the various priests and scholars who have lived here before me. They have grown to me as former lovers of one's mistress, horrible existences haunting with dreamed kisses the lips she presses to your own.' By the end of his third season in Aran the visitor is telling the islanders that he is going back to Paris to sell his books and his bed (the elementary furnishings of his life), and then coming back to grow as strong and simple as they among the islands of the west. The next year, in self-ironizing counterpoint to his own romanticism, he also records the advice of the young men to him, that he should marry a fine, fat island girl who would have plenty of children and not be wasting his money on him.

But it is when alone, as he is for long hours, that the visitor enters into his own ecology of Being, finding his introspective way to that oneness with the natural world he divines in the island culture. He begins to understand the island nights and the distinction they lend to those who work by dark; he spends time by himself near the shore in darkness so absolute he cannot see or realize his own body and exists only in his hearing waves and smelling seaweed. He lies on the cliff-edge and experiences something of the revelation of inanimate vastitude Synge tried to express in his first notebook; he seems 'to enter into the wild pastimes of the cliff, and to become a companion of the cormorants and crows'. (A draft for the Aran cliff episode goes further than this Wordsworthian empathy: 'I fulfil a function like the litchen and the grass, and my thoughts are older than the stones about me' – but this illumination is not developed.) And if he were to become part of this island universe, it would at the last treat him with dignity and accept him into its own element: 'This death, with fresh sea salt in one's teeth, would be better than most deaths one is likely to meet' – a thought the first notebook elaborates into a painfully realistic prevision of the death that would face Synge himself: 'to struggle in soiled sheets and thick stifling blankets with the smell of my own illness in my nostrils and a half paid death tender at my side till my long death battle will be fought out'.

Thus three identifications are being asserted: of the islanders with the island, of the visitor with the islanders, and of the island with the visitor. But none of these is without its painful contradictions, and Synge is true to those as well. Sometimes it is the Aran people who do not live up to the vision he has of them. The claim that the waves forbid the existence of clumsy or foolhardy men on the islands is undermined by the anecdote in Part I of a half-drunken crew rowing the visitor 'at an absurd pace' in a currach slowly filling with water from a leak which they had 'with their usual carelessness' neglected to mend. Often the Araners are distracted by the outside world from their island natures: 'Yet it is only in the intonation of a few sentences or some old fragment of melody that I catch the real spirit of the island, for in general the men sit together and talk with endless iteration of the tides and fish, and of the price of kelp in Connemara.' Synge could imagine better Aran men than these, and eventually he had to create his Araners of the mind, in *Riders to the Sea*. At the same time the visitor, in common humanity, cannot but listen sympathetically to the islanders' economic problems. 'The price of kelp in Connemara', in particular, was to be a question of heart-rending importance for the Aran Islanders Synge depicted in his 1905 articles on 'the distress' in the Congested Districts, but for the visitor in Aran in 1898 such a question was only an interruption, part of the deplorable but inevitable intrusion of the mainland which was coercing and seducing the islands away from their essence. The most aggressive instance of this coercion is the eviction party of sweaty policemen who contrast so horribly with islanders as cool as seagulls; the most beguiling of the seductions is the shrill handbell calling the womenfolk to a meeting of the Gaelic League. The absurdity of applying mainland law to the seagull-islanders and of charging them rent for the rock they perch on is manifest; the teaching of written Irish is ominous, for it heralds the death of their oral culture and the clogging of their language with the dross of modern life.

But even if the outside world leaves them alone and uncorrupted, can the islanders really be at home in 'a universe that wars on them with winds and seas'? In the last two sections of the book Synge describes repeated scenes of anguish over deaths by drowning, which evidently affected him deeply.[26] The account in Part IV of the woman dying of typhus, while her menfolk row off into mist and wind in a vain quest for help, ends with the visitor talking with the old folk around the fireside about the sorrows of the people until late in the night. Coming from a funeral, he watches fishermen at work with a dragnet on the shore, and feels that they are all under a judgment of death on sea or land, and will all be battered naked on the rocks or buried with another such fearful scene in the graveyard as he has just witnessed. The islanders' symbiotic pact with nature, then, leaves them helpless when it is broken, in the absence of civilization's support.

The visitor's own aspiration to oneness with the island community is problematic too. During his second stay he realizes how far away from him these people are: 'They like me sometimes, and laugh at me sometimes, yet never know what I am doing.' The cultural spaces between him and the islanders seem impassable: 'They have the same emotions that I have, and the animals have, yet I cannot talk to them when there is much to say ... On some days I feel this island as a perfect home and resting place; on other days I feel that I am a waif among the people.' And (in Part IV) it is not just he himself with his insufficient Irish who is excluded, but the whole civilization that he was born into: 'I became indescribably mournful, for I felt this little corner on the face of the world, and the people who live in it, have a peace and dignity from which we are shut for ever.' Similarly his attempts at direct communion with the island itself can lead him into dark moods:

> After a few hours [of walking in the storm] the mind grows bewildered with the endless change and struggle of the sea, and an utter despondency replaces the first moment of exhilaration ... The wind is terrific. If anything serious should happen to me I might die here and be nailed in my box, and shoved down into a wet crevice in the graveyard before any one could know it on the mainland.

Here is the bad death, grim alternative to the heroic sea-change he had proposed for himself as an Aran currach-man, during his first rhapsodic immersion in island life. From his early days in Inis

Meáin the visitor records a striking dream, in which he is seduced into an ecstatic dance by music tuned to a forgotten scale, that becomes a vortex annihilating all outside itself and changes suddenly to shrieking agony. The dream hardly bears the theory it is burdened with: 'Some dreams I have had in this cottage seem to give strength to the opinion that there is a psychic memory attached to certain places' – which reads like a perfunctory nod to Yeats.[27] Synge's mind was too positivistic to entertain the mysticism of AE's *The Earth Breath* either (and he confesses in the first notebook that he is too profane and sophisticated to see 'the small gentry' with which the islanders' island is swarming at night). If this dream represents the blissful and deadly dance of union with nature, it also enacts the rebellion of the individual intelligence against such pantheistic self-obliteration.

Thus it seems that there is a painful contradiction between the necessity and the impossibility of each of three identifications constituting wholeness, between the visitor, the islanders and the island itself – or between the individual, the community and the natural world, if we may read by the light of the question Synge asks himself in his notebook, on taking leave of the island after his first rapturous appropriation of it: 'In this ocean, is not every symbol of the cosmos?' And it is on the site defined by this triangle of tragic conflicts that Synge, in one sentence near its beginning, conjures the spirit of his book:

> The continual passing in this island between the misery of last night and the splendour of today, seems to create an affinity between the moods of these people and the moods of varying rapture and dismay that are frequent in artists, and in certain forms of alienation.

Here the island, the islanders and the writer are as one, subject to the manic-depressive regime of the Atlantic. It is the swift and transitionless alternations of emotional weather that give his book its characteristic texture, and this is no mere surface phenomenon or stylistic finish, but a structure deeper than the fourfold division of the work or of any analysis of it by themes. This structure expresses itself in miniature in the exquisite portrait of a young island girl whom he salutes across the chasms that divide them, as a kindred soul:

As we sit on stools on either side of the fire I hear her voice going backwards and forwards in the same sentence from the gaiety of a child to the plaintive intonation of an old race that is worn with sorrow. At one moment she is a simple peasant, at another she seems to be looking out at the world with a sense of prehistoric disillusion and to sum up in the expression of her grey-blue eyes the whole external despondency of the clouds and the sea.

In this passage we are surely looking into the face of Synge's Aran herself.

NOTES

1 The largest of the three islands is called Árainn (the obsolete locative case of *ára*) or Árainn Mhór (*mór*, 'big'); the latter name was anglicized as Aranmore or Arranmore. Nowadays the name Aranmore is reserved for the island off County Donegal. Perhaps it was to avoid confusion with the Donegal island that the Ordnance Survey in 1839 introduced the name Inishmore for the big island, in line with the anglicized forms of the neighbouring islands' names, Inishmaan and Inisheer, and despite the fact that there was then no Irish form Inis Mór ('big island') to be anglicized. Sadly the dull backformation Inis Mór is now widely used even by native Irish speakers, and the euphonious Árainn is neglected. Inis Meáin, anglicized as Inishmaan, means simply 'middle island'. The name of the third and smallest island has been rather corrupted; anciently it was Inis Oirthir, 'island of the east', and the form now recommended by the Ordnance Survey, Inis Oírr, anglicized as Inisheer, is an attempt to represent the current pronounciation while remembering the old meaning. Synge often refers to it as the south island, and to Árainn as the north island – the island chain runs from east-south-east to west-north-west.

2 Etienne Rynne, 'Dun Angus: Fortress or Temple?' in *An Aran Reader*, eds Breandán and Ruairí Ó hEithir (Dublin, 1991).

3 E. Hacket and M. E. Folan, 'The ABO and RH Blood Groups of the Aran Islanders', *Irish Journal of Medical Science*, June 1958.

4 The Reverend Simon Digby, Protestant archbishop of Elphin, had acquired half of Aran in 1713, and Robert Digby bought out the other

half in 1744. At the time of the Great Famine of 1847 the landowner, Miss Elizabeth Francis Digby of Landenstown, Kildare, was criticized for sending only two tons of meal as relief to her hungry tenants. According to local lore, Miss Digby visited the islands once, when a dance was held in her honour on a stretch of smooth limestone near Cill Mhuirbhigh; there was a spot known as Miss Digby's Steps by the harbour in Cill Éinne, but otherwise little was known of her by the islanders. A niece of hers had married Sir Thomas St Lawrence, third earl of Howth, in 1851, and when Miss Digby died in about 1894 the two daughters of that marriage, Henrietta Eliza Guinness (sister-in-law of Lord Ardilaun) and Geraldine Digby St Lawrence, inherited. The islands were acquired from the St Lawrences and the Guinnesses by the Land Commission in 1922.

5 Oliver J. Burke, a barrister who visited Aran for this purpose, wrote the first book on the islands, *The South Isles of Aran* (London, 1887).

6 George Petrie (1790-1866) represents the transformation of Celtic antiquarianism, with its armchair speculations about the Druids and the Lost Tribes of Israel, into a recognizably modern archaeology based on investigation of sites. He was also President of the Royal Hibernian Academy and published an important collection of Irish traditional music. He visited Aran and made the first study of its monuments in 1822, and again in 1857 with the British Association expedition, when he collected many folksongs and painted an almost expressionistically contorted view of Dún Aonghasa on its precipice, now in the National Gallery of Ireland. From 1835 to 1842 he directed the Topographical Department of the Ordnance Survey of Ireland, for which the great scholar John O'Donovan (1806-1861) travelled the country recording ancient monuments, placenames and traditions.

Dr William Wilde (1815-76), Dublin's leading eye and ear surgeon, was President of the Royal Irish Academy and catalogued its collections. He conducted the British Association's visit to Aran in 1857, and was knighted in 1864 for his services to the Irish census. His wife Lady Jane Wilde wrote patriotic poems and books on folklore, and their son was the famous and infamous Oscar.

7 Kuno Meyer (1858-1919) studied at Leipzig. While lecturing on German and Celtic at Liverpool, 1884-1906, he travelled widely in Scotland, Wales and Ireland and founded the School of Irish Studies in Dublin in 1903. He succeeded Zimmer in the chair of Celtic Philology at Berlin in 1911. Heinrich Zimmer (1851-1910) was in Aran in 1880 and supported the Land Leaguers at a public meeting; he published a paper on St Enda in 1889.

145

The eminent Danish linguist Holger Pedersen (1867-1953), professor at Copenhagen, published his *Comparative Grammer of the Celtic Languages* in 1903-13. The folktales he took down in his own phonetic script from the old man who was later to be Synge's guide in Árainn, have recently been deciphered and published (*Scéalta Mháirtín Neile: Bailiúchán Scéalta ó Árainn, Holger Pedersen a thóg sios sa bhliain 1895*, ed. Ole Munch-Pedersen, Comhairle Bhéaloideas Éireann, Dublin 1994).

Pedersen's disciple Franz Nikolaus Finck spent four months in Aran in 1894-5 researching his thesis, which was published as part of his two-volume *Die Araner Mundart* (Marburg 1899). An Aran-born writer, the late Breandán Ó hEithir, has disintered from this work a saying, 'Ní bhéarfainn broim dreóilín ar dhuilleog cuilinn agus is beag an puth gaoithe é sin!' ('I wouldn't give the fart of a wren on a hollyleaf, and it's the small puff of wind *that* is!') – which the linguistic anarchs of Synge's plays would be hard pressed to emulate.

The American linguist and antiquarian Jeremia Curtin (?1840-1906) was reputed to know seventy languages. As Secretary of the US Legation in St Petersburg he studied and translated from Slavonic languages. In 1883-91, with the Bureau of Ethnology of the Smithsonian Institute, he worked on North American Indian languages. His *Myths and Folklore of Ireland* appeared in 1890.

8 Fr Eugene O'Growney (1863-99) first visited Inis Meáin in 1885 as a student at the Catholic seminary of Maynooth; he became Professor of Irish at Maynooth in 1891 and began to publish his famous *Simple Lessons in Irish* in 1893.

The Gaelic League was founded in Dublin in 1893 by 'half a dozen nonentities', as Douglas Hyde, its first President, put it. Its policy was to foster an 'Irish-speaking Ireland', and the inspirational dedication of these early cultural revolutionaries can be judged by the contrast between the late nineteenth century, when Irish-speaking parents in collaboration with the National Schools were actively beating Irish out of their children, and the early decades of the twentieth century, when up to 75,000 people were trying to learn the language and participating in Irish dancing and folklore classes, festivals celebrating Irish culture, and Irish games. The League was progressively politicized by such members as Patrick Pearse, and Hyde retired in 1915 when it declared, against his wishes, that it stood for a free Ireland. He was replaced the next year by Eoin MacNeill, then in prison for his part in the 1916 Easter Rising. Writing for the *Manchester Guardian* in 1923, Hyde summarized the influence of the League as follows:

The Gaelic League grew up and became the spiritual father of Sinn Féin, and Sinn Féin's progeny were the Volunteers, who forced the British to make the Treaty. The Dáil is the child of the Volunteers, and thus it descends directly from the Gaelic League.

The young Patrick Pearse visited Inis Meáin in 1898 and set up an Aran branch of the Gaelic League; the attendance of seven hundred people at its inaugural meeting in Cill Rónáin included a large delegation from Inis Meáin. (See *The Gaelic League Idea*, ed. Seán Ó Tuama, Dublin 1972, and for the Aran branch, the League's own organ, *Fáinne an Lae*, 20 August 1898.) Pearse, who proclaimed the Republic of Ireland in 1916, and his teacher colleague Thomas MacDonagh were among the leaders of the Easter Rising executed by the British.

9 The factual framework of my account of Synge and his family is drawn from the standard biography by David H. Greene and Edward M. Stephens, *J.M. Synge 1871-1909* (revised edition, New York and London, 1989).

10 Quoted in Dr William Stokes, *Life and Labours in Art and Archaeology of George Petrie* (London, 1885).

11 Synge's substantial attainments in the knowledge of the Irish language and its literature, together with his changing attitudes to the policies of the Gaelic League, are discussed in detail in Declan Kiberd, *Synge and the Irish Language* (London, 1979).

12 George Steiner (*After Babel*, New York and London, 1975) writes, 'MacKenna gave his uncertain physical and mental health to the translation of Plotinus' *Enniades*. The five tall volumes appeared between 1917 and 1930. This solitary, prodigious, grimly unremunerative labour constitutes one of the masterpieces of modern English prose and formal sensibility.'

13 This account of his visits to Aran is based on Synge's diaries and notebooks in the manuscripts department of Trinity College Dublin. The fullest of the notebooks (4385), used on his first visit and corresponding to the first and longest section of *The Aran Islands*, has been usefully transcribed by Marek van der Kamp ('An Authentic Aran Journal'), M. Phil. thesis, TCD, 1988). On Synge's second visit he used some pages from a notebook (4384) started years earlier in Paris. I have referred to 4385 and 4384 as the first and second notebooks respectively. A third notebook (4387) contains mainly folklore material used in Part IV of his book, and a fourth (4397) also has some notes from his fourth visit.

14 The twenty-three surviving photographs of Aran have been published in *My Wallet of Photographs: The Photographs of J.M. Synge*, arranged and introduced by Lilo Stephens (Dublin, 1971).

15 Not *The Life of Guy de Maupassant*, as the standard biography has it!

16 The 1800s were a period of extreme want in the islands because of the potato crop failures and a fall in kelp and pig prices; many tenants owed six to nine years' rent. There were repeated attempts to collect this money together with a collective fine of £452 that had been imposed on the tenantry for damages to stock and property during the Land War of 1880/81. In January 1898 a rent-collector with an escort of fifteen constables was driven off the big island by a crowd of 300 islanders. In May a rent-collecting expedition to Inis Meáin was thwarted by a sudden storm, but in June the forces of justice returned, with the results Synge witnessed. These seem to have been the last evictions on the island. (See Antoine Powell [an island author], *Oileáin Árann, stair na n-oileán anuas go dtí 1922*, Dublin, n.d., but *c*.1983.)

17 B.N. Hedderman, *Glimpses of My Life in Aran*, Part I (Bristol, 1917).

18 J. Masefield, 'John M. Synge', *The Contemporary Review*, April 1911.

19 Marie Bourke, *Painting in Focus: 'The Aran Fisherman's Drowned Child' by Frederick William Burton* (Dublin, 1987).

20 The Hon. Emily Lawless (1845-1913), daughter of Lord Cloncurry, published her best-known novel *Grania: The Story of an Island*, set in Inis Meáin, in 1892; her other works include poetry, historical studies and biography. Synge read *Grania* during his first visit to Aran, and in his notebook criticized the superficiality of her knowledge of the islands.

21 *The Collected Letters of John Millington Synge*, ed. Ann Saddlemyer, 2 vols (Oxford, 1983).

22 Synge mentions the story of the Connemara man hidden by the islanders in Part I of *The Aran Islands*, and in a draft of this passage he adds, 'Another story is told here of a highway robber who escaped from his prison and hid himself away among the people in the Connaught hills ... At last two girls were arrested on a charge of harbouring him, and he gave himself up to clear them. This happened recently.' The Connemara man was the son of a poor farmer called Ó Máille and was born about 1838 in Callow, west of Roundstone, where his story is not quite forgotten. According to local lore collected early in this century (Tomas Ó Máille, *An Ghaoth Aniar*, Dublin, 1920), he was a handsome athletic man, the pride of the neighbourhood, but his father was a quarrelsome drunkard. When the son wanted to plant some potatoes, the father tried to stop him by

grabbing his 'loy', or spade, and in the struggle had an attack and seemed about to die, and young Ó Máille took to the hills. (A very circumstantial account of the quarrel and of Ó Máille's wanderings in Connemara is preserved in the manuscripts collection of the Department of Irish Folklore, University College, Dublin, among material collected through local schools in 1937-8.) After eluding the police for several months, he crossed to Cill Rónáin, where he was sheltered by a woman relative (who, it is still remembered in the island, was living next door to the Atlantic Hotel at the time of Synge's visit). Because he was so distressed by what he had done, and was talking to nobody, the islanders tried to cheer him up with parties, dances and cardgames – hence, it is said in Aran, his reputation as a 'playboy'. Word of his presence reached the authorities, so the islanders took him to Inis Meáin, and when the police surrounded the cottage in which he was sheltering there the man of the house let himself be captured in his place. After living rough for a time, Ó Máille got away to Tralee in a boat carrying potatoes from Árainn, and signed on as a sailor in a ship for America. He revisited Galway as a ship's captain two years later.

The other case was that of James Lynchehaun (c.1858-c.1937), a wild and unpredictable school-teacher who had already been arrested for a minor assault and jumped bail before the period of the crime that made him famous. In 1894 he was facing eviction by Mrs Agnes MacDonnell of Achill Island, County Mayo, who had been his employer. Her stables burned down one night and during the confusion she was assaulted and left dreadfully battered, with her nose nearly bitten off. Later that night her house burned down as well. She accused Lynchehaun of the assault (and he was probably behind the burnings too). He was arrested, escaped from the police, was hidden by distant relatives, including a young female cousin, in a hole in their floor under a dresser, was discovered and rearrested, tried and condemned to life imprisonment. He became celebrated in ballads and in newspaper reports as 'the Achill troglodyte'. In 1902 he made a most ingenious and daring escape from Maryborough Gaol and got away to America. When arrested there he claimed his crime was political, and with the support of the Irish nationalist community avoided deportation. He revisited Achill in disguise in 1907 and returned safely to America, despite having been briefly detained by the local police over a break-in. Later he returned to Achill again, was arrested and released after a few months. It seems he died in Girvan, Scotland. In *The Playboy of the Western World* he is mentioned as 'the man that bit the yellow lady's nostril'. 'Yellow' here means English, as in the derogatory name for an Englishman, Seán Buí, 'yellow John'; Mrs

MacDonnell had English connections. (See James Carney, *The Playboy and the Yellow Lady*, Swords, County Dublin, 1986.)

23 The typescript, together with an earlier draft, is no. 4344 of the Synge manuscripts in TCD Library.

24 Mary C. King, *The Drama of John Millington Synge* (London, 1985).

25 I wronged Synge here. The maidenhair fern is the *dúchosach* (black-footed) in Aran. But I will let the error stand, as I have subsequently written it into the structure of my *Stones of Aran: Labyrinth* (Dublin, 1995).

26 Synge has been criticized by the anthropologist John C. Messenger not only for 'primitivism' and 'nativism' but for projecting a tragic world vision on island life (*Inis Beag, Isle of Ireland*, New York, 1969; *Inis Beag Revisited*, Salem, Wisconsin, 1989; 'Islanders Who Read', *Anthropology Today*, April 1988). Messenger, in the course of his researches in Inis Oírr in 1959-60, reckoned up that there had been only four sea accidents, with the loss of but twelve lives, in that island since 1850, and states that Synge's claim that every family has lost men to the sea 'reflects not only his masochism but the broadness of kinship reckoning'. Amazingly, the world of Synge scholarship seems meekly to have accepted this rebuke. Quite apart from any too subtle considerations of the exact reality-status of Synge's verbal creation, it should be pointed out that Inis Oírr is another island, and that his remark on drownings are closely linked to specific incidents – two due to drunkenness in which four lives were lost, a drowning of three men of one family 'a few years ago', the destruction of fishing boats in Killeany Bay, and another loss of a young man whose funeral he attended. Synge also reports the realism of an islander's view of the use of fear: 'A man who is not afraid of the sea will soon be drowned, for he will be going out on a day he shouldn't. But we do be afraid of the sea, and we do only be drownded now and again.' And when that 'now and again' comes, which is the more adequate response – the anthropologist's statistics or Synge's prose, as resonant as the keening of the grief-stricken relatives?

27 In view of this theory it is odd that the only dream Synge's diary records from Aran was of a riot in connection with the Dreyfus case, which was agitating Paris at the time.

10

Listening to the Landscape

On the other edge of the Atlantic there is an island roughly the shape and size of Manhattan, called Árainn, one of the three Aran Islands, off Galway Bay, where I lived for many years. From it I could see the quartzite peaks of Connemara, on the north of the bay, and the grey limestone plateau of the Burren, on its south. It seems strange now to be talking about those quiet little places, here in this roaring city, on the edge of this vast continent. And to be discussing in New York the language, Irish or Gaelic, that is still spoken in Aran and Connemara, but only by a few thousand people, in fact to be bringing you merely a few words from the local dialects of that language, words that are falling into disuse – perhaps that needs some explanation. My excuse must be that I came to that narrow island and that dying language from the great cities and the great languages of Europe, and found in them something that I am still trying to understand, and am anxious to pass on. Heard something, I should say, rather than found. The language and the place, the landscape, spoke with one tongue, and spoke of something that is in danger of being forgotten by the busier languages and places of the world.

To get over an initial embarrassment about it I should also explain that the fairly fluent if grammatically limited Irish I picked up when living in Aran has decayed a good deal over the last few years when I have been living in an English-speaking part of Connemara and although I have no difficulty in reading and understanding Irish I fear to speak it in public, lest my pretention to know something about Irish placenames look absurd. If I am to declare what the Irish language, and in particular the placenames, have meant to me as a wanderer in that language's natural habitat, I must rely on your forbearance.

I'll begin with some moments – which in my memory have become symbolic – of my first encounters with Irish, after M and I
moved from London to the Aran Islands twenty years ago. One of
the first remarks the village blacksmith, Mícilín an Gabha, made to
us after showing us round the bare, damp, cottage we had rented
from him in Árainn, was that the wild geese flying southwards
over the island in the autumn make every letter of the alphabet in
the sky; first a huge A, then a B, and then, as he put it, 'a burst of
them' make a C. He thought this was remarkable, since those
geese had never been to school. I would have thought it remarkable too, but the best I ever saw the wild geese do in all the
autumns we spent in Aran was the occasional *síneadh fada*, the
stroke marking a long vowel in Irish writing. But the idea of the
sky's teaching us the language remained with me. The Irish language as an emanation of the land of Ireland, of that segment of
the earth's surface and its moody skies, is the theme I want to
explore tonight.

Micilín spoke English competently, but his sentences, sparse,
short and sturdy, seemed to rise up out of a continuum of *sotto-
voce* murmurings like jutting rocks in a foaming sea. This flux of
obscure phonemes, I realized by degrees, was Irish, from which his
English was being translated, with great loss. By listening to him,
and to the men chatting with him at the forge while their ponies
were shod, I began to pick out words, and so identify topics, even
if what was said about these topics was still carried away from me
by the streams of sound. I remember a significant step towards
acquisition of understanding. I had asked an old man the name of
a certain well – for the absurdity of my *curriculum vitae* is that I
started collecting Irish placenames before I could understand Irish
– and he had told me it was Tobar an Asail, the well of the
donkey. And then he added: '*Thit asal isteach ann fadó.*' ('A donkey fell into it long ago.') It was the first sentence of spoken Irish,
outside the classrooms of Irish courses, that I completely understood. *Thit asal isteach ann fadó.* As dense and foursquare as a
limestone block, a stone from the ruins of the past – but with that
mysteriously evocative momentary prolongation of the word *fadó*.
The voice of history itself, telling how all things fall.

Another moment, from a later stage of the process: I was going
into Inis Oírr, the smallest of the Aran Islands, in one of the local

boats called currachs – flat-bottomed canoes that can be run up onto a sandy beach. At that period the old cargo ship that served the islands used to hang about off shore while the currachs came out and ferried both goods and passengers to the beach. A very calm, silent afternoon – it must have been out of season as I was the only non-islander in the boat. As we neared the strand the men lifted their oars and the currach hung motionless, little waves running in under it, clucking, like chicks under a hen. The islanders were exchanging murmurs, so quietly that if I had not learned some Irish I might not have realized anything was being said at all. They were discussing the individual waves, looking for one a little bigger than the rest on which to run the currach up onto the beach so that I could leap out dryshod. I heard the man in the prow whisper to the man in the stern, *'Fan nóiméid, tá ceainnín beag eile ag gobadh aníos fút anois'* ('Hold on, there's another little one pushing up under you now'). A still moment, drifting on a neaptide of time – and then a surging stroke of the oars and they were shouting at me to jump: *'Anois! Amach leat go tapaidh!'*

These images I am offering you – the wild-goose chase of the alphabet in the sky, the waves whispering to each other under the currach, the donkey uttering *seanchas* from the well – are little myths, to tempt you to hear the language as if it were spoken by the landscape. For me it was so from the beginning, as I shall explain. But is there any more defensible, objective truth in the idea of a deep connection between a landscape and its language? Is it in any way more true of Irish than of, say, French or German? An Irish philosopher, John Moriarty, recently told me that among the things that had not happened to the Irish language were the Renaissance, the Reformation and the Enlightenment. If this be true it is so only with many partial exceptions and qualifications. But, letting ourselves be swept along with the huge generalization, it would mean that Irish is a language less dominated by the prestige of the book, less individualistic in its stance towards the absolute, less hospitable to analysis, than those neighbour languages which were the immediate sites of these cultural upheavals. And these upheavals, these floods of thought, not only left rich deposits in those languages, but swept much away that had come to be seen as obsolete and valueless, and which we now feel the want of. So the obverse of these limitations might be that Irish is more eloquent by the fireside than in the lecture hall, more apt to conviviality than solitary self-definition, happier in the phenomenal and emotional world than among abstractions. Of course in any living language there are speakers and writers who swell its vocabulary and bend its structures. Life, for a language, is continuous self-transcendence. Nevertheless, each language has its own core of native strength and sweetness, and perhaps in the case of Irish this is to be identified with its immediacy to experience, and in particular with its closeness to the land. If in the following examples I concentrate on land of a stony nature it is because of Ireland I only know Aran, the Burren and Connemara, which are all of stone, and if in the Irish language I concentrate on nouns, it is because I only know nouns, having picked up them up like so many coloured stones.

Stones, then. *Cloch* (stone) is a fine word, a solid, lumpy two-fistfuls of sound. I love also the expressive suite of words for different sorts of stony place: *clochar*, *clochrach* or *cloithreach*, *creig* (in Aran a *creig* is an area of bare limestone pavement; the plural is *creigeanna*, but I have heard the magnificent form *creigreachaí*), *cragán* or *criogán* (which is something between a *creig* and a field), *leac* or *leic*, meaning a flagstone or flat sheet of rock, with the plural *leacrachaí*, and *leacht*, which usually means a cairn or monument but in Connemara can mean the same as *leac*. Also: *scairbh* and *screigín*, both meaning rough stony places, and *scailp* (in Aran a *scailp* is usually a fissure in the limestone, but can be any sort of stony declivity or hole), with the marvellously rugged plural *scalprachaí*. Aran is of course the headquarters of these harsh words in *cr* and *scr* and *cl*, the islands being totally composed of *creigeanna* and *scalprachaí*. Many of the little green fields of Aran have been reclaimed from bare rock by spreading sand and seaweed on it year after year to build up the soil. Tomás Ó Direáin, brother of the well-known Irish language poet from Aran, Máirtín Ó Direáin, has a little poem about an Aran man reclaiming a *leic*, a flat sheet of rock, beginning

> *Féach é ina sheasamh ar an leic,*
> *Atá liath agus lom*

(See him standing on the flag/ which is grey and bare)

and ending with nursery-rhyme simplicity:

> Le allas a bhaithis
> Le fuil a chroí
> Déanfaidh sé talamh
> As na scalprachaí.

(With the sweat of his brow, with the blood of his heart, he will make land out of the – *scalprachaí*! I defy anyone to find an adequate translation for the word.) Nursery rhymes can be explosive, though; they have to be handled carefully. Here we have 'land', the earth, being made out of the blood of the heart – the blood of self-sacrifice through labour, not the blood of self-sacrifice in battle, the blood Patrick Pearse thought would warm the heart of the earth, but disturbingly reminiscent of it. In talk about land and language, there is always a whiff of this third element, blood, and the three have historically made up a deathly stew. This dark context of my theme is one that, having glanced into, I must now step around – with perhaps this note of caution to myself: When talking about the land or the landscape speaking, do not forget that this is only a metaphor, suggestive in some contexts and baleful in others, and that in fact the speaking is made up of the speech acts of countless individuals, each one in its unique historical and social setting. My own 'listening to the landscape' has included listening to hundreds of farmers, housewives, fishermen, shopkeepers, and the odd professor of Irish too.

The most immediate connection between language and reality, the one first made by children and by language learners, is that of naming things. Placenames are the interlock of landscape and language. As mentioned, I started collecting placenames in the Aran Islands before I could understand a word of the language; this was perhaps because Micilín the blacksmith was so anxious to impart his knowledge of them. This zeal for communication of the lore that it seemed was no longer finding an audience in the local community, and so was discharged on me, demanding of me that I take note and record it for ever, is an imperative force I have felt again and again over the twenty years of work that grew out of those initial conversations in the smithy of Aran. This work was not what I had in mind when I came to Ireland; there is an element of compulsion in it, something I did not know of in myself, perhaps still do not know of, which answers to something in this landscape. Or perhaps the landscape saw me coming. So in my diaries for that first winter in Aran I find notes on the boundaries or mearing walls of villages whose names I have spelled out in *ad hoc* English phonetics, with scrappy explanations of the names, some of them completely misunderstood. It is usual to have a degree in Irish, and to know something of Old Irish too, before tangling with the complexities of placenames. Of course as I became aware of the difficulties I took to consulting experts. Most of the obscure or arguable cases have been submitted to the judgement of several specialists – the result often enough being several different opinions, or rather suggestions, for no one who knows the subject would be dogmatic about interpreting a name without visiting the place itself. Armchair speculations about the meaning of placenames, without visiting the locality to hear the exact pronunciation and to observe the topography or any other salient characteristics of the place, are necessarily inconclusive.

This is because placenames are semantically two-pronged; they not only have a referent, like any proper name, *i.e.* the place they denote, but most of them also have a connotation; they make a condensed or elliptic remark about the place, a description, a claim of ownership, a historical anecdote, even a joke or a curse on it. And so they may only reveal their meaning in the physical and historical context of the place. When I was mapping Connemara I was puzzled by the names of two uninhabited townlands out in the wide expanses of the bog: Tullaghlumman More and Tullaghlumman Beg. A *tulach* is a small hill – in Connemara most *tulacha* are sizeable drumlins in fact – but these areas were labyrinths of lakes in level bogland. According to John O'Donovan, who was the Ordnance Survey's expert on placenames for the first survey in the 1830s, Tullaghlumman meant 'Lomán's hill' – for whenever O'Donovan could not otherwise interpret a placename he would derive it from some personal name, and he invented an amazing number of peculiarly named persons in the process. But one day I was out walking the bog with a shepherd from Roundstone, and when we stopped to catch our breath and admire the view he pointed out a rocky knoll in the distance, and said 'That's Tulach Lomáin.' It was a very small eminence, only noticeable even in the huge encircling flatness of bogs and lakes because of a large outcrop, a sheet of bare rock, on one side of it. Back at home, in the dictionary I found the word *lomán*, rock outcrop, evidently from *lom*, bare. So a very minor feature, but one visible from afar, a useful landmark to shepherds, had given its name to a large area. On that same day we passed a small lake up on the side of a steep hill, called Loch Roisín na Róige, a name nobody could explain or translate for me. Climbing beyond the lake, we followed a little ravine cut by a streamlet that flung itself down waterfalls, which my companion told me was called the Róig. And that solved the crossword puzzle of the landscape, as if a 'down' word had given me the vital letter in the 'across'; for *róig* means a sudden rush or attack, and where this aggressive little stream drops into the lake a little peninsula or *roisín* has been built up out of the stony material it has ripped out of the mountainside. Loch Roisín na Róige, the lake of the little point of the Róig or onrush; it encapsulates the dynamics of the geography. For me it is also a memento of a vigorous day's walking and talking with one of Connemara's mountainy men.

Interpreting such placenames sends me to the dictionaries; the landscape examines me in the language. Often, though, the dictionaries cannot help, as particular usages are so localized as to have escaped their nets. Here's an interesting example from the biggest of the three Aran Islands, Árainn itself. The word *scrios* occurs in dozens of placenames in the western half of Árainn, where it apparently means a broad expanse of land not much broken up by field walls; Micilín tells me one could say *'Nach breá an scrios talún atá agat!'* ('What a fine *scrios* of land you have!') I haven't heard it anywhere else. There is Scrios na gCapall, the *scrios* of the horses, Scrios Buaile na bhFeadóg, the *scrios* of the milking-pasture of the plovers, and Scrios an Teach Beag, the *scrios* of the small house. (Grammatically speaking, it should be Scrios an Tí Bhig, but Aran placenames are not so fussy about genitive cases as the grammar books, and who am I to correct them?) I haven't found any connection between this usage and the various dictionary meanings of the word *scrios*: destruction, scrapings, a light covering of soil *etc.* Another highly localized word from Aran is *creachoileán* or *creachalán*, applied to a number of big slab-shaped offshore rocks, rather grim-looking and dangerous, and all well-known to the currachmen; there's An Creachoileán Mór, the big *creachoileán*, and

An Creachoileán Báite, the drowned or submerged *creachoileán*, for instance. Tom O'Flaherty, Liam O'Flaherty's brother, in one of his stories of Aran fishermen, renders *creachoileán* as 'rock of woe' (as if from *creach*, ruin, loss *etc.*), but I don't know its true derivation, nor of any instance of it outside of the Aran Islands. Some of these dialect words have other senses elsewhere. In the west of Connemara everyone would understand an *imleach* to be a glacial hill, a drumlin, whereas in other parts of the country, and in the dictionaries, it means marginal land. A *caorán* in south Connemara is a small roundish hill of moorland; elsewhere it is a moor in general. In the Aran Islands a *réalóg* is an unenclosed patch of good land in the middle of a *creig*; the word is still understood in Inis Meáin in this sense, but not in Árainn, although it occurs in dozens of placenames there. I particularly relish this linguistic parochialism, as part of the connubiality of land and language; these are words one learns, not from the resources of the library, but from the woman carrying her milkpail up to the cow on the *caorán*, the farmer who has his sheep on the *imleach* or his potatoes in the *réalóg*, or from the fisherman who nearly got drowned off the drowned *creachoileán*.

Of course I could be wrong about any one of the placenames I have published, even if no one else is in a position to prove it. I don't mind putting question-marks by the names on my maps; and if I have made mistakes, I have at least recorded the material on which someone better equipped than myself can make a better guess. But if I waited until academically impregnable certainty is attained, there would never be a map. However, I keep a special copy of each of my published maps, on which I note my cartographical sins of omission and commission as they come to light; I call it the Black Copy. There will always be another edition, an afterlife in which these things can be made good, or at least a more informed guess can be made.

Can certainty be reached? There is a myth of ultimate authority for the placenames of Ireland, recorded in a Middle Irish work of the twelfth century, *Agallamh na Seanórach* or *The Colloquy of the Ancients*. This tells of how St Patrick meets a band of tall men with huge wolfhounds, who it says were not people of one time or one epoch with the clergy; in fact they were the last of the Fianna, the followers of the Celtic hero Fionn Mac Cumhaill, in their immense old age. They wander all round Ireland with the saint, telling him the name of each place and the story behind the name. At the end of each story St Patrick calls for his scribe and says, '"By thee be it written down all that Caoilte has uttered," and written down it was.' This represents the handing-over of the land and its meanings by paganism to the new religion, a profound symbolic linking of the historical and modern to its timeless legendary hinterland, enacted in terms of placelore. St Patrick, bishop, is the guarantor of the truth of the interpretations inscribed under his watchful eye. Note the patriarchal significance of the saint's episcopal staff here, as the ultimate symbol from which all others derive their stability of meaning. But the saint's staff or *bachal*, the shepherd's crook, is itself a question-mark. There is a tempting resonance in the idea that all interpretations are open to question, that certainty is endlessly deferred. One hears of the 'death of the author', the impossibility of grounding literary readings in the intentions of the writer – and no author is as deeply under the sod as the originators of placenames. But, to be sensible, in the majority of cases one can arrive by historical and linguistic inquiry, by guesswork and emendation, by hook or by St Patrick's crook, at what we might as well call truth.

At the same time, misinterpretation is part of the life of a placename. I heard recently of a Connemara farmer who was expounding the local placenames to a visitor; after a series of fascinating elucidations he summed up by saying grandly that the farmer without Irish is a stranger on his own land. Unfortunately, on examination, most of his derivations were duds, linguistic impossibilities. Nevertheless they were genuine meanings, one- or two- or three-word poems the man had grown out of his own land. We are all prone to error, we are all strangers on our own land. As language changes course like a river over the centuries, sometimes a placename gets left behind, beached, far from the flood of meaning. Then another meander of the river reaches it, interpreting it perhaps in some new way, revivifying it. The sound may have to be bent to allow this to happen. Eventually the original meaning may be for ever irrecoverable, or it may only be accessible to the learned. Locally, or at a personal level, it is still a name, a pointer, a misdirection perhaps, to the place. How many times could it happen, that the sound and the sense do this dance around each other? Corruption of the name, it is called; but corruption is fertility.

In Ireland O'Donovan himself, the greatest Irish scholar of his age, presided over the systematic corruption of Irish placenames. He was working for the Ordnance Survey (the section of the Army charged with mapping the land, under British rule, in the 1830s) and after the surveyors on the ground had noted down the placenames from the locals as best they could, it was O'Donovan who checked the earlier textual and cartographical sources, and, having decided on the correct Irish form of each name, wrote down not the Irish but the anglicized form that was to appear on the map; it was the great betrayal, for as he himself noted, many of these names become very indistinct when transcribed in English phonetic values. Of course O'Donovan personally was not the originator of government policy in the matter; this process of anglicization had been going on since Strongbow, was not challenged until the rise of the Gaelic League a century ago, and still proceeds today. But emblematically we may take the Ordnance Survey's reduction of the placenames to meaningless syllables of English as the second great trauma of the sense of place in Ireland. Brian Friel's *Translations* is the mythical expression of this second fall. The first, St Patrick's appropriation of the ancient Celtic lore, was traumatic in that the words, the names, recorded by St Patrick's scribe – that is, by the whole historical process I am taking him to symbolize – do not have the meaning they had for the followers of Fionn Mac Cumhaill. The landscape of the Celts was inhabited by the wonders and terrors of nature. When one of the Fianna in *The Colloquy of the Ancients* tells St Patrick that if the leaves of the wood had been gold, the generous Fionn would have given them all away, he is talking about the magnanimity of autumn. The gods and giants and magical animals that inhabit and give their names to the mountains, forests, marshes and springs are not distinct from the moods and potencies of those places themselves. But in St Patrick's redaction, the version transmitted to us by the missioners of monotheism, the wisdom of these many gods is reduced to fables, to amusing tales, to placenames. Then comes O'Donovan, a few minutes later, as it were, and further reduces the placenames to sounds emptied even of their residual meaningfulness, to whispering husks.

Is all this just two steps in the advance of reason? An example: Glasgeivnagh Hill in the Burren. The anglicized map-name tells us nothing, not even how we are to pronounce it. Behind it lies the Irish *Glas Ghaibhneach*, meaning the grey cow. The legends of this fabulous cow concern its inexhaustible productiveness. No vessel could be found that it could not fill with milk, until someone determined to outwit its good nature tried milking it into a sieve. When it failed to fill the sieve the cow died of mortification. The waterfalls that drop from the grey-green limestone hill of Glasgeivnagh into the lush little valley called Teeska are *Seacht Srotha na Taosca*, the seven streams of the overflowing. The hill itself with these silvery outpourings is the cow and its unfailing milk, and not just that but an image of the nurturing Earth itself, in its vulnerability to abuse and insult. Placenames then are the last faded ghosts and echoes of powers and words of power we have let lapse almost into oblivion. With such consequences as this, that just across the valley from the hill of the sacred cow, at Mullaghmore, the authorities want to build a visitors' centre for the coachloads of tourists, right in the middle of an exquisite and unspoiled landscape. That would be the real milking of the Burren.

But even anglicization is not enough to flatten the life out of a name entirely. Yeats's 'lake isle of Innisfree' is I suppose *Inis Fraoigh*, island of heather; but the attraction of his little poem has a hidden source in that syllable 'free'. One doesn't dream-visit his isle for its heather but for its freedom from the cares of the city. That selective amplification of the name's previously unnoted resonance is the imperious act of a major poet. But in the Irish names, and particularly in the west where the language still lives or at least has not long withdrawn, and the names are still pronounced properly even if not comprehended, we are surrounded by poetic acts as by the flowers of the field. I always record local opinions of the meanings and origins of placenames, even though some professionals would regard this as naive credulity. In the east of Connemara there is a townland called Doirín na gCos Fuar, the small wood of the cold feet. Why, I do not know; a *cos* can be a small measure of land, and in south Connemara '*na cosa fuara*' is a term for very poor people; but maybe neither usage is relevant here. Fortunately the locals have the complete explanation. It seems that once a shepherd went into this wood in search of lost sheep, and he was attacked and eaten by a bull; all that was ever found of him was his two boots, with the feet still in them. A macabre invention, indelibly connected with an otherwise unremarkable place. Though in fact the name has other associations for me. I remember first visiting Doirín na gCos Fuar when I was mapping Connemara. An uninhabited wasteland of cut-away bog, dark ranks of conifers in the distance, the autumn afternoon dimming and rain in the air; it looked intolerably dreary, and I had to steel myself to leave my bike by the roadside and set off to tramp across it. At the very first step off the road my foot sank into liquid mud, and as I felt it oozing down inside my wellingtons I thought, '*Doirín na gCos Fuar!*'

Thus we, personally, cumulatively, communally, create and recreate landscapes – a landscape being not just the terrain but also the human perspectives on it, the land plus its overburden of meanings. A placename is a few words piled up to mark a spot, draw attention to it, differentiate it from the unmarked; a few stones that fall down after some generations, perhaps for someone to pile them up again, into a different shape. There is a difference between a mere location and a real place, between a placename and a map reference; there may even be conflict between them. Iorras Beag in Connemara, the hill in whose evening shadow I live, clarifies this issue for me. This is the westernmost of Connemara's hills; beyond it is only a low-lying stony peninsula, and rocks and breakers and the Atlantic horizon. The top of the hill is an inchoate terrain of criss-crossed fault-valleys and fretful pinnacles. At twilight in particular this is a disorientating, spooky place; wherever you stand, there is another peak looking over your shoulder. One of these almost-summits is relatively distinctive, though: An Goibín Géar, the sharp little gob or snout; it sticks out at one side of the hill and once you have had it pointed out and named by a local inhabitant, it is a landmark on the skyline above the village. It is not marked on the Ordnance Survey maps, so I made a point of climbing up to it and standing on it to take some compass bearings of landmarks in the surrounding lowland in order to pinpoint it for my own map. But my compass seemed to have been turned inside out; I could not make head or tail of the bearings I was getting. Later I mentioned this to a geologist and he explained that such a peak attracts lightning, and here the rocks must have been magnetized by a lightning strike. This added to the interest of An Goibín Géar for me. The act of naming, or of learning its name, strikes a place like lightning, magnetizing it, attracting observations and the accumulation of placelore. But in this instance the point of enlightenment had become a place of bewilderment. Among the dancing peaks of Iorras Beag, An Goibín Géar resisted my attempt to locate it. Perhaps others long before me had felt this shape-shifting quality of those summits, for another of them is called Tower an Phúca. I think the English word 'tower' is used here and in other hilltop names, rather than the Irish *túr*. The *púca* is of course a sort of fairy; it is the goatish practical joker of the Celtic spirit world, that sneaks up behind you, suddenly shoves its head between your legs, carries you off on a wild caper around the countryside, and dumps you, dizzy, in some distant glen, as in the south Connemara song, *Marcíocht an Phúca*, the ride of the *púca*.

Now a few years ago the Ordnance Survey made an attempt to quell this riot of place, by building a little concrete pillar on one of these anarchic summits of Iorras Beag, with a socket on its top in which a radar-like instrument could be firmly and indubitably fixed for measuring the distance to identical pillars on neighbouring hills and offshore islands. This highly accurate triangulation was a first step towards the production of a new range of maps, which are being derived by photogrammetry, *i.e.* by computer analysis of stereoscopic pairs of aerial photographs. I pile on the technological agony only to heighten the contrast I want to draw, the contradiction between true place, with all its dimensions of subjectivity, of memory and the forgotten, and 'location' as established in terms of latitude and longitude or of a six-figure map reference or some other objective, uniform schema. High-tech cartography is a wonderful procedure, and we all draw directly or indirectly on a fund of objective geographical information, which has to be underpinned by an exact topographical data base. It was necessary that that summit be located with such accuracy; and it has been located to within an inch – to within an inch of its life, in fact. One climbs a mountain, drawn instinctively by the magnetism of the highest point, as to a summit of personal awareness, awareness of oneself as a point in relation to as much of space as can be grasped within a maximal horizon. Thus a mountain top is one of the most sensitive spots on earth, of our feelings for the earth in all their depth, elevation and comprehensiveness. A concrete stub demeans it, in a way that the traditional hilltop cairn does not, that stone memory-bank of all the people who have clambered up to that height. So the Ordnance Survey should find some technical fix to minimize the intrusion of the regime of location on that of place. A compromise could of course be found. We all need the topographic fix, and the occasional fix of immensity – of something that perhaps transcends my theme of the nameable and the knowable.

Does that sound like the complaint of some hypersensitive aesthete or intolerant environmentalist? I hope not, for my aim is deeper. Enquiring out placenames, mapping, has become for me not a way of making a living or making a career, but of making a life; a mode of dwelling in a place. In composing each of the placename instances I have given you into a brief epiphany, a showing forth of the nature of a place, I am suggesting that what is hidden from us is not something rare and occult, or even augustly sacred, but, too often, the Earth we stand on. I present to you a new word: 'geophany'. A theophany is the showing forth, the manifestation, of God, or of a god; geophany therefore must be the showing forth of the Earth. In the west of Ireland there is a language and a placelore uniquely fitted to the geophany of that land, with its skies full of migrating alphabets, waves that conspire to lift the currach ashore, its mountains like teeming udders, its foot-chilling bogs, the donkey's bray of its history, its ancient words piled on hilltops. My work is possible thanks to what I have grasped of the geophanic language of Ireland. My work thanks that language.

I I

Four Threads

The folk of Aill na Caillí used to say that the heron shrieks on
moonlit nights because it is frightened by its reflection in the
water. This fact, which I heard from the last man to leave this now
deserted coastal hamlet in the south west of Connemara, would
seem to lead one immediately and deeply into the lives of his vanished neighbours and their forebears. Nevertheless the generalities
of historical geography are needed for its full appreciation. Fishing
and mollusc-collecting in Cuan na mBéirtrí Buí, the bay of the
yellow oyster-bank, sailing to Roundstone and farther shores of
Galway Bay with turf cut from their commonage, feeding the
patchwork of tiny pastures and potato plots around their cottages
with seaweed shorn off the rocks, the villagers were as dependent
as the heron on the complexities of creek and reef, sandbar and
mudbank, neep-tide and spring-tide. I am told that when an unusually high tide would wash into the cottage nearest the landing
stage, the woman of the house would just pick up the glowing sods
of the turf fire and put them in the iron pot hanging on the hook
above the hearth until the waters turned and trickled out under the
door again. People lived as intimately as fleas in the skirts of the
sea, and died there too, unknown to the outside world. Theirs was
a harsh and hungry world; the labour necessary to keep life going,
to satisfy the landlord's agent, demanded every daylight hour.
Strength was a virtue. A certain round boulder lying on the shore
by the landing stage challenged the young men to lift it, prompted
boasts about their fathers or grandfathers who had lifted it. The
fear of physical failure, of eviction, emigration or the workhouse,
must have hung in the night-hours like a cry of despair.

The great resource of these people, their principal comfort, was
an intellectual one: talk, the telling of stories, endless commentary

on places and people they knew or had heard of. A close-woven web covering the bare landscape, this rehearsal of lore, a warm and comforting cloak of familiarity the land pulled around itself against the cold night. In Aill na Caillí (the name means the cliff of the hag, where perhaps the 'hag' is the green cormorant, not the wise or wicked old woman), the cottage by the landing stage was the resort of the local talkers and listeners; no doubt when the tide came into the house conversation was hardly interrupted for a second by the unusually wet visitor. The people especially prized by these gatherings would have been of two sorts; first, those who made things happen, who generated histories, good or bad, by their energy, courage or rashness, their wit or luck; and then those who could transmit the store of words, the passing boatmen who often spent the night there unlading cargos of rumour, the pedlars who walked the roads and whose anecdotes were the best of the goods they carried, the old men and women who had traveled through time, who remembered genealogies and derivations.

'Express a life that never found expression'; Yeats's command to Synge, on dispatching him to the west, was absurdly Anglo-centric, as Synge must soon have realized; for the life of the common people was not waiting for the English-speaking littérateur to express it; it was and long had been expressing itself volumi-nously, through words and music. But this oral culture was obscured for the outsider not just by the difficulties of the Irish language in its various dialects, but by its dependence upon a back-ground of local lore, the assumed familiarity of its audience with placenames and personalities, microgeographies, microhistories. What I am trying to recapture is how the people of Connemara felt their countryside, how they read it. It was like a book in fineness of detail, closeness of print; every corner of it conveyed a message, held a memory. Also it was like a board-game or a card-game – you knew every place and person by repute in all their relationships; if you did not, you took steps to complete your hand, your set of pieces. An old woman I have heard of would walk a dozen miles to get a verse of a song she didn't know. I am hooked on this game too – after seven years of research, I still go to absurd lengths to fill in some little corner of my jigsaw puzzle of Connemara.

I will illustrate this density of reference through stories and verses about four names much talked-of in nineteenth-century

Connemara: those of a smuggler, a rebel priest, a land-agent family, a wandering rhymer. But time itself is shrivelled and feeble-witted nowadays, and we have not the patience to sit by the smoky turf fire with the rain dripping through the thatch, while a language we no longer understand mutters and hawks and spits in the ashes, and stops to redden its clay pipe. Therefore I translate, and abbreviate, and document, and contextualize.

THE SMUGGLER

I begin with the famous Captain George O'Malley, An Caiptín Máilleach as he is known in Irish, born in 1786 in Ballynakill or Baile na Cille, 'the village of the church'. Connemara in general was more prosperous then than in later years, and that remote north-western corner has patches of a mellower geology than the rest; green hills of glacial till and sheltery valleys of limestone-derived soils soften its asperities. Also, its coastline, its deep and winding inlets running to the foot of trackless mountains, might have been drawn by nature with smugglers in mind. So, the O'Malley ladies and those of their neighbours such as the Coneyses of Streamstown and the O'Flahertys of Renvyle, went in silks, and even common boatmen sported extravagant high hats brought in from Guernsey. It was not until the 1820s that new roads allowed the influence of civic authority into the region, and the inhabitants blamed the roads for the subsequent economic decline. In fact the cycle of years of 'distress' and those of mere chronic want, that culminated in the Great Famine, was ushered in by the agricultural depression following on the end of the Napoleonic Wars, the collapse of kelp prices when alternative sources of alkali became available to Britain, and the coincidental disappearance of the herring shoals that had brought an international fleet of fishing boats to Killary Harbour. These changes must have given the memories of Captain O'Malley's most active days a varnish of nostalgia even while he lived.

Two songs attributed to the Captain are still sung in Connemara, one of them in praise of his boat, the other in praise of himself. The traditional singing of the west of Ireland, called *sean-nós*, the old way, sounds strange to our ears as it uses modes other

than the major and minor ones we are familiar with, but it is worth
persevering and learning to appreciate its expressive qualities.
These are uniquely allied to the rich and complex phonetics of the
Irish language. Hear the difference between 'Captain O'Malley'
and, properly pronounced, 'An Caiptín Máilleach' – it is as if the
syllables of Irish have more space inside them. In fact there are
Irish words so spacious you could hold a *céilí* dance in one syllable
and a wake in another, without mutual interference. The art that
explores these spaces inside words is *sean-nós*. In print, and in
translation, I can only explore the outsides of such words.

'An Caiptín Máilleach'[1] is a series of scenes from a smuggling
voyage. The first verse gives the course, by various islands and
headlands; the Captain makes fine music out of the placenames:

> *Thart le Rinn an Mhaoile, sios 'un Crua' na Caoile,*
> *An Cloigeann le n-a thaobh sin is Trá Bhríde ina dhiaidh.*

Renvyle (how their quality is lost in the anglicized forms of these
names!), with its castle that one of the Captain's forebears Grace
O'Malley half-felled with a cannon-shot from a galley; Cruach na
Caoile, now called Deer Island, uninhabited in the Captain's time
except for a herdsman watching over the red deer the Martins of
Ballynahinch bred there; Cleggan, where a martyred saint picked
up his severed head (*cloigeann*), washed it and put it back on; Trá
Bhríde, Bridget's strand, the fishing village that was to lose sixteen
of its menfolk in the sudden storm of 1927 – it would take a book
to unpack the stories in these names. Then, as the Captain steers
his boat past the Aran Islands, the breeze becomes a gale, waves
roar and flash, the sky quakes and fog thickens; if the planks could
speak they would tell a dreadful tale of how only they stand
between the crew and death. The crew are looking at the Captain's
forehead for signs of hope, but all he can do is to carry on under
sail while the boat still floats. His hands are torn from endlessly
hauling ropes, the skin and flesh are pulled off the bones – but if
the Son of God has decreed their death there's no avoiding it, and
they'll all go to Paradise together:

> *Tá mo lámha stróicthe go síoraí ag tarraingt rópaí,*
> *Tá an chraiceann 'gus an fheóil tóigthe amach on gcnáimh;*
> *Ach más é an bás a gheall Mac Dé dhúinn, cen gar atá dhá shéanadh,*
> *Acht a ghoil go flaithis Dé dhúinn ar aon stáid amháin.*

Then, the storm having abated, they land their cargo of Jamaica rum, tobacco and silks; he can have whichever girl he sets his heart on, the ship is shaken from stem to stern but what does it matter, they'll finish the song and drink their dram. Finally he relives the dangers they have overcome – water-guards, revenue cutters, spies, treacherous pilots – but: 'I am George O'Malley, a sound man of Grace's stock – My cargo was landed with ease, no thanks to any of them!'

Ach is mise Seóirse Ó Máille, fear maith de bhunadh Ghráinne -
Cuireadh i dtír mo lucht go sásta, agus ná raibh maith acu dhá chionn.

Years ago I came across an old reference to a manuscript auto-biography of Captain O'Malley said to have been written in the workhouse at Westport where he died in 1865. But, having heard the very groaning of planks and clapping of sails echoed in the words of his song, it was difficult to credit the existence of any such work; as a creature of stormy myth he seemed as unlikely as the Flying Dutchman to have left tangible documentation of himself. However, when I was mapping the Captain's haunts I made a point of asking the local inhabitants for any knowledge they had of him, and one day to my amazement Eileen O'Malley of Cleggan answered me by producing a weighty boxful of paper – the Captain's memoirs, in seven volumes each of three or four hundred closely typed pages. This huge work has never been pub-lished, and I subsequently learned that at least two scholars have played with the idea of editing it for publication and have retired defeated by its verbose braggartry, as I myself have been. This typescript copy, evidently made many decades ago, had been passed down to Professor T.S. Ó Máille of University College, Galway, as head of the O'Malley clan. The next time I called in on Tomás, as I did now and again in search of counsel on prob-lematic placenames, I discussed the document with him. He was dubious of its genuineness; he felt that the Captain was unlikely to have been able to write, and that much of it was inherently incred-ible. Indeed the Captain's adventures during the Napoleonic Wars – when he is pressed into the English navy, captured by a French privateer, imprisoned in the Tower of St Malo, and later with hundreds of other prisoners marched in chains hither and thither about Napoleon's collapsing empire – or in the Caribbean where his shipmates persuade him, much against his conscience, to lead them in leasing a ship for a season of piracy, in which they are very successful until they lose all their loot to a bigger pirate vessel – might perhaps prove to have been lifted from other memoirs. However, I can vouch for the accuracy of the references to people and places in the early chapters; his adversarial dealings with Captain Morris of the navy, his involvement with the Coneys family in the basking-shark fishery, and above all, his father's relationships with his financial backer, Anthony O'Flaherty of Renvyle, place George O'Malley in the real Connemara of the early nineteenth century.

But for me, obsessive topographer, the document is chiefly valuable for exactly situating the place of George's birth, which had eluded all my local enquiries, and for the curious detour through the Otherworld by which it does this. It was clear from various hints and conjectures I had come across that the O'Malley home was near Keelkyle in Ballynakill parish, but nobody could confirm this, much less identify the site of the house. The memoirs certainly point to Keelkyle, though without naming it. George's earliest memory is of watching his father sailing into his home bay pursued by the coastguard cutter, and turning his boat suddenly to dart through a narrow passage between an islet and the shore and head out to sea again, leaving the coastguards to blunder on and run aground on a sandbank – whereupon he magnanimously comes back, throws them a rope and hauls them off, a gallantry of which they are so appreciative that they shake his hand and ask no questions about his cargo. The course of this adventure inscribes itself without difficulty on the map of Ballynakill Bay. But a more precise clue (pointed out to me by the historian Sheila Mulloy, who has looked into the memoirs) is the reference to a fairy hill on his father's land and 'within eighty yards of the hall door'. Now there is in the townland of Keelkyle at the head of the bay a curious abrupt knoll between the coast road and the sea (almost opposite a craftshop that advertises itself as 'possibly the best craftshop in the west', and is therefore known as the Possibly Shop). The knoll is called Dúinín Mór, and although I never heard locally that it was regarded as a dwelling-place of the fairies, this was formerly a familiar fact; indeed, according to a story preserved in the Department of Folklore in University College, Dublin,[2] a Clifden man going by on his way to Letterfrack intervened to stop a fight between two men, who turned out to be the respective kings of the Dúinín Mór fairies and those of Cathair an Dúin, an Iron-Age promontory fort on the Renvyle peninsula, also regarded as a fairy fort. The quarrel, like so many in Connemara, was over seaweed-gathering rights, and the traveller undertook to mediate:

> 'I'll settle the question for you,' said the travelling man, 'if you accept.'
>
> 'We're happy to accept,' said the pair of them.
>
> 'Well,' said the man, 'let the people of Dúinín Mór come and cut seaweed from Letterfrack west until they come as far as Gob an Rosa, and let them go across the bay there and cut the seaweed opposite Gob an Rosa on the Leitir side and round by Damhros until they come back to Dúinín Mór again. And the Cathair an Dúin people,' said the man, 'they can cut the shore west of Gob an Rosa and then cross the bay to Leitir and cut that shore until they come to the Cora, the place where the Dúinín Mór people started to cut on the Leitir side.'
>
> 'We're satisfied,' said the two kings. 'We'll accept that.'

So Dúinín Mór was a well-known factor of the supernatural economics (and tales about it no doubt had an ideological role in local power-politics); hence we now know pretty exactly where the Captain was born. It might seem odd to fix a human address by reference to a fairy dwelling, but the aura of the uncanny can outlast historical memory. In fact, although the knoll is no longer thought of as a fairy fort, it is still a locus of the numinous. In 1987 a statue of the Virgin Mary was installed in a little 'grotto' on its roadside face, and shortly afterwards reports that the statue was moving caused crowds to gather. Men in suits of fundamentalist darkness materialized, I remember, to oversee the devotions and control the traffic jams. They were servicing a cult older than they knew.

THE REBEL PRIEST

Despite the sturdily nationalistic tone in his memoirs, Captain O'Malley seems only to have been caught up accidentally by the history and politics of his times. But the Connemara he grew up in was full of refugees from that history. In 1798, forever known as the Year of the French, General Humbert's expeditionary force landed at Killala in Mayo, and initiated a rebellion against British rule that was crushed with great brutality. Many of the rebels fled from Mayo, where the British yeomanry were hunting for them; some got away to France, probably with the help of George O'Malley's father and other smugglers, while others lurked for years in the mountain fastnesses of Connemara.[3] One of them was a Johnny Gibbons, who hid out in a *scailp* or cave, still called Scailp Johnny, on the forested hillside of Kylemore near Ballynakill. In the end he foolhardily went back to Mayo to attend a wedding, and while he was asleep someone soaked his pistols in water and sent for the redcoats. When he was about to be hanged, he cried out, 'Ah Connemara, my five hundred farewells to you; no treachery would have come to me had I stayed with you!' In the aftermath of the Mayo rising the chief prosecutor of the United Irishmen, as the rebels were called, was the Honorable Denis Browne, brother to Lord Altamont of Westport House, and he went about his task of having people hanged with such enthusiasm he earned the nicknames Soap-the-Rope and Donncha an Rópa. The blind poet Raftery, the most famous itinerant rhymer of his time, curses him in a song about the men on the run in Connemara.[4] The verse is very fierce; he says he'd like to shake hands with Denis Browne, not out of friendship but to string him up with a hempen rope and stick a spear in his big belly – and threatens that many of the lads driven overseas would be returning in uniform, with a French drum beating for them:

> *A Dhonncha Brún is deas chraithfinn láimh leat*
> *agus ní le grá duit acht le fonn do gabháil,*
> *cheanglóinn suas thú le rópa cnáibe*
> *agus chuirfinn mo spiar i do bholg mór.*
> *Mar is iomdha buachaill maith a chuir tú thar sáile*
> *a thiocfas anall fós is cúnamh leo,*
> *faoi chultaí dearga agus hataí lása*
> *is beidh an droma Francach ag séinm leo.*

In another verse he names some of the men on the run, describes their sufferings out in the bogs 'under thirst and dishonour, and the cold of night', and cries 'shame' on those who didn't help them, for unless Christ wills otherwise, they will succumb.

Tá Johnny Gibbons is ár nAthair Maol're
agus iad á gcaomhúint amach faoin móin,
faoi thart is faoi easonóir is fhuacht na hoíche
is níl fiú an bhraoin di acu ná dram lena ól.
Ní mar sin a chleacht siad ach fuíoll na bhfuíoll
agus shoraidh díofa nach dtug aire dó,
is rímhór m'fhaitíos mura bhfuil ag Íosa,
go mbeidh siad síos leis, agus tuilleadh leo.

There are caves and traces of former cottages associated with the many escapades of this Athair Maoilre, or Father Miley, whom Raftery mentions, scattered over the region from Clifden to Carna, and one can still pick up fragments of his story from living mouths. Fr Myles Prendergast was an Augustinian friar from Murrisk in Mayo, who joined the French on their landing at Killala. After the defeat of the rebellion, he and Johnny Gibbons and another man of the Gibbons family were imprisoned in Castlebar. The story of their escape was recorded in the 1930s from an Irish speaker in Carna:[5]

> When Father Miley was in prison he and the Gibbonses cast lots to see which of them would knock out the gatekeeper. It fell to Father Miley, but he didn't intend to kill him. The gatekeeper was asleep. They had no weapon but a sledgehammer and he hit him on the head with the sledgehammer thinking not to kill him but put him into a deep sleep or a faint. It happened that he killed him with the blow. They took the key off him, opened the lock, and the three of them escaped.

Father Miley and his companions made their way to Connemara, where, according to one of Denis Browne's anxious reports, Valentine Jordan and other rebel leaders who had returned from exile in France 'resided openly and in perfect security with a number of other inferior rebels resident there'. In another letter, Browne writes, 'It is my duty to repeat to your Excellency that this Province is not safe while Connemara is a secret asylum for outlaws of all descriptions.' Despite Browne's offering considerable rewards for their capture, in 1803 he had to report that

> there are still in the mountains of Connemara John Gibbons (Jnr), Fr Myles Prendergast and Valentine Jordan, whom it would be

very desirable to arrest and send away. Gibbons is mad, Jordan feeble and penitent, and the friar the only one that could again do harm, being a most daring character of desperate courage and some influence arising from his sacred function.[6]

Indeed it seems that Fr Prendergast was recognized as the parish priest of the western parish of Moyrus, and near Clifden (or rather, since the town of Clifden did not exist at that time, near the hamlet of Ballinaboy just south of it), there is a glacial boulder, a huge cube of ragged marble, on which it is said he used to celebrate the mass. It stands on a dry patch in the middle of a very wet bog, a place from which any soldier or suspicious person could be seen while still far away. Again according to the Carna folklore, a spy tracked the priest to a house in Doire Bhrón, a few hundred yards from the mass rock, and Father Miley, guessing that this man's intentions were not friendly, shot him. Recently a local historian enquired about some stones sticking up in the bog close to the old bridle-path by Doire Bhrón, and got the reply, 'That's the grave of the man the curate shot!'[7]

The many stories of Father Miley's sojourn in Connemara add up to a tale of mounting weariness and despair. Always fearful of treachery, he would shift from valley to mountainside, from house to cave, at any rumoured sighting of strangers. The yeomanry were quartered at Ballynahinch, but it was Ballynahinch that held his only hope of peace. Richard Martin, who was the largest landowner in Connemara as well as being the Colonel of the local Volunteer regiment and Galway's representative in Parliament, offered to get Father Miley a pardon from the government, for although the Martins were by that period anglicized gentry, their relationship to their tenantry was still coloured by the ancient mutual attachment of clan and chieftain, and their Protestantism was skin-deep, a cover adopted in order to be able to hang onto their estates at a time when Catholics' lands were being expropriated. But Father Miley would not accept a pardon unless his fellow outlaws were included, and that could not be done, and Martin could only advise him to move on, to the peninsula of Iorras Aintheach in south Connemara.

One of Martin's bailiffs, Liam Barra, owned a shop in Carna, the principal village of that quarter, selling salt, ropes, tar and so on to the fishermen, and had the genial habit of offering a free hornful of poitín to anyone who could drink it. One day Father Miley was drinking in the shop with another bailiff, and they quarrelled. The two bailiffs seized the priest and tied him up in the cellar, and went off to fetch the Yeomanry. But while they were away a servant-girl called in another man, who crept into the cellar and cut him free. Father Miley ran off along the shore, pursued by the Yeos, and his subsequent escape is still retold, with as much fidelity to place and personal names as in this version from the 1930s:

> He went down the slope eastwards. There were two big hookers beached at the mouth of the river. The anchor of one of the boats tore the priest's calf and cut it badly. All the same he was able to walk with it – he had to – until he came to a kelp kiln that was being burned in Roisín na Maithníoch. A man of the name of Faherty was burning the kelp. The Faherty man himself saw the army and they coming. Faherty told him to take off his coat and his 'coroline' (a high hat), so that he would put them on himself and take the army for a run. 'Let you stay here with the seaweed covering you,' he said.
>
> Father Miley took off his things and hid himself under the seaweed. Faherty put on the priest's coat and hat. He went off eastwards over the mountain making for Cill Chiaráin. He kept on until he reached Ros Dúgáin on the edge of the sea in Coill Sáile. He went into a house there and told them that he had run in place of the priest, and the hard case he was in. The man of the house told him to take off the hat and coat and that he himself would hide them. There was a basket of potatoes on the floor and they were eating a meal. They told him to sit at the basket like the rest of them and it wouldn't be known that he was not one of the household.
>
> It wasn't long before the army came. They enquired had they seen any man in black clothes going by. The man of the house said that they had seen him, that he was gone off with one of the boats that had just sailed from the beach, that he had heard the stranger calling to the boatmen, asking them to take him to Béal an Daingin on the other side of the bay. The army went on as far as Inbhear Ros Muc but they didn't get any boat that would follow the boat that had gone out, and they didn't get any news of Father Miley either.[8]

Nicknames of two families commemorate this adventure; the famous nineteenth-century strongman Seán an Chóta (of the coat) was the son of the man who had changed coats with Father Miley, and as late as the 1930s a descendant of the man who had freed him from the cellar was called Colm an tSagairt (of the priest). In the version of the story I heard from a pious old lady in Coill Sáile, the Faherty is an old man, and says that since his life is nearly finished anyway, it would be better if the Yeos caught him instead of the priest; and Father Miley accepts his reasoning – an interesting moral point.

In any case, Father Miley lived to minister to his flock until the 1840s, making a living by playing the bagpipes at weddings. He used to write out the Gospel according to St John, for people to wear around their necks as a charm. He was once seen taking off his hat when caught in a hailstorm, to let the hailstones strike his head as a penance. In his old age, when he had been called upon to anoint a man dying after a faction fight at the fair of Ballinaboy, he said that that was the last of his services for God. He was living in a little cottage in Gowlaun near Clifden when the Yeomanry found him at last, and he was so decrepit that they left him to die in his own good time. His colleagues in the rebellion of 1798 had by then long gone abroad or died or vanished into obscurity. A verse from a lament[9] for another of these rebel refugees can be their epitaph:

Is gurb as Cill Álaidh a ghluais an dé-smál
A dhíbir sinn ó chéile,
Na Francaigh a thíocht go hÉire,
Mo léan agus mo chrádh!

From Killala came the blast of misfortune
That drove us asunder,
The Frenchmen's coming to Ireland,
My grief and my sorrow!

THE LANDLORD'S AGENT

Throughout all such times of adventure and tragedy and song, the business of earning the rent, and collecting the rent, went on.

Over 160,000 acres of Connemara belonged to the Martins of Ballynahinch, but successive profligate generations had left the estate deep in debt long before 1845, when the onset of the Great Famine made it impossible to extract money from the tenantry. In 1847 new legislation placing the burden of famine-relief schemes on the local landowners completed their downfall. Thomas Martin died of a fever caught when visiting his former tenants in the workhouse at Clifden, his daughter fled the country, and the huge desolation that had been their estate passed into the hands of the financiers to whom it had been mortgaged, the Law Life Assurance Society of London. Whereas the Martins are said never to have evicted anybody, their successors knew that their only hope of selling the land for a profit was to rid it of superfluous human beings, and so they energetically carried on with the clearance the Famine had begun.

Law Life Assurance, a faceless, distant abstraction, has left no trace in Connemara lore that I know of, and its representative in oral history is its land-agent, George Robinson. George came to Connemara in about 1857. He had previously been employed as a civil engineer at Shannonbridge, where he had married Rebecca, daughter of the Protestant minister of Aughrim and a descendant of the Martins and Wood-Martins of Sligo. The former Martin residence, which is now the almost glamorous Ballynahinch Castle Hotel, was then a plain two-storey house looking down through a few trees to a lake; as a surveyor a few years earlier had reported,

> There is a good field, not of land, but of rocks and water, to be worked upon, and the scene might be made truly a 'Highland House', but up to the present time the *cutting* and *carving* that has taken place, and the *unfinished* and *poverty stricken* state of everything around the Castle, has only weakened the natural romanticness of the spot.[10]

Although the Law Life Society furnished the house with battlements in about 1858, cannyness still outweighed romantic sentiments in prospective purchasers' minds, and the estate remained on their hands until a London brewer, Richard Berridge, bought it in 1872. Thus the Robinsons occupied the Castle up to that date, and probably until 1885 when they built a fine bay-windowed mansion near Roundstone, for George became agent to the

Berridges, who themselves did not opt for residence in those increasingly dangerous times.

The society the family grew up in was as bleak as its setting. Two photographs by the well-known William Lawrence of Upper Sackville Street, Dublin, have been preserved by the Robinsons' descendants (whom I have got to know on the strength of our common name). One shows the Protestant chapel a mile or so away from Ballynahinch on the Galway to Clifden road. Not a tree or shrub mediates between the pretty little Gothic-revival building and the windswept boglands around it. The occasion is surely the inauguration of the chapel in 1865, for about seventy people line the drive up to the chapel, facing the eye of the future, and behind them a long stretch of the road is occupied by waiting horse-cars and carriages. All the beleaguered gentry of the Round-stone and Clifden area would have mustered for this show of solidarity, for Connemara had been racked by sectarian strife ever since the Reverend Alexander Dallas had been blown in from England by the ill wind of the Famine to fight the priests for the souls of the hungry. One needs a lens to individuate the tiny figures: the minister in his shovel hat and cassock, the ladies pyramidal in poke bonnets, mantles and crinolines, the gentlemen all stiffly vertical and extended upwards by tall top hats, the Robinsons' butler Old Burke bringing up the rear with one of his young masters, and three men dressed with propriety but immediately identifiable as 'natives' by the way they sprawl against the gable of the chapel, near the bellrope they have probably just finished pulling. These last remind me of the contemptuous nickname the Catholics of Kingstown near Clifden had for their neighbour who performed the same office for the little Protestant chapel there: 'bell-slasher'.

The other photograph, perhaps taken on the same day, shows the Robinson family posed on a slope which one can deduce is that now occupied by balustraded garden steps and hydrangea beds opposite the front door of Ballynahinch Castle. No such charms existed then; patches of stone show through the poor, strawlike grass, and the only other vegetation is a gaunt tussock of hazel scrub farther up the slope. George is on the left, Rebecca on the right, and the nine children between them, despite the formality of their grouping, seem to have started from their father's loins in a disconcerting rush. George's body looks undersized, angular, his trouser-leg strained by one acutely bent knee, the other leg doubled uncomfortably beneath him. His top hat has been put aside; one can see his receding hairline and anxious eyebrows and drawn cheeks. His longish beard is frosted. Rebecca seems more settled, matron-formed in her striped blouse and vast dark draperies of skirt, but her face is set and unsmiling. The three teenage daughters – known as the Rose, the Lily and the Ivy, says family lore – are artistically displayed, straw hats in their laps, each with her face at a different angle to the camera. Only the middle one seems happy with her looks, though (and she did become a beauty, as later portraits of her witness, including one by Oscar Wilde's friend Frank Miles, who thought she excelled another of his sitters, the Jersey Lily herself). The light tones of the girls' dresses are set off by the dark formality of the two male youngsters behind them. One of them, hand in pocket, manages to lean back in an almost raffish pose despite his tightly buttoned waistcoat and the sharp upward stabs of his collar-points. The other, Henry, who will succeed his father as Resident Magistrate and agent to the Berridges, already mirrors him in attitude and expression, but is as yet unmarked by his cares. And set into this composition here and there are the three younger children and the baby, all glancing askance at the camera in apparent foreboding and mistrust. Despite their architectonic grouping, the family looks fragmented, forlorn. Too much of the surrounding vacancy is shown. The top of Benlettery Mountain rears behind them, as bare as a skull.

Were it not for these images, I would have little idea of George Robinson as a person, rather than as that figment of ideological history, the wicked land-agent, for the only view I have of him from the side of the oppressed is of some absurd, semi-mechanical creature. In his autobiography *Mise*, the nationalist and revolutionary Colm Ó Gaora describes the journey he made by foot when he was young, from his native Ros Muc to Tourmakeady in Mayo.[11] Passing through the lonely valley of Mám Trasna, he thinks of the gruesome and mysterious slaughter of the Joyce family there in 1882, and quickens his steps to Pairc an Doire, where another memory disturbs him:

> It was near this place that *seanRobinson* [Old Robinson] was shot one day. He was coming by pony-car with a couple of policemen

when he was fired on. Damned bad luck it was that every inch of
him was armour-plated [*plátáilte*] except his head. The shooters
were so keen and eager they aimed to put the lead into his heart.
The shot didn't touch him there, because he was plated. The
police who were there to guard him were so drunk they couldn't
draw their guns or get out of the car.

Robinson's own view of the job that exposed him to such
dangers is clear from a letter he wrote in 1875 to Dublin Castle,
concerning 'an outrage which has been perpetrated on this Estate,
near Oughterard'. Certain leases having fallen in, on the tenants'
deaths, Robinson had it in mind to 'readjust and square the lands',
that is, to put higgledy-piggledy smallholdings together into viable
orderly farms. The obstacle to such improvement was the usual
one of there being undertenants in possession. Young Henry
Robinson had called on them with the sheriff to offer them an
arrangement by which they could become temporary caretakers of
their farms until new agreements should be drawn up, but their
parish priest had refused to let them agree to this proposal, saying
that both Isaac Butt, the nationalist MP, and Archbishop McHale
of Tuam had advised tenants not to sign such agreements. So the
sheriff had evicted them, but did not put out their furniture, and
in one case, 'moved with compassion', did not remove an infant in
a cradle. That night the families all broke into their homes again,
and George was advised that, as legal possession had not been
obtained (had young Henry been insufficiently forceful in not
putting out the furniture?), it would have to be taken again. So
George himself called on the undertenants, accompanied by the
sheriff and the local Justice of the Peace:

> We went first to the house of John Sullivan of Garranagry a man
> aged about eighty years. Mr Jackson, the Sheriff and I strongly
> advised him to consent to be put in as caretaker & not allow his
> furniture to be removed. His reply was that he would not sign any
> caretaker's agreement, that he would pay his rent, & that the fur-
> niture might be removed as soon as we liked, he then walked out
> of his own accord & possession was taken by the sheriff. In the
> course of an hour or two we received intelligence that the poor old
> man had died.
> In the meantime we went from house to house offering the
> same terms but receiving the same answer, – they dared not sign

caretakers' agreements as the priest had ordered them not, and had moreover taken their money stating that he would settle with me. After having taken possession of all the houses we returned to the village of Garranagry where we found the priest & with him a mob of I should say two thousand men & women. On our arrival he addressed me & stated that the old man had been murdered & that he would swear informations before a Magistrate ...

The verdict of an inquest, to which Robinson and his colleagues were not called as witnesses, was that John Sullivan had died as a result of rough handling in being put out of his house. Robinson claims that this finding was contrary to fact, and calls on the authorities to hold a sworn investigation into the whole transaction. What the outcome was I do not know, but such incidents must have been part and parcel of George's professional life in those dreadful years of class and sectarian strife.

By the time of the Land War, when the peasantry's sporadic and pathetic acts of terrorism were being co-ordinated into a political campaign by the Land League, agents and bailiffs had to go about their business with large escorts. In 1880, when ejectment notices were served on a number of Roundstone tenants, forty police confronted a crowd of three hundred armed with pitchforks, the Riot Act was read, and eighteen arrests were made.[12] A couple of years later, when thirty-two Roundstone families were evicted for arrears of rent, the echo of cannonfire from gunboats in the bay underlined the gravitas of the proceedings.[13] But if the Robinsons were *plátáilte* their property was vulnerable; on the night of 27 November 1879 three of their bullocks were driven over a cliff into the sea near Roundstone, and seventy-six sheep and two rams were killed or injured.[14]

Evictions on the Berridge estate continued until at least 1894, and as Henry Robinson was also agent for the Digbys who owned the Aran Islands, he would have ordered the eviction that J.M. Synge witnessed there as late as 1898. Nevertheless, with the passing of the Land Acts leading to large reductions in rent from the mid-1880s, and the developmental work of the Congested Districts Board from 1891, the worst of times were over. George, who died in 1890, hardly saw them, but Henry is remembered in ways that suggest the good old days rather than the bad, probably because he outlasted the Berridges and became agent to the Land

Commission when the estate was bought out in 1914. The planta-
tion of beeches and pines he wrapped around Letterdyfe House,
his home just north of Roundstone, has prospered, shadowing the
house too darkly but mellowing the stern magnificence of the
village's famous outlook. In the harsh terrain of Connemara,
mature woodland is historically synonymous with landlordism, and
those trees are still 'Robinson's Wood'. Henry's sheep, on the hillside behind the house, used to be watched over by one Mattie
O'Donnell, and Mattie's grandson, himself a shepherd, has told
me a story that shows Henry in benevolent mood. One day Mattie
was attending the Clifden cattle fair, and Robinson offered him a
lift back to Roundstone in his pony-car. As they were rattling
along the track that winds across the immense bog between
Clifden and Roundstone (a labyrinth of lakes and streams that only
the shepherds know), O'Donnell said, 'Let me down here and I'll
go and get a hare for my dinner.' Robinson was amazed, and said,
'How will you kill a hare, with no gun and no dog?' O'Donnell
replied, 'If I don't get him on the run, I'll get him some other
way.' Robinson was sceptical; he said, 'Well, if you can meet me at
Lydon's Bridge (which is on the road into Roundstone) with a
hare, I'll give you five pounds.' Of course five pounds would have
been a fortune to O'Donnell, who had, as they say, a long weak
family to support. So off he went into the bog, and he crept up to
a place where he knew a hare would be lying in its form (a hare
makes a hollow in the heather for itself, into which it fits exactly
and invisibly, called its form), and he tiptoed up and grabbed the
hare, and carried it in his two hands across the bog until he came
out on the road again just as Robinson was coming round the corner in his pony-car. Robinson looked at him and said, 'If that's not
Mattie O'Donnell it must be his ghost!', and true to his word,
next time he was at the bank, he got Mattie the five pounds.

So, the Robinsons are not totally locked into their historical
roles as ogres; something of their whims and oddities is preserved.
In one of their eminent namesake Sir Henry Robinson's books of
reminiscences I found this:

Another instance of queer so-called humour I remember when I
was staying on a wet wintry day in Murphy's Hotel, Oughterard.
Walter Seymour, the secretary of the Grand Jury, a very peppery

gentleman with a wooden leg, was staying in the house, and also a
large land agent, a namesake of my own, Henry Robinson of
Roundstone. Seymour pulled his chair close in to the fire and,
with foot on the fender and the wooden leg on the hob, fell fast
asleep, and he snored so loudly that he irritated Henry Robinson,
who was trying to wind up the accounts of his day's collection. To
put an end to this disturbance, Robinson went to the fireplace and
piled the turf sods around the wooden leg on the hob, and then
went back to his work. Very soon the leg ignited, burned for a
while, and at last with a loud crack split up, waking Seymour,
who at first didn't know what had happened, and hopped about
the room on the sound leg with the other crackling and burning
merrily under him. Robinson proceeded to remonstrate with
Seymour, 'Ah now, will you stop your pranks?... That's a dangerous thing to do, man; you might burn the house down.'[15]

And so on. The local carpenter is called in, and replaces the
burned leg with a huge hourglass-shaped thing four feet long;
Seymour protests he isn't a piano. ... The story goes down well
when I retail it in Roundstone, and perhaps when all Henry Robinson's oppressions have been forgotten, his contribution to the
grotesqueries of Connemara will be relished still.

To wrap up my worrying about the Robinsons, I quote a verse
of a song about *carraigín*, an edible seaweed Connemara people
used to gather on the shore and sell in Galway market. I have
never heard it sung, or met anyone who knows the rest of it, but
this much is remembered:

> *Dá mbeadh dhá mhaide rámha*
> *Agus báidín agam fhéin,*
> *Rachfainn ag baint charraigín*
> *Is á thriomú leis an gréin.*
> *Bhéirfinn taoscan dhe go Gaillimh*
> *Agus taoscan ar an tráen,*
> *D'iocfainn cíos le Robinson*
> *Is bheadh brabach agam fhéin.*

> If I only had two oars
> and a rowboat of my own,
> I'd go and gather *carraigín*
> and dry it in the sun.
> I'd send a load of it to Galway

and another on the train;
I'd pay the rent to Robinson
and keep the profit for my pains.

So Robinson didn't extort the last penny, at least in the softer,
latter times. For the honour of the name, I'd like to think so.

ITINERANT RHYMER

Thinking of the different trajectories out of which I am seeking to
reweave the old Connemara – O'Malley's exuberant wake, Father
Miley's hare-like startings, the Robinsons' staid mainroad clip-clop
– it seems unlikely that any two of these persons ever met. But the
prodigious life-span and roving habit of Colm de Bhailís, craftsman
and poet, may well have brought him under the notice of all of
them. Hitching a lift to Aran in a turf-boat, he might have seen the
Captain's sloop flying before the revenue cutter; he might have
been aware of an anxious stirring in the loft of one of the isolated
cottages he worked in; he might have had to step respectfully off
the road and doff his cap to *seanRobinson* or even to Master Henry.
Born in 1796, two years before the people of outer Connemara saw
the French fleet go by to Killala, as is still remembered, and dying
in 1906, when the tenants of the Berridge estate were boldly press-
ing for the land to be divided between them, he saw the country go
down decade by decade into the pit of the Great Famine, and its
agonizingly slow recovery.

Colm de Bhailís lived in the south Connemara island of Garomna – five or six square miles of bog, its rim transformed by the
labour of generations into a lacework of plots and pastures. Since
poverty has compelled the inhabitants not only to dig away the peat
for sale as turf to Galway city and Aran, but to cut and dry the
'scraw', the surface layer of living vegetable matter, for their own
fuel, the underlying granite is now naked and gleaming, or covered
only in a thin straggly web of heather and furze. And, like many
eroded landscapes, this is one of severe beauty; sometimes in the
long days I spent exploring it I stopped and stared, confounded by
its sharp horizons biting at the sky, its lakes reflecting high-piled
emptiness. The ragged stone walls of the de Bhailís potato gardens

are still pointed out among little hillocks in the far south-western corner of the island. Nowadays Garomna is linked by causeways via two other islands to the mainland, but in those days to walk out of the island it was necessary to wait for the exceptionally low ebb-tides that follow the new moon or the full moon, and then to slip and stumble over half a mile or so of seaweed-covered rock and mud. During the Famine many people died while waiting thus to escape from the island, waiting for the moon. I have been shown their graves, little heaps of stone on the stony shoreline.

Such is the background of the poet whom Patrick Pearce described as 'a naive, sprightly, good-humouredly satirical personality, a peasant living among peasants, who sings like the lark from very joyousness and tunefulness of soul.'[16] And under that good humour the realities of deprivation show, like bones sticking out. 'Amhrán an Tae', the song of the tea, is a comic dialogue between wife and husband, she addicted to tea and he to tobacco.[17] He says, 'Musha, you're always talking about tea, and when you have it no one else sees any of it; be off and get me some tobacco or I'll give you a touch of the spade-handle!' She replies, 'How can I do that but by selling two chickens that laid yesterday? The stuff you got on tick at Christmas isn't paid for yet, and that's running short for the children.'

An Fear	*Maise, bionn tusa i gconaí 'cur sios ar an tae,*
	'S an lá bhios sé agat, ní fheictear a'at é;
	Imigh leat 's faigh tobac dam ar mhaithe leat féin,
	Nó roinnfidh mé leat feac na lái!
An Bhean	*Cia an tslí atá a'am-sa? Cá bhfaighinn-se duit é,*
	Acht ag ceangal dá chirc a raibh ubh aca aréir?
	Rud a thóg tú faoi Nollaig, níor íoc tú fós é,
	'S tá an méid so sách gann ag na páistí.

After a dozen verses of argument they go to law, and end up as laughing-stocks; 'But,' says Colm, 'I suppose the children died':

Ach ceapaim gur cailleadh na páistí.

A story about Colm is told in the Aran Islands, where he used to do odd jobs (he had a great reputation for building chimneys that drew well). On this occasion he was in Inis Meáin, the middle island, where he had work to do on several houses. It was the custom in those days to do a few hours' work before breakfast. Colm finished the job on the first house before breakfast time came, and the woman of that house assumed, or pretended to assume, that he would get his breakfast in the next house. But the people there took it that Colm had had his breakfast already. So Colm worked away quietly for a bit, and then he turned to the man he was working for and said, 'What is the name of this island?' 'Why, this is Inis Meain!' he replied. 'Ah,' said Colm,

> 'Inis Meáin, inis gan 'rán
> Inis gann, gortach;
> Tabhair leat do chuid 'ráin
> An lá 'mbeidh tú a' dul ann,
> Nó beidh tú an lá sin i do throscadh!'

[Inis Meain, island of hunger and wanting. / Have bread in your pocket / The day you make your visit, / Or you'll spend that whole day fasting.]

The poet's satire was a fearsome weapon in the Gaelic word-world, and Inis Meáin has never forgotten Colm's little verse. Perhaps that is why its penury has not stopped it being the most hospitable of places, as Synge found when he stayed there.

Tailoring, I am told, was the easiest trade to take up in the old days, for all you needed was *siosúr, miosúr 's méaracán*, scissors, tape-measure and thimble. Tailors were often despised as being unfit for hard physical work. Once when Colm was working in a house in Ros Muc, there was also an itinerant tailor there, a miserable little fellow nicknamed An Bás, death, and Colm was annoyed to find that he had to share a bed with him. The next day the woman of the house promised Colm a quart, no less, of poitín if he would make up a poem about the tailor before bedtime. The result, 'An Bás', is one of his best-known productions. He praises the house highly: 'If I were to pass the whole of spring there, I'd think it but a fortnight – But it's there they made me up a bed / in which to talk with Death.'

> Dá gcaithfinn ráithe an earraigh ann
> Comharfainn nach mbeinn seachtan ann,
> Acht is ann a coireadh leaba dhom,
> Ag cómhra leis an mBás.

Talking with death must have been a familiar domestic situation for Colm de Bhailís, who outlived his wife and his son and must have seen most of his neighbours starve. In 1901 Colm went into the workhouse at Oughterard; he was so old that, although his songs were still sung, most hearers would have assumed their author was long dead. But by that time the outside world was beginning to take an interest in the Gaelic oral tradition, and the Gaelic League had been set up to revive the dying language. Patrick Pearse, who often visited Ros Muc and had heard Colm's songs there, discovered to his surprise that their author was still living. He raised a subscription, the Gaelic League bought a cottage for the ancient poet, and his works were written down and published for the first time. But Colm's health soon failed and he had to return to the workhouse hospital, where he died at the age of 110.

One could say that Colm de Bhailís and his like represent the last step in the decline of the bardic tradition: from the great Munster poets of 'Hidden Ireland' one descends to blind Raftery sitting in the drinking houses of Galway, 'face to the wall, playing tunes to empty pockets,' in the words of a verse attributed to himself – and then, down with a bump, the step one had forgotten at the foot of the stairs, to the rustic wit of Colm de Bhailís. But this is no doggerel; his jaunty rhythms and rhymes lend themselves to singing, and, more to my point, his themes grow out of the stony Connemara ground itself. I end with a glance at his best-known song, 'Cúirt an tSrutháin Bhuí', the court of the yellow stream. A peculiarity of many of these old songs is that, to make any sense of them, one has to know circumstances of their composition not explicit in the song itself; the song is the kernel of a nut, the shell of which is a dense fabric of personal histories and place-names – not always the most digestible of stuff, but without it the kernel loses its savour. The 'yellow stream' of this song is a tiny thread of water running out of the bog between two hills in the island of Leitir Móir. Colm was caught in the rain there once, and made himself a little shelter of sticks and clods of grass. Then, to pass the time, he made up a song praising this 'court' in wonderfully high-flown terms:

Is deas an féirín gheobhtha gléasta
Cúirt an tSrutháin Bhuí,

Ar talamh déanta ar dheis na gréine
I bhfoscadh ó 'chuile ghaoith,
'Bhfuil a ghairdín pléisiúir le n-a taobh
A dhéanfadh óg de'n aois,
'S go bhfuair na táinte bhí gan sláinte
Fóirithint ann le mí.

[How fine an ornamental treasure, / Is the Court of the Yellow
Stream, / Built on land blessed by sun / And sheltered from the
wind. / So that the pleasure garden by its side / Would make the
old feel young, / While hosts of invalids / Found succour there
for a month.]

And so on it goes, heaping up extravagances for verse after verse:
Queen Victoria is mad with rage since hearing praise of its roof,
sailing ships with favouring winds bring the Queen of Sardinia, all
is prepared with golden gates and company fit for a king, and
finally Martin Luther himself comes begging for pardon at the
Court of the Yellow Stream. The strange thing is that this fantasy
is sung to an air of passionate, almost tragic intensity. But one
could understand the implicit tragedy to be the disproportion
between these people's material circumstances and their life-capa-
bilities. The poet of south Connemara ended in the workhouse, but
he had built a house, a Court in fact, that no agent could raise rent
on, and the artistry that goes into singing its merits, even today, is
as glorious as the furze that blossoms on his granite island.

* * *

In trying to convey something of the old, gossipy, intimacy
between this countryside and its inhabitants, I have had to patch
the cloak of oral history with evidence from document and photograph, for the inter-generational conversation, which persisted
through the Famine and to a degree survived the retraction of
Irish into its present narrow quarters, has been broken up by our
easy comings and goings and our well-fed indifference. I would
like to offer Connemara its lost memories, but fear to denature
them; I am troubled by my translation of the homely glow of the
turf fire, in which each thing is only the more richly what it is for
being half shadows, into the even, comparativist, light of a computer screen with its implicit worldwide connections. However,

today's Connemara breathes the global gale of information, and if
there is any way home for a contemporary society to a known
landscape, it detours all over the earth's surface. Perhaps, though,
we have to eke out the concept of home to cover all that route. If
the old Connemara is irrecoverably lost and no equivalent can be
constructed, my four left-over threads from it can serve only on
that wider loom.

NOTES

1 *Amhráin Chlainne Gael*, collected by Micheál and Tomás Ó Máille
(Dublin, 1905; republished, ed. William Mahon, Indreabhán, Connemara, 1991).
2 The original Irish is quoted in *Hidden Connemara*, ed. Erin Gibbons
(Connemara West Press, 1991).
3 Richard Hayes, *The Last Invasion of Ireland* (London, 1939).
4 'Na Buachaillí Bána', in *Raiftearaí: Amhráin agus Dánta*, ed. Ciarán Ó
Coigligh (Dublin, 1987).
5 *Annála Beaga ó Iorrus Aithneach*, collected by Seán Mac Giollarnáth
(Dublin, 1941); my translation.
6 Quoted in Hayes, *op. cit.*
7 Information from Ruairí Lavelle, Clifden.
8 Mac Giollarnáth, *op. cit.*
9 'Aifi Mhac Ghiobúin', author unknown, in *Micheál Mhac Suibhne agus
Filidh an tSléibhe*, ed. Tomás Ó Máille (Dublin, 1934); my translation.
10 Thomas Colville Scott, *Connemara after the Famine: Journal of a Survey of the Martin Estate, 1853*, ed. Tim Robinson (Dublin, 1995).
11 Colm Ó Gaora, *Mise* (Dublin, 1943, 1969); my translation.
12 *Galway Vindicator*, 12 June 1880.
13 Kathleen Villiers-Tuthill, *Beyond the Twelve Bens* (Clifden, 1986).
14 *Galway Vindicator*, 5 May and 2 June 1880.
15 The Rt Hon. Sir Henry Robinson, Bt, KCB, *Further Memories of Irish
Life* (London, 1924).
16 *An Chlaidheamh Sholais*, 8 August 1903.
17 *Amhráin Chuilm de Bhailís* (Dublin, 1904, republished 1967).

12

Botany – a Roundstone View

The view from Roundstone, or from Errisbeg, the hill overlooking Roundstone Bog – consists mainly of heather, and so I'll restrict myself to heather today. I will describe a sort of chain dance of plants and humans, interlinked by their roles in the odd history of discovery of the rare species of heather found here. This then is a cultural ecology, with comic interludes.

For the amateur like myself the identification of these rarities is tricky. Here's the trick. Hold the specimen in one hand and insert the following key:

1 Much the same as any other heather	2
Same but bigger	*Erica erigena*
	(Mediterranean Heath)
2 Spelling mistake in Latin name	*Daboecia cantabrica*
	(St Dabeoc's Heath)
Vericaceous	3
3 Not to hand	*E. ciliaris* (Dorset Heath)
Just like any old heather	*E. mackaiana* (Mackay's Heath)

The reason you don't have *E. ciliaris* in your hand is because it's only found in one spot, which is a state secret, and it's illegal to pick it. In general these Ericas are best told apart by their extreme similarity to the common sort, *E. tetralix*.

I cannot deal with their ecology, their curious Atlantic distribution, the puzzles of whether or not they show up in the pollen record since the Ice Age, or any of the sensible questions that make them endlessly fascinating to botanists. Instead I'll tell the story in which they figure in conjunction with some human characters. I start with the tall one, *E. erigena*, which used to be called

E. mediterranea, and also *E. hibernica*. In English it is the Mediterranean Heath, though its affinities are more coastal Atlantic than Mediterranean. However, I can reveal that its real name is French Heath. At least, a shepherd here has shown me a little stream valley on the north east of Errisbeg called French Heath Tamhnóg. A *tamhnóg* is a small *tamhnach*, a patch of cultivated or cultivable land in the middle of a bog. This patch may have been cleared as a summer milking pasture, a 'booley', in the old days, but now it's a small forest of Mediterranean Heath, and no doubt some farmer or shepherd heard from a visitor and misremembered its name. Apparently this plant was first collected by the great Welsh Celticist and natural historian Edward Llwyd, who visited Connemara in about 1700. Then it was rediscovered here by J.T. Mackay, the director of the TCD botanical garden, in 1830. Those pioneer botanists didn't do things by halves; Mackay sent a hundred and fifty samples of it to Sir W.J. Hooker at Kew. When Robert Shuttleworth, a young English medical student acting on Mackay's behalf, came here in the following year, he collected a cartload of it. However, there was and is plenty; as Shuttleworth writes, 'I found *E. mediterranea* covering a very large extent. My young guide told me that on St Patrick's Day the whole bog was white with it.' Oddly enough it did have a use, which is still remembered. A botanist called Tomlinson writing in 1910 records that 'the heath had in many places been ruthlessly uprooted, and was lying about in withered heaps'. He subsequently discovered that this had been done by the small farmers of the surrounding lowland in order to procure suitable bunches for potato 'Spraying' purposes, most of those concerned being too poor to purchase spraying machines.

That 'young guide' mentioned by Shuttleworth could have been Roundstone's native botanist, William McCalla, to whose grave all botanists visiting Roundstone make pilgrimage. My information on him is drawn from papers by Alan Eager and Maura Scannell, and by Charles Nelson. McCalla's father kept the hotel here; he was a retired veteran of the Peninsular Wars against Napoleon, a Scot, and a great drinker. Roundstone was largely a Scottish foundation. The Scots engineer Alexander Nimmo, who designed the harbour here for the Fisheries Board and planned the road system of Connemara, bought the lease of this area and sublet plots to people who would build houses along the street; he is also said to have brought in Scots fishermen and fishwives. There was soon a Presbyterian community here, and young McCalla, who was born in about 1814, was educated to be a teacher in a Presbyterian school nearby, funded by the Martins, the big landlords of Connemara. The various botanists who stayed at his father's hotel, and the interest caused by the discovery of *E. mediterranea*, may have influenced him to study botany. Soon the experts were finding him an invaluable guide and a source of specimens. Then he began making his own discoveries. Collecting litter for his cattle one day he noticed a slightly different heather on a hillock called Na Creaga Móra, in Roundstone Bog a few miles north of the village. When Charles Babington, the Cambridge botanist, visited in 1835 McCalla took him to see *E. mediterranea*, and the next day showed him the new heather. Babington was very impressed by McCalla; he wrote that 'this young man, although labouring under very great difficulties, has by his own exertions, and with an almost total want of books, obtained a very complete knowledge of the geology, mineralogy, conchology, and botany, of the neighbourhood of Roundstone'. Babington also sent samples of the heather to Mackay, who forwarded them to Hooker at Kew, saying that McCalla 'promised to be a useful person in the country.' Eventually it was named *E. mackaiana* after Mackay, who one could say was indirectly responsible for its discovery through his encouragement of McCalla.

However, McCalla was not content just to be Mackay's 'useful person in the country'. He soon went to Dublin and worked under the botanist David Moore for the Ordnance Survey, but after a few months he was dismissed for giving away specimens of finds to Babington and William Thompson. That seems harsh punishment for a minor indiscretion; perhaps the naive young Connemara man had strayed into the field of some professional infighting.

After that he worked supplying specimens to Dr Scouler of the Royal Dublin Society, and then at Scouler's suggestion he wrote to Hooker at Kew proposing himself as leader of a botanical expedition to New Zealand. Hooker was impressed enough to agree to pay him at the going rate of £2 per hundred species, even though his testimonials were mixed. Moore wrote that McCalla was an indefatigable collector *etc.*, but 'he wants industry, taste, and a due sense of honorable and faithful motives. So much so that I fear he will lose many of his specimens after they were collected and statements by him will require to be received with the very greatest care.' Scouler was prepared to finance the expedition, or at least to put up the £20 fare to New Zealand, and another £20 for 30 reams of paper. However, McCalla never quite got around to setting off. Scouler was annoyed to find that he had started collecting algae for sale and had caught a cold in the process. He felt that McCalla was perfectly honest – and unlike his father never touched the drink – but 'he is far too simple and from his ignorance of business habits apt to be imposed upon.' Scouler still hoped that 'this wild man I have caught in Cunnemara' would soon be on his way – but a couple of months later McCalla was again under doctor's orders at Malahide, having got soaking wet gathering algae. Eventually Scouler wrote to Hooker that he had given up on McCalla, whose 'incorrigible habits of procrastination and his cowardise ... have worn out my patience. He made it a point to do nothing today which could be deferred until tomorrow and to do nothing for himself while there was a chance of someone else doing for him.' McCalla candidly agreed with this assessment, acknowledged that Scoulter was justified in withdrawing his patronage, thanked him, promised to repay the money he had received, and came home to Roundstone. His big adventure was over.

After that he worked on his algae, on which he was an expert, and in 1845 published the first of two volumes on the topic, which won him a silver medal. In the following year another of the rare heathers was discovered, probably on Na Creaga Beaga, the small crags, the next hummock to the west of Na Creaga Móra, the big crags, where *E. mackaiana* grew. A visiting botanist found the plant, but it was McCalla who identified it as the Dorset Heath. These were the Great Famine years; Connemara was being depopulated. Yet there were still visitors, and McCalla made a bit of a living selling them prepared specimens of the locality's famous flora, until, in 1849, he was carried off by the cholera epidemic that followed the Famine. He was aged thirty-five. His tomb is in the Presbyterian churchyard, up the lane to the north of the Protestant church. The chapel, the Kirk, itself was knocked down some decades ago, and McCalla's tomb is the most notable of the few that are still traceable. But it is in danger of falling down; and it would be fitting if the botanical community made a move to re-store it.

An odd fact about *E. mackaiana* is that it was discovered in Spain just months after its discovery in Ireland. That's an impressive victory for the theory of Morphic Resonance – you remember that some years ago this theory was propounded to explain such observations as that once a new chemical substance has been crystallized for the first time, it suddenly becomes easy for laboratories all over the world to do the same; similarly once something abstract has been thought out in one place, the same idea will strike elsewhere. This all comes about through the propagation of morphic fields, fields of pure form, through space. If you prefer something less exotic than Morphic Resonance, it would be interesting to enquire out the personal networks, interlinking with the Roundstone one I am talking about, centering perhaps on Hooker, which by spreading general ideas about classification and specific floristic expectations, brought the discriminating gaze of botany to bear on the same rare plant at the two ends of its range at the one time.

I skip back to the discovery of *Erica ciliaris*, the Dorset Heath. (I am basing myself here on an article by the late Professor Webb.) Everything combined to make this discovery harder and harder to credit. First, in 1839 a Mr Nash of Cork had sent out specimens of three rare heaths he said had been found in his own county. When Babington unexpectedly visited Cork and wanted to see these marvels, Mr Nash's excuses were varied: the site for *Erica ciliaris* he said had been ploughed up; that for *Daboecia cantabrica*, St Dabeoc's heath, had been burnt over; that for *Erica mackaiana* had been destroyed by baryta mining. Then J.F. Bergin found the unfamiliar heather in Roundstone bog that McCalla identified as *E. ciliaris*, and later McCalla showed it to another botanist, J.H. Balfour of Edinburgh, who very briefly announced its existence in an article in *The Phytologist* in 1853. But thereafter for a long time, although several eminent botanists came to search for it, none saw the plant, and doubts arose. So Balfour came back to try to confirm the record, and got very confused as to which bridge he had found it near, along the road across the bog north of Errisbeg. Eventually he came to the conclusion that he had identified the correct bridge, but the stream there had now been banked and the site destroyed. Subsequent writers were of the opinion that Bergin had been 'the victim of an imposition' (was McCalla the suspect?) and that Balfour's specimens had been mislabelled in the Edinburgh herbarium. *Erica ciliaris* was thenceforth filed among 'unverified records and missing plants'.

When David Webb was working on the distribution of *E. mackaiana* in Roundstone Bog, he kept an eye open for other things too, and became convinced that the *ciliaris* record was incorrect. Then in 1965 he accompanied a student, Michael Lambert, to a place where the latter had noted some 'very large *E. mackaiana*' – and it turned out to be *E. ciliaris*. (The version I heard was that Webb and his students were standing in the bog, and Webb said he didn't suppose there was much chance of finding *ciliaris* among all these thousands of acres of heather, and one of the students said, 'What about this?' – pointing at their feet – and there it was, immediately identifiable, of course, by its being just the same as all the rest.) Now, there are only about five tussocks of it, covering an area the size of a tabletop. It is more or less where Bergin claimed to have seen it, but the site only matches Balfour's description if one assumes he was completely muddled when he mentioned a bridge nearby. Is it the same colony, that has been stumbled on three times in a century and a half? It was nearly wiped out by a fire shortly after Webb's rediscovery of it; it is also very vulnerable to disturbance and even to the interest of professionals, who all want just a little sprig of it. A local naturalist has told me that to ensure its survival he has taken bits and planted them on various islands: I think he is lying, but future finds of it might be suspect, and so might the present known station. Did McCalla have access to specimens of *ciliaris*? Might he have been tempted to use them to renew his flagging career? A libellous suggestion about Roundstone's native son! Roundstone Bog has been repeatedly traversed by experts engaged in mapping the distribution of *E. mackaiana*, and no other *ciliaris* sites have ever come to light. The one known station is close to the road, which looks suspicious. On the other hand if it were not close to the road it would most likely never have been seen.

Botanists will not reveal this location to the casually curious. I had to persuade a botanist – we'll call her Erica – to show me the site, which she would only do on condition I was blindfolded. So off we went in her all-terrain vehicle for hour after hour, driving round and round, me bouncing around in the back with the Kalashnikovs and machetes; I don't know where we went, but three times I smelled Guinness and fish and chips. Then we walked round and round in the bog for hours. Eventually she said 'This is it!' I was very moved. I can't describe the plant, since the blindfold was not removed; but, to trip over, it feels subtly the same as any other heather.

Meanwhile, mapping the exact distribution of *E. mackaiana* continues to attract a lot of effort; I'm not sure why. Praeger, David Webb, Maura Scannell and David McClintock, Charles Nelson, and several others, have added to the sum of knowledge on the question; now Micheline Sheehy-Skeffington has just shown me the latest distribution map of it in Roundstone Bog, from Errisbeg to the edge of Clifden, compiled by her student Liereke van Doorslaer. The original site was on the bog road about halfway from Roundstone to Clifden, and the known range has gradually been extended both north and south of the bog road. This has led to it becoming the best known and most controversial plant in the history of Connemara since, say, the potato. Partly because of these rare heathers, the area of lowland blanket bog south of the bog road has long been designated an Area of Scientific Interest. Then in 1987 the ASI was extended to take in an area of bog – the same bog – north of the bog road. This was done by the scientists of the Office of Public Works' Wildlife Service. However, the OPW bureaucrats then left the redrawn maps sitting in their out-trays until January 1989, and did not even inform the County Council. They excused themselves later on by saying that they were short of staff and the index to the maps wasn't ready. Unfortunately in that period some businessmen of Clifden decided the town needed an airport, and that the ideal site was on the corner of the bog nearest to Clifden. Three months after they had applied for planning permission and when their scheme seemed to be well airborne and had gathered enthusiastic local support, it was discovered that the airport site was within the new bounds of the ASI. Of course ASIs as such had no legal standing, but the Council tended to adopt them into the County Plan, and European funding was being sought, so in practice the ASI designation grounded the scheme. A mighty row broke out; single-handedly the OPW by its inefficiency had created an anti-environmentalist backlash in Connemara. For us local environmental activists it was a difficult time; we cursed the OPW but had to fight their battle for them to preserve the bog from this intrusion. After a judicial review, which the Clifden businessmen quite deservedly won, the whole ASI system nationwide has been declared unconstitutional, and is now being replaced by a new sort of designation.

The airport company had, of course, had to commission an Environmental Impact Report. The bit of bog in question was examined by botanists and zoologists and other sorts of 'ists from REMU in Cork, and lo and behold REMU's conclusion was that in general this was an uninteresting corner of the bog, whose loss would not be of significance. The REMU botanist did not notice any *E. mackaiana* on the site, although the nearest known station at that time was only a few hundred yards away – but the Connemara National Park personnel looked over the site as well, and found acres of *E. mackaiana*, together with its hybrid with *E. tetralix*. The Environmental Impact Report therefore ended up with this embarrassed mention of the plant: 'This heather, including its hybrid *E. stuartii* and St Dabeoc's Heath, were identified by OPW personnel and validated by REMU personnel.' Perhaps it was REMU who were the more in need of validation. Of course, then, *E. mackaiana* became a pawn in the arguments for and against the airport – not an easy argument to conduct on our side, for the airport lobby quickly grasped the essential scientific fact about the stuff, that it's indistinguishable from ordinary heather. It certainly didn't obviously count as interesting 'wildlife'. As one woman said to me, 'If the Wildlife Service is so keen on the place why don't they buy it and put some wildlife on it?' Wildlife is zebras and elephants, not heather. Another airport supporter used to perform at the public meetings they held in all the villages; he would wave two bits of heather to prove that *Erica mackaiana* grew all over the mountain behind his own house miles away at Letterfrack. This ridiculous plant it seemed was standing in the way of progress. A poem was written about it in the local paper; I'll give you a few lines from it:

BOTANICAL PRISONER
Now the voice of Bureaucracy thunders yonder,
I have set a boundary to the nation,
I don't cherish my children equally.

The prognostic perception of Parnell and Pearse perishes,
Homo sapiens has a captive audience
A prisoner of *Erica mackaiana*.

The airport scheme did not get planning permission, and I can tell you *E. mackaiana* wasn't Connemara's favourite plant; it became the symbol of obscurantist and incomprehensible intellectuals and especially of 'self-appointed experts' with funny foreign names like Matthias van Schouten, who were denying Connemara its place in the twentieth century and wanted it to be depopulated by emigration and overgrown with heather. I think, though, *E. mackaiana* will never again bloom as it did that summer. The highpoint was its appearance at the annual Clifden fancy-dress ball: the prize for the best costume went to someone dressed as *Erica mackaiana*.

That concludes this Roundstone set-dance of human beings and heathers. In the last figure, a human takes the appearance of a heather which already bears a human's name.

13

Through Prehistoric Eyes

A raven materially outweighs a peregrine falcon – but in the scales of honour, the invisible scales of air poised above a precipice, the falcon is predominant.

I witnessed this one spring a few years ago, in the Twelve Bens, the mountains at the core of Connemara. I was accompanying a friend who was researching the breeding birds of high stony and boggy places, in an exploration of a magnificent valley called Gleninagh which runs up into the heart of the mountain range from the east. The cliff, hung like a great curtain between two peaks of its south-western perimeter, boasts the longest rock climb in Ireland: Carrot Ridge, so named from an episode in which more carrot than stick had to be used to get a certain climber up it. No combination of carrot and stick would induce me to try, but I have walked along the top of it, the col called Mám na bhFonsaí, or the pass of the rims. On this occasion, as we approached the foot of the cliff, a pair of ravens flew out from a crevice high up on its left-hand side, and my bird-man remarked that since the ravens had not built their nest in the prime site, the very centre of the cliff, we could expect to find peregrine falcons nesting there. And sure enough a peregrine falcon soon appeared over the top of the cliff – a much slighter bird, a fluttering dot against the bright sky, insignificant until you noticed how fast it was crossing your visual field – and it dived at the ravens once or twice in a perfunctory way, not seeking to damage them but just to remind them of their place.

In the good old days that the Prehistoric Society* exists to commemorate, there would have been a pair of golden eagles on

* To which this talk was addressed.

the cliff as well; but the principle of precedence would have been the same; these things were settled long before human eyes were turned up to them.

It had already been a rich day's walk. Coming up the track past the valley's only farmhouse, we had seen the menfolk of the Bodkin family planting their potatoes. Bodkin is an ancient name in County Galway; the family came in with the Normans. However, I don't believe they have been in Gleninagh for more than a few generations, although to see them building spade-ridges, that ran at forty-five degrees up the hillside and seemed to be composed of nothing but stones, one had an impression of a way of life of chthonic immutability. Farther on, we sat down to drink our coffee, on the sunnier flank of the valley. As we rested, my eyes went straying, grazing with the sheep and spring lambs, across the floor of the valley; and were brought up short by a row of little bumps on the profile of a low ridge a few hundred yards away. Something regular, it seemed, something organized, con-trasting with the sprawling topography of the bog; evidently worth investigating. We splashed across wet places and climbed the bank, which proved to be a glacial moraine crossing the valley; the stream meandering down the valley has had to cut a sharp little ravine through it, about fifty feet deep. And there on the crest of the ridge was a line of six boulders; roundish, sack-shaped, glacial boulders of quartzite. There was no doubt about which way the line pointed; the largest – it was only waist-high – being at one end, and distinguished from the rest by the streaks of white quartz in it. I knew enough to recognize this as a Bronze Age site – there is another very fine alignment in north-west Connemara, and a smaller one in the Joyce Country to the east – and I was excited by the discovery, because nothing of the Bronze Age had at that time been found in central Connemara. So I busied myself pacing it out and taking its compass-bearing, playing the amateur archae-ologist instead of using my eyes. The orientation was about south-south-west, and did not appear to me to be of much importance, because the line was pointing vaguely at the high wall of moun-tains. In any case I was prejudiced against the idea of the astro-nomical significance of such structures, which I felt was often merely the projection of the archaeologist's suppressed supersti-tions onto the sensible folk of the prehistoric past.

Unfortunately, my rationalism had blinded me to the evidence of my eyes. Later on I showed the Gleninagh stones to Michael Gibbons, who has made a lot of archaeological discoveries around Connemara of recent years, and he noted that they do not just point vaguely at the mountains, they point precisely at the col, the high pass between two peaks, above the precipice. And, revisiting the site on midwinter's eve, he observed that the sun sets neatly into that cleft in the horizon, when viewed from the alignment. I returned to Gleninagh myself the next midwinter, to pay my respects, and indeed apologies, to this phenomenon. At two o'clock in the afternoon the sun was already sliding down into the gap between the peaks. The sky around it was dazzling, eating away the black profile of the mountains. It was very difficult to see what was happening, the blaze of light was so intense; light was bouncing off the boulders like grasshoppers. The valley was flooded with gold, the Bodkins' farm was picked out in vivid detail, and, hundreds of yards farther up the bracken-invaded hillside behind it, traces of potato ridges, that must have dated back to pre-Famine days when the valley carried a larger population, were equally insistently present, as if the moment were transparent, X-rayed, visibly built up out of layers of the past. Time, in our everyday experience, does not consist of such moments; they are as rare in the general flux as grains of gold in the gravel of our Connemara streams. Perhaps the high light-levels of classic lands produce more of these intoxicating instants in which one feels that all history has been harvested, pressed out and fermented into the wine of the now; but they do occur even here, and sometimes with almost painful sharpness, when a low shaft of sunlight under cloud cover or between mountains transfixes the scene and pins it to the retina. The same must have happened in the Bronze Age; it's a matter of the eye's physiology.

By a quarter past two the sun was just above the bottom of the col, and exactly in line with the row of boulders. It was a spectacular conjunction of energy and matter. I had no idea how to photograph it, but in the viewfinder of my camera it looked like sword-in-the-stone fantasy-fiction. Is it fantasy to believe that, at a level below all cultural constructions and reconstructions, I was experiencing the same illumination that any embodied mind would have been subject to at this place three or four thousand years ago to the minute? But I was confused and distracted by my delight in having discovered the site – something worth telling the Prehistoric Society about! – and irritation that I hadn't been first with its essential interpretation. And so, to peel off those layers of ego-investment and recover the structure of the experience, as an index of human continuity and community since prehistoric times, is my aim in this paper.

The conjunction I have described would be peculiar to midwinter solstice; at any other time of year the sunset would be further round to the west. But why had this particular site on the valley bottom been chosen? Consider the situation from the point of view of the sun – a great blind eye that has seen through prehistory, will stare down history and overlook whatever comes after that, but which has never seen darkness, neither night nor the least patch of noontide shade. The sun's view embraces the illuminated disc of the earth; as the earth turns the Twelve Bens travel in an arc across that field of view towards its north-eastern limb. Just as the mountain peaks are beginning to obscure the sun's access to the valley behind them, the col between them swings into line and opens up the valley floor; then that window closes by degrees, and the mountains roll on towards the edge of night and sink over it. Now watch the same process through the eyes of the peregrine falcon high in the light-filled air above the mountain-tops. In spring there would be morning sunshine on the cliff-face, but in midwinter it is perpetually dark. As the sun sinks to the southwest the evening shadows of the mountains spread across the valley. A silhouette of the two peaks and the col becomes clearly accentuated for a while, and creeps across the broad meander-plain and the moraines, and begins to climb the opposite slopes. The point of that shadow-profile corresponding to the bottom of the col is well defined for perhaps an hour or so and traces out a lengthy locus. Anyone standing on any point of that locus will see the midwinter sun set uniquely into the V of the col. If the alignment had purely practical purposes – marking the day from which one starts counting the days of the year, so that one knows when to put the crops in, when to expect the salmon running upstream and the goose-flocks migrating northwards, *etc.*, – it could have been placed anywhere on that line across the valley.

Thus the practical astronomy of horizons is not enough to

determine the positioning of the stone alignment. But on that locus of possible positions, the actual one, the crest of the moraine, is undoubtedly the one any of us would have chosen; and here we can feel sure that we, too, are seeing through prehistoric eyes. For the eye, alert to spatial balances, visual discontinuities, the rhetoric of visibility, of seeing and being seen, vastly predates all cultural constructions on that organic basis. (In the eye, I include as much of the image-processing, pattern-recognizing, neural networks of the visual cortex as is necessary to make good my argument.) The eye is evolution's answer to a potential visual field that is a Darwinian arena of life-opportunities and death-threats. Centrality and marginality, openness and closure, balance and imbalance – these states were branded into our nervous systems as fraught with potentialities long before they were conceptualized. The words I use to convey a sense of this place as elevated above and central within the arena of the valley, respectful but not self-abasing before the cirque of mountains, are modern metaphors for ancient phenomenologies. So: this site marks the intersection of an astronomical constant with a constant of human spatial awareness; it is in itself ceremonious, observant of the geometry of humanity and the heavens.

Of course only one boulder is needed to mark such a point, given some such distinctive profile of the horizon; the five extra boulders are redundant, part of the generous redundancy that constitutes human culture. They are an indication that there was ceremony attached to the observation of the midwinter sunset from this point. Nobody could fail to be awe-struck by the spectacle, and no doubt the forces it marshals – the sun, the mountain peaks, the battle of light and dark – were apprehended religiously. Right next to the alignment is a roundish depression, a few yards across and a few feet deep. I had assumed that this was a kettle-hole, a place where a block of ice left over from the waning of the glacier had melted *in situ* on the moraine. But, if so, why does the only such pit happen to be exactly here? Mike Gibbons suggests that this may have been where precious objects were ritually deposited. And the Bodkins, straightening their backs from their potato ridges, tell me that people used to dig for treasure there, long ago. The Bodkins, although not the absolute aboriginals of this valley, probably know more of their secrets than we ever shall.

But whatever their religious and practical dimensions, the placing of these boulders was an aesthetic act, a response to the sense of place and balance I have credited the prehistoric eye with. The choice of this spot pulls all the forces of the valley together and knots them into a form one can grasp. I'm not talking ley-lines or anything mystical here; nothing more mysterious than art, which is mystery enough for me. A site has been created, around which the terrain assembles itself into a landscape – that is, an area apprehended by the eye, taken from a vantage-point. The concept of landscape, we know, is of modern origin, and its connections with Enlightenment objectivity, with the portraiture of estates and the perspectivism of power-relations, have been much discussed; but the roots of its possibility are in the nature of the eye, an organ trained by stick and carrot to command a sphere of vision.

Calendrical functions and religious conceptions wither away with time, but a well-founded aesthetic intervention can grow in stature indefinitely. This privileged site articulates more of the dynamics of the valley than the Bronze Age could have known. Thus, the line of boulders points us back to the precipice, which is where they themselves came from. The precipice is part of a corrie, a glacier's nest. Imagine the building of this nest, long before humans came here. The prevailing winds off the Atlantic are driving snow over the mountain tops, and the snow is settling and freezing in that sheltered, shadowed, north-east-facing hollow. And then the accumulated mass begins to slip downhill under its own weight. As it inches away it plucks fragments of rock out of the slope behind it. A crevasse opens up between the rear of this newborn glacier and the hillside; more snow drifts into the crevasse, freezes, welds the ice-body to the rock-face again, so that more stones are ripped out. So, over centuries and millenia, the slope is eaten back into a cliff, and the corrie is excavated. The glacier advances, sweeping all before it, so that the valley itself is widened and deepened and given its characteristic U-shaped cross-section. And all that rock is slowly dragged away by the ice, and deposited in the sea or in terminal moraines many miles away.

But then the climate changes. Melting-back of the glacier snout outpaces the downhill slippage of ice. Periodically, the retreat of the ice-margin is stalled; for centuries at a time, the glacier pours out its load of crushed stone along a certain front, building up a great bank of till across the valley. Thus the ridge of the moraine I have described marks a point of temporary balance between those two huge processes. Finally the glacier retires to its nest, and dwindles and dies. The raven and the peregrine begin the sequence of their springtime ritual battles. Human beings, perhaps after thousands of years of farming there, select the stones to build the alignment, from among the countless fragments torn off the mountainside by the glacier and scattered in the valley bottom. They toilsomely drag them up onto the moraine and set them in position – a position carefully chosen after much observation and perhaps already consecrated by some slighter structure. And that act of selection brings the whole valley and its force-field into aesthetic oneness. For the first time. The mountains themselves are 460 million years old, and the moraine was built ten or fifteen thousand years ago, but it was in the Bronze Age, say four thousand years ago, that this focusing of the terrain into a landscape took place – an event of a new sort, an act characteristic and perhaps definitive of humanity of all times and all places.

In fact I am tempted to boast that, in the whole prehistory and history of the valley, there have been two creative events; the first, the setting-up of the alignment, the second, the rediscovery of its significance. However, I must note a slight discrepancy, to see if it amounts to a loose link in my argument. The midwinter sun actually misses the very lowest point of the col; it passes just a degree or two above it and vanishes behind the mountain slope on its west. Part of that discrepancy represents a small change in the orientation of the earth's spin over the last 4000 years, due to the gravitational influence of the other planets; for just as a child's top nods and wobbles, so the earth's axis bows all around itself in a cycle lasting 26,000 years, and the depth of the bow varies slightly, in another cycle lasting 40,000 years. The angle between the plane of the equator and the plane of the earth's orbit round the sun – the obliquity of the ecliptic – has decreased by about half a degree since the Bronze Age, so that the midwinter sun now rides a little higher in the sky than it used to. Thus the whole vast system has got slightly out of focus since the alignment was built. But realizing that fact is like readjusting the focus, toning up the valley once again, bringing it into sync, not just with the order of the seasons but with the earth's orientation in the cosmos.

As to the preservation of such a landscape: evidently the first necessity is to keep the sightlines clear, the rays of connection uninterrupted. Obstacles can spring up with amazing rapidity if one is not vigilant. In this country we are particularly afflicted by sitka spruce and interpretative centres. Not that I'm against all such centres – the Céide Fields pyramid seems to me to effect in itself a focusing, valid in that stupendous landscape of sprawling bogs and streeling clouds. But as for the accursed Mullach Mór, it would have been not so much an interpretative centre as an interruptive centre. Interpretation calls for a knowledge of the language, and since the language of the Burren includes such terms as strangeness, and silence, and mystery, obviously foreign to the mentality of those who wanted to site the centre out in the area to be interpreted rather than in one of the nearby villages, all it could have offered would have been an impertinent interruption. The Mullach Mór scandal makes one wonder if the idea of an interpretative centre is of devilish origin. It is the devil of commercialism and commodification who takes one up into a high place, and shows one a landscape, and says, 'All this can be yours, cognitively, if you will only fall down and worship me.' Anyway, such a modest site as this I have described in Gleninagh – I know I have interpreted it as the very fulcrum of the universe, but it is indeed a modest site – needs no interpretation. It is in the best sense an interpretative centre itself, it is the stance from which the relationships of the terrain can be sensed even before they are theorized, as the Bronze Age well understood.

So, its conservators, apart from simply ensuring the physical integrity of the stones and their uninterrupted dialogue with the skyline, have to look to the general metabolism of the landscape. It might seem that, as yet, there are few problems in the wild recesses of Connemara; due process of Nature seems to be the rule. The raven and the falcon re-establish their primordial pecking order each spring; the lambs bleat, the stream meanders, the Bodkins build their stony potato ridges. But – to pick up one clue to a hidden distemper – this year in the stream, which is one of the headwaters of the Ballynahinch River, famous since mediaeval days, there were no salmon spawning. On this fishery, according to Roderic O'Flaherty, writing in 1684, '... experience was made how the salmon hath still recourse from the sea to its first offspring; for here, eighteen salmon were marked, with a fin cut off each of them, at their going to the sea, and seaventeen of them were taken next season, in the same place, coming back'. And now, for the first time in many thousands of years, the salmon no longer has recourse to its own origin. One of the reasons for this is European Union policy. The farmers of 'disadvantaged areas' such as Connemara cannot compete with New Zealand in the cheap raising of lamb; so they are helped out with grants, headage payments of so much per ewe. There is little market for the end-product, neither the meat nor the wool, at present, but it is still profitable to collect the grants. The result is overgrazing. (I am not pointing the finger at the Bodkins; I know nothing of their stocking levels. This is a general observation about Connemara and other rain-soaked western mountain regions.) Thousands of sheep − more than have ever been seen there before − are eating the heather down to the ground, and incidentally are suffering and dying in the winter and spring; then the rainstorms are breaking up the shallow exposed peat layer, and the streams are sweeping it away, and the delicate pebble beds the salmon need to lay their eggs in are burdened with mud and rubble. There is an outcry, mainly from the commercial point of view, about the decline of the salmon and sea-trout fisheries (the sea-trout suffer from a veritable Gordian knot of environmental problems). People enjoy killing salmon, and Connemara's gillies and hoteliers live by holding their coats and praising them mightily when they succeed, and the rest of us let them stand rounds when flushed from their triumphs. This is, to say the least, interruptive of that silver ring, the life cycle of the salmon, that we glimpse in pools and waterfalls when its recurrent destiny interlinks it, too often fatally, with our own world. Even in Bronze Age eyes, I am sure, the king of fish was more than a source of food and cruel fun. But when the grants system is amended, as it will be, if only in the interests of the economy, will the farmers turn to the sitka spruce? I dread to see the forestry ploughs go into the valley of Gleninagh. Several other superb valleys of the Twelve Bens and the Maumturk Mountains have great rectangular sticking-plasters of forestry on their cheeks. Without going farther into the maze of ecological interactions, I think I have made the point that to preserve a prehistoric sacred landscape it is necessary to preserve what we still have, of the nature that gave it its meaning. Otherwise, what we pass on is a poignancy of regret, a reproach.

One might think that, to a conservationist, time, both past and future, is the problem, for if, in considering the preservation of ancient sites, we are humbled by how old they are, we might well also be abashed by how young they are, these objects and relationships between objects, that we are supposed to hand on in wholeness to future centuries, to millenia, perhaps to timespans of geological magnitude. But in so doing, we are hardly just playing the pedagogue, informing and improving the mind of futurity. That we entertain this stupendous project of conservation must mean that we still preserve, in ourselves, an openness to present space as well, a reverence before the play of forces a site such as this in Gleninagh celebrates.

In this talk, the ceremonies of raven and falcon, the setting sun and the shadow of the mountain, the salmon seeking out its origins, the glacier disgorging its burden of rock, the changing obliquity of the ecliptic, have been both metaphors for and instances of the processes of nature, the genderless mutual engendering of time and space. And in presenting them in terms of retinal images, of optical geometry, I have been insinuating the idea that the eye itself has its religion, its sense of relationship to the whole, anterior to, underlying, and outlasting all other cults. I fear that these six boulders in Gleninagh, like six precarious stepping stones, are leading me too far out into the Ineffability of the Absolute, but instead of underpinning all I have said with a reference to innate, pre-cultural, Chomskyesque universal spatial grammars, I will suggest that spacetime is the irreducibly general religious object we share with the Bronze Age and with all future inheritors of the prehistoric eye. And with that, before I fall and drown, I will be silent.

14

Taking Steps

Pausing to catch my breath near the top of Derryclare Mountain in Connemara a few years ago, I turned to look across the boggy plain below that stretches southwards and breaks up into islands scattering out into the Atlantic. A few miles away, Cashel Hill, an isolated pyramid not as high as Derryclare, arose out of these lowlands, dark against the light-flooded distances. I noticed that, from where I stood, the top of it was exactly level with the ocean horizon. That meant that a straight line drawn from my eye to the summit of Cashel Hill would go on to graze the curve of the Earth's surface, like a tangent to a circle. Surely, I thought, I could calculate the radius of the Earth from this observation, given the height of Cashel Hill and the height of the point I was now at, which I could read off a map. So, when I got home that evening I drew a few little diagrams, and resurrected from my schoolday memories one of Euclid's theorems about circles, and found that, indeed, the calculation would have been quite simple, had I remembered to mark on the map where I was when I made the observation, which, unfortunately, I had not done.

However, I have no intention of reclimbing the mountain in order to find that spot again, since it is only the theoretical possibility of the calculation that excites me. Further, I now realize, I have no need to refer to maps for the heights and distances needed for the calculation; there is near my house a long level stretch of road with a clear view of both Cashel Hill and Derryclare Mountain; I could walk, say, a thousand paces along this road, and take sightings of the two mountains from either end of that distance, and with a bit of trigonometry arrive at rough estimates of all the data I need. Thus I could calculate the size of the Earth in terms of my own pace, without recourse to maps, astronomy or even the magnetic compass. Of course the result would be highly inaccurate, but that is not the point; obviously if I really need to know how big the Earth is I can look it up in an encyclopaedia. What is of value in the thought-experiment is the relationship it brings into consciousness between my body and the globe of the Earth.

Perhaps one reason this might seem significant to me is that for over twenty years now I have been living in and exploring with manic attention a rather limited patch of that globe: the Aran Islands off Galway Bay, the Burren on the south shore of the bay, and Connemara to the north of it. And if the countless footsteps I have taken in these three terrains have not in some sense carried me beyond their horizons, if the work I have done there does not have that wider relevance, then I have cast away a large proportion of my life.

The published outfall of these years comprises three maps, of Aran, the Burren and Connemara, a number of booklets and essays on the history, placenames and folklore of these places, and a fat, two-volume book devoted to just one of the Aran Islands, Árainn itself. Since the second volume of this book, *Stones of Aran*, has now appeared, and I have no interest in taking the mapmaking techniques evolved as part of my response to specific places and turning them like a torchlight on some other territory, and no idea at present of how to create a work of literature out of my vast accumulation of material on Connemara, this present period is one of retrospection and evaluation for me. And I have to start on that task from where I am at this moment, writing this letter.

The nearest thing to me is the cat, Nimma, asleep on my lap as she usually is whenever I'm typing. Warm cat and humming Apple Mac are inseparable sensations for me. A small terrier, Squig, is lying by the radiator. At the other end of the room my partner in life and in business – I'll call her M as I do in my writings – is pecking out a column of VAT figures. This cosy, homely, efficient set-up is called Folding Landscapes; it publishes the maps and some of the shorter prose-works. There are windows along two sides of the room, and the other sides are internal glass screens that reflect the windows, so that Folding Landscapes itself is enfolded in the landscape, or the landscape is folded into it like eggwhite into batter. All around me I see sample rectangles of

Connemara; the waters of Roundstone Bay, silvery grey today with
a wind-driven crosshatching of darkness, and beyond them dim
purple silhouettes of mountains, the Twelve Bens, their heads
thrust into banks of cloud. Our workspace is at sea level; I sometimes have to break off to watch an otter eating a fish on the rocks
of the foreshore, yesterday there was a red-breasted merganser
appearing and disappearing among waves, and once we were able
to look down on a little auk, blown in from the ocean, submarin-
ing just below the windowsill. When the wind is strong from the
east, spray taps on the pane; twice, when a prolonged gale pushing
water into the bay has coincided with an equinoctial spring tide,
the sea has seeped through the floor, leaving the carpet feeling like
sphagnum moss underfoot and spoiling a few books, but doing no
lasting harm. On summer evenings, with a full moon rising from
the hills across the bay, glimmers of reflected moonlight ripple
across our ceilings. On still frosty winter nights the outside looks
in at us balefully; the bay seems brim-full of black poison, the
reflected moon a stream of livid necromantic symbols swimming
towards us and dissolving as they reach our shore. I love living
beside these glamorous tides, living on the edge of the habitable
habitual.

In reality we are much more sheltered here in Connemara than
we were on Aran, where we spent most of our time between
leaving London in 1972 and coming to the mainland in 1984.
There the storms broke unimpeded against our cottage, the whole
fetch of the Atlantic behind them. As we learned on our very first
day – it was mid-November when we arrived – an Aran squall of
hailstones cannot be faced; one has to turn one's back, shrug the
shoulders up over the ears, and creep in under a field-wall until it
is over. That move from West Hampstead, from a life that had a
structure and impetus quite uncoupled from the seasons of the
year – I had been pursuing a career in an unprofitable but presti-
gious avant-garde sector of the visual arts, while M was studying
and working in arts administration – to Aran, where weather ruled
over practical affairs such as whether or not the steamer arrived
from Galway and there might be bacon or sugar in the shops, and
tended at first to dictate our personal lives, our moods, our deci-
sions to walk or read or stay in bed, precipitated me – and I can
only follow my own story here – into a directionless state in which

I was prey to anxieties and obsessions. But it was the place itself that suggested a way out. Aran is extraordinary in so many ways – its limestone polished by glaciation into a mirror of geological theory, its floral rarities flourishing the characteristics by which they might be looked up in Floras of the Aran Islands, its rambling, ramifying paths like invitations to explore, the Irish language teasing with inimitable sounds and cryptic, Celtic allusions – that I was soon lured into trying to understand the island, by its promise that this project could never reach an end. Accumulating impressions in a diary, I became a writer; and then, noting placenames and routes and locations on paper, a cartographer.

My first crude map of the Aran Islands has led onto better-informed versions, and also to maps of the other two great terrains visible from Aran: the limestone uplands of the Burren with its countless remnants of all prehistoric ages, and Connemara of the riddling coastlines and interior solitudes. But I have not set myself up as a regional rival to the official mapmakers, the Ordnance Survey, and this for two reasons. First, I need the Ordnance Survey's topographical accuracy as a basis for my own constructions of these landscapes; I do not want to spend my life remeasuring the toothy perimeters of these tiny fractions of geography, and my net is spread to catch other features of the world, including the otherworld itself as it shows itself through folklore and legend in this one. And secondly, the usual conventions of map-symbolism – the precise-looking smoothly sweeping contours, the generalized colour-coding of areas for height or vegetation-cover, the hard-and-fast line of high water mark, to mention but a few, all useful in particular contexts – add up to a spurious claim of universality and objectivity, and I am ready to trade in some of this scientistic legibility for a measure of freedom of expression, room to doubt.

Perhaps it is only in hindsight that I can justify my choices of technique in such terms. Nevertheless it does strike me now that these black-on-white maps, in which shingle banks and beaches and bogs and crags and lake water and mountain heights are all represented through thousands of dots and dashes and twiddles and twirls, are elaborate disclaimers of exhaustiveness. Everywhere are these minute particulars of ink, mimicking the rough, the grainy, the oozy or the dazzling, the sensuous modalities of walking the Earth's surface; while, equally everywhere, the white, the abyss of the undiscovered, shows through. Also, it occurs to me that there is at least a coherence between this style of drawing and a cluster of images that surface everywhere in my writing, centering on the human pace, the step taken, as in the beginning of this present letter. Though I have probably taken more steps about and on my three western marches than most of their born inhabitants, I have not put down roots in any of them. Roots are tethers, and too prone to suck up the rot of buried histories. I prefer the step – indefinitely repeatable and variable – as a metaphor of one's relationship to a place. The big book I have spent most of my Irish time on, *Stones of Aran*, is through-composed in terms of steps; the first volume, called *Pilgrimage*, being a walk round the coast of the island; the second, *Labyrinth*, working its way with incredible tortuosities through the interior. Another, shorter work is called *Setting Foot on the Shores of Connemara*. This controlling imagery is not entirely something I have freely chosen to elaborate, and it could become a knot-garden I have to cut my way out of. Perhaps I do need to quit these worn ways and trodden shores, to test these ideas elsewhere, to travel in search of that impossibility, the view from the horizon.

I know that the step, which is only one in a linked set of images of lateral extension – the walk, the path, the labyrinth, the spider's web – is not some poetic flower picked of my own creative fancy by the wayside of my life, because, looking back, I see it implicit in the work I was doing in London. One of these, a project that was never realized in fact, I called a structured arena; it would have been a concrete floor in the form of a frozen wave-pattern, the regular distances from wavetop to wavetop imposing a choreography on one's walking across it. Now it seems to me like a prevision of the bare limestone crags I loved to walk across in Aran, on which one's paces pick up a pattern from the regular alternation of deep fissures and smooth surfaces of rock. Another London work, also strangely like my later experience of Aran, consisted of a hundred simple geometric shapes cut out of board, a yard or so across, black on one side and white on the other, which were exhibited on a black floor in a blacked-out gallery; as the public – participants, not spectators – found these shapes and turned them over, so a dimly luminous terrain was formed and reformed underfoot. This was called 'Moonfield', because it was inspired by those almost indecipherable black-and-white TV images of the first moon-landing. How long ago it seems, how antiquated and dusty, that 'great stride for mankind!' I wrote about it at the time in terms of lunar paradoxes: 'One flies towards a symbol of inconstancy, ambiguity and madness, to alight on a surface of weatherless scientific candour; after the longest voyage one steps from the space-craft into an indoor environment, that of the hermetically sealed, sound-proofed, sterilized laboratory; the first exploratory step alters what is to be explored more than a million years have done.'

Then there was a work only a few visitors to my studio saw, for it was done when I was already withdrawing into myself from the London artworld: a yard-long white rod, hanging vertically in the middle of the room, very still, suspended by a multitude of taut coloured threads. This represented for me then a single pace taken towards the centre of the earth. Now it rhymes mysteriously with my experience on Derryclare Mountain.

Clearly, then, a devotion to footsteps was something I carried with me on that decisive step from city to island. Indeed a related image comes back to me from much earlier days. I must have been eight or nine – old enough anyway to have learned that the Earth spins in space, and seemingly to have picked up Newton's Law that action and reaction are equal and opposite – when it occurred to me one day that it was the effect of all the people walking on it that made the globe turn. I soon realized, of course, that the net outcome of those multitudinous tiny impulses in all directions would be zero. That was my rational mind forming itself, by closing itself. Now I can open it again to that image of the world's endless random turnings under the feet of its inhabitants. Since it seems that such thoughts came with me to these western corners, perhaps I do not need to go beyond present horizons to test them further. Perhaps I will not travel. But mentally I am already turning the globe, this way, that way.

Sources

ISLANDS AND IMAGES
This is a lightly reworked version of an essay written for *The Geographical Magazine* (London, December 1976) to mark the publication of my first map of the Aran Islands. Several themes in it concerning the big island were subsequently enlarged upon in *Stones of Aran*. I have added some anecdotes from my diary, that lapse of time now authorizes me to publish, about the two smaller islands. Of course many changes for good and ill have taken place since the period I am describing. The original title has been restored (it appeared as 'Aran Surrounded by Water', which annoyed me at the time but now seems quite acceptable).

SETTING FOOT ON THE SHORES OF CONNEMARA
Written in London in 1981 as a private memorandum, according to my diary, 'to convey the strangeness of my experience, & the degree to which it seems to happen inside me, as if the people I met were my own creations. But what seems graspable when I lie dreaming back over it sifts away like fine sand between my fingers when I sit down before the cold clattering typewriter.' I am happy that Antony Farrell later carried it off to inaugurate Lilliput's list (*Lilliput Pamphlets* / 1, Mullingar 1984).

THE VIEW FROM ERRISBEG
This piece formed the Connemara and Aran chapter of *The Book of the Irish Countryside* (Town House and The Blackstaff Press, 1987). I have curtailed some historical material dealt with in greater detail in 'Space, Time and Connemara'.

CROSSING THE PASS
The Burren chapter of *The Book of the Irish Countryside* (1987). I have amended one or two obsolete remarks, rearranged some other material slightly, and thrown in a badger for good measure.

5 SPACE, TIME AND CONNEMARA

Written for my *Connemara*, Part 1, *Introduction and Gazetteer*; Part 2, *a one-inch map* (Folding Landscapes, Roundstone, 1990). It was also published in *Éire-Ireland* (Vol. XXIV No. 3, St Paul, Minnesota, Fall 1989) with unforgivable sub-editorial blemishings, and, restored, in *The Mayo Anthology* (ed. Richard Murphy, Castlebar, 1990). The title of this brief and tender evocation of a little patch of territory imitates another, the awesome comprehensiveness of which inflamed my childhood ambitions, though I was and am quite unable to read the work in question: the cosmologist de Sitter's *Raum, Zeit, Materie*.

6 INTERIM REPORTS FROM FOLDING LANDSCAPES

This appeared in *The Bulletin of the Society of University Cartographers* (Vol. 20, No. 1, Reading, June 1986) and in *The American Geographical Society Newsletter* (Vol. 9, No. 1, New York, 1989). I have recast one or two passages to avoid overlap with other essays in this volume. As to the trifling formula into which I sought to compress all the pathos and challenge of cartography, I had left it unsupported, as a minor infraction of the bounds of the literary ('Never apologize, never derive!'); however, I will risk a line of proof here. If S is the scale of the map, then T cannot exceed St, and M is at best m/S. Hence $MT \leq mt$, which is a fixed amount given one's means of representation. There is a teasing parallel with the Uncertainty Principle here.

7 A CONNEMARA FRACTAL

A talk given at the first Conference of the Centre for Landscape Studies in University College, Galway, 1990. A short version was published in *Technology Ireland* (Vol. 23, No. 3, June 1991), and a fuller one in *Decoding the Landscape* (ed. Timothy Collins, Galway, 1993). The reminiscence of Besicovitch and the attempt to explain fractional dimensions have been added more recently. In fact this piece seems still to be in evolution; it could become a book on Connemara, or on various other things.

8 ON THE CULTIVATION OF THE COMPASS ROSE

Another very private meditation started in about 1979 and taken up again in 1990. It later came in useful as an intervention or interruption in a debate of mind-numbing cautiousness as to the proper definition of cartography that was occupying the professionals; I sent it to *The Cartographic Journal* with the suggestion that 'Cartography was the cultivation by graphic means of the compass rose', and was as surprised as I was delighted that it was accepted (Vol. 29, No. 1, British Cartographic Society, June 1992). It also surfaced in *Decantations: A Tribute in Honour of Maurice Craig* (Dublin, 1992).

PLACE/PERSON/BOOK

The introduction to my edition of J.M. Synge's *The Aran Islands* (Penguin Twentieth-Century Classics, London 1992).

LISTENING TO THE LANDSCAPE

A talk first delivered at the 1992 Merriman Summer School, 'Something to Celebrate: The Irish Language', and published in *The Irish Review* (No. 14, Belfast, Autumn 1993); the present version was given at Ireland House, New York, in 1994.

FOUR THREADS

This piece originated as 'Secret Connemara', a talk with slides and cassette recordings of folksongs, my contribution to the 1994 Toronto Conference (strangely entitled 'The Haunted Ark') of the Canadian Institute of Irish Studies; in recasting it as an essay I have added a layer of self-questioning.

BOTANY − A ROUNDSTONE VIEW

Concocted to amuse the Botanical Society of the British Isles when I persuaded them to hold their 1994 AGM in Roundstone. Published in *Irish Botanical News* (No. 5, February 1995).

THROUGH PREHISTORIC EYES

The keynote address to the sixtieth anniversary conference of the Prehistoric Society, held in University College, Dublin, in September 1995.

TAKING STEPS

A retrospect, conceived as a 'Letter from Ireland' and broadcast on BBC Radio 4 in January 1996.